Wars Without Flags

Wars Without Flags

How AI, Cyber Armies, and Mercenaries Are Redrawing Global Power

By

Rowan Hale

Vij Books
New Delhi (India)

Published by

Vij Books
(Publishers, Distributors & Importers)
4836/24, 3rd Floor, Ansari Road
Delhi – 110 002
Phone: 91-11-43596460
Mobile: 98110 94883
e-mail: contact@vijpublishing.com
www.vijbooks.in

ISBN: 978-93-90349-69-2 (PB)

This book was developed using advanced writing tools to support the drafting and ideation process. All content has been thoughtfully curated, refined, and reviewed to ensure quality and relevance.

Contents

Introduction

Wars Without Flags

The history of war is usually written in the language of nations. Armies wear uniforms, flags signal allegiance, and battles are recorded as contests between sovereign states. For centuries, the image of a battlefield has been one of clear lines—identifiable soldiers, declared wars, and hierarchies of command. But in the twenty-first century, this clarity has dissolved. Violence is no longer monopolised by the state. It has leaked across borders, seeped into networks, and been repackaged as a commodity for sale to the highest bidder. The wars of our time are fought without flags.

To understand this transformation, one must first grasp how extraordinary the old order appeared in the first place. Political theorists such as Thomas Hobbes and Max Weber framed the state as the entity with the "monopoly of legitimate violence." That idea underpinned the modern system of international relations: states alone had the right to make war, and their armies embodied the sovereign will. Yet this notion, while powerful, was always more myth than reality. History is filled with condottieri, pirates, auxiliaries, and militias that blurred the neat lines of state authority. Still, the illusion of monopoly endured, reinforced by the rise of disciplined standing armies and bureaucratic states in the nineteenth and twentieth centuries. That illusion has now collapsed.

Today, the command of violence resembles a marketplace rather than a monopoly. Mercenaries and private military companies operate alongside state forces. Militias function as governments in miniature, often with more credibility than the regimes they challenge. Hackers in anonymous collectives can paralyse a nation's critical infrastructure or sway its elections. Artificial intelligence, once the stuff of science fiction, increasingly guides drones, analyses intelligence, and generates disinformation at speeds beyond human capacity. The ability to wield decisive force no longer requires a state; it requires capital, skill, networks, and code. Power has been outsourced.

This book examines that outsourcing, not as a collection of isolated phenomena but as a coherent shift in the architecture of global power. The decline of state monopoly and the rise of a privatised, digitised, and algorithmic landscape of conflict are not accidents of history. They are the logical consequence of globalisation, technological acceleration, and the fragility of many states. To grasp this new terrain is to see how international politics is being redrawn before our eyes, often invisibly, and why traditional categories—war and peace, soldier and civilian, ally and enemy—no longer suffice.

The stakes are high. Wars without flags are not merely new methods of fighting old wars; they redefine what war itself means. If battles can be waged through keystrokes rather than tanks, if loyalty can be purchased like a subscription, if machines can decide life and death without human oversight, then the frameworks that governed centuries of conflict—laws, treaties, moral codes—are thrown into disarray. This is not just a military problem; it is a political, ethical, and civilisational challenge.

Consider the reach of mercenaries in the modern age. In Africa, private contractors fight insurgencies while extracting resources, entrenching both profit and instability. In the Middle East, militias backed by regional powers redraw the balance of influence without ever raising a national flag. In the shadows of the Cold War, covert armies operated as proxies, preparing the ground for the deniability and subcontracting that now dominate the twenty-first century. Meanwhile, in cyberspace, mercenary firms sell surveillance tools to governments and corporations, blurring the boundary between national security and commercial espionage. What once seemed like separate developments—militias, cyberattacks, private armies—are in fact threads of a single fabric: the unravelling of the state's exclusive hold on force.

Technology accelerates this process. The digital battlefield is borderless; a hacker in one country can disable power grids on another continent. AI systems enable operations at scales and speeds human commanders cannot match, while deepfakes erode trust in what is real. The very nature of sovereignty is tested when invisible code, rather than visible soldiers, determines outcomes. Cities like Kyiv, Lagos, and Hong Kong have already become theatres where kinetic violence, digital disruption, and psychological warfare collide. For the first time in history, wars can be fought simultaneously on the ground, online, and in the minds of millions of civilians.

This shift demands a new vocabulary of power. To speak only of armies and treaties is to miss the networks of actors—contractors, hackers, corporations, algorithms—that shape today's conflicts. The wars of our time are as much about finance, data, and legitimacy as about territory or ideology. Investors profit from prolonged instability; tech firms become arbiters of truth; civilians are conscripts in psychological campaigns whether they wish to be or not. Violence has become modular, portable, and purchasable. The battlefield has become the marketplace.

Yet these transformations do not only expose vulnerability; they expose paradoxes. Democracies, with their openness, are uniquely vulnerable to manipulation, yet they hesitate to adopt the authoritarian controls that might secure them. States denounce mercenaries and cyberattacks while quietly employing them. Artificial intelligence is celebrated as a tool of efficiency while raising profound questions about accountability: when an autonomous weapon kills, who is responsible—the coder, the commander, the machine? Wars without flags thrive in these grey zones, exploiting ambiguity as much as weaponry.

This book is written not to alarm but to clarify. We are living through a profound reordering of violence and power. To treat it as peripheral, or as a temporary distortion, is to misread the century we are entering. The conflicts of the past were mapped in borders; the conflicts of today and tomorrow will be mapped in networks. Sovereignty, legitimacy, and security are being renegotiated, not in treaties but in contracts, algorithms, and deniable operations. To navigate this new world, one must see the continuities with history as well as the novelties: mercenaries are not new, but their integration with global finance is; propaganda is ancient, but AI-generated disinformation transforms its reach; covert wars have long existed, but the scale of cyber armies makes them systemic rather than exceptional.

As you turn the pages ahead, you will encounter mercenaries who reshape governments, militias who provide more effective governance than states, hackers who wage wars without stepping onto battlefields, and algorithms that change the calculus of life and death. You will see how violence has become both democratised and commercialised, and how the traditional anchors of international order—law, morality, sovereignty—strain under the pressure. Above all, you will see how invisible wars, fought without flags, are redefining what it means to live in a world where conflict no longer begins with a declaration and may never end with a treaty.

The chapters are designed to build upon one another, tracing the erosion of the state's monopoly on violence, the rise of private and proxy armies, the emergence of cyber mercenaries, the deployment of artificial intelligence, and the profound consequences for democracy, accountability, and sovereignty. By the end, we will consider not only how wars are fought but how societies can adapt, protect themselves, and perhaps even redefine security for an age where the boundaries between war and peace no longer hold.

Wars without flags are not an aberration of the present; they are the shape of the future. They will not wait for governments to catch up, nor for treaties to be signed. They will continue to evolve in real time, across continents and networks, influencing the lives of ordinary citizens in ways both visible and hidden. To understand them is not an academic exercise. It is a civic necessity, a moral responsibility, and an urgent call to reimagine what safety, power, and freedom mean in the twenty-first century.

This book is an attempt to provide that understanding. It does not claim to have all the answers, but it seeks to give the reader the tools to ask the right questions, to see the unseen, and to recognise the forces reshaping our world. Wars without flags are already here. The challenge is whether we can recognise them, confront them, and adapt before the ground shifts beneath us completely.

Chapter 1

The End of the State's Monopoly on Violence

The story of modern politics has often been told through the lens of control—control of land, control of resources, and, above all, control of violence. For centuries, philosophers and statesmen alike assumed that the defining feature of the state was its exclusive claim to wield legitimate force. Thomas Hobbes, in the seventeenth century, famously envisioned a Leviathan to whom individuals ceded their natural right to violence in exchange for security. Max Weber, centuries later, would refine this idea, asserting that the state was the entity that "successfully claims the monopoly of the legitimate use of physical force within a given territory." These formulations shaped the very foundations of international order and political science. The modern state, in this telling, is not merely a geographical container of people but a unique authority that distinguishes between lawful and unlawful violence. To challenge that authority was to undermine the state itself. Yet from the start, this idea was more of a stabilising myth than a historical fact. What Hobbes and Weber offered was not an empirical description but a normative aspiration, a principle that justified why citizens should obey and why the state should govern. The actual history of warfare reveals a persistent reliance on mercenaries, militias, auxiliaries, and proxies. The monopoly, in other words, was never absolute. It was always constructed, always fragile, and always subject to erosion when circumstances demanded.

Take the mercenaries of Renaissance Italy, the condottieri, who hired their services to city-states such as Florence, Milan, or Venice. These companies of soldiers were essential to the maintenance and expansion of urban power, and yet they owed no allegiance to the state that employed them. Their loyalty was to contract and profit. The condottieri became so powerful that they often dictated terms to the very rulers who paid them, sometimes even switching sides mid-conflict if the price was right. Far from undermining the state system of the time, they were integral to it. Mercenary forces did not exist on the margins; they were central players in the geopolitics of their age. Nor was their use confined to Europe. Colonial empires relied heavily on auxiliary forces, from Indian sepoys in British service to African askaris under German command. These forces were indispensable to imperial conquest and control, yet their existence directly contradicted the notion of a monopoly on violence. They demonstrated that states could expand their reach not by centralising force under one flag, but by subcontracting it to those already embedded in local contexts. What mattered was not the purity of sovereignty but the efficacy of control.

The persistence of such practices reminds us that the neat lines drawn in political theory rarely map onto reality. The so-called monopoly of force was less a description of how violence was managed than a claim about legitimacy. States attempted to present themselves as the sole arbiters of lawful violence, even while outsourcing or supplementing their armies with mercenaries and allies. The doctrine said one thing; practice revealed another. What Weber called "legitimate" force was often legitimised only after the fact, once victory had been secured. Defeat, by contrast, rendered any use of mercenaries suspect. History, in this light, reads less as a story of monopoly than of improvisation—of rulers cobbling together coalitions of soldiers, militias, and contractors to achieve their aims.

If the early modern and colonial periods show us the reliance on mercenary power, the Cold War illustrates how deeply states institutionalised the outsourcing of violence. Far from a contest confined to two superpowers and their armies, the Cold War unfolded as a sprawling web of proxy wars, insurgencies, and covert operations. The United States and the Soviet Union rarely confronted each other directly; instead, they funded, armed, and trained militias across Africa, Asia, and Latin America. The CIA sponsored guerrillas in Afghanistan and paramilitary groups in Central America; the KGB and its satellites supported revolutionary movements from Angola to Nicaragua. These hidden armies fought brutal wars on behalf of distant patrons, embodying a model of violence that was deniable, decentralised, and devastatingly effective. The Cold War was, at its core, a masterclass in how states could maintain the appearance of monopoly while outsourcing the practice of violence to others. Superpowers maintained the illusion of direct control while simultaneously dispersing violence through networks of clients and proxies.

It is tempting to believe that the end of the Cold War marked a return to order, a reassertion of the state as the primary wielder of force. In reality, the end of bipolar rivalry removed the structures that had contained many of these networks, leaving a residue of militias, warlords, and contractors who were no longer tied to superpower sponsorship. Globalisation then accelerated the erosion of monopoly. The integration of markets, the proliferation of small arms, and the spread of digital technologies made it easier for non-state actors to organise, fund, and arm themselves. Weak states found themselves unable to control their territories, while strong states discovered that subcontracting violence was cheaper, more flexible, and often politically less costly than deploying their own armies. At the same time, the rise of private military companies offered governments and corporations alike a new mechanism for securing interests abroad. Violence became a service to be contracted, regulated by contracts and capital rather than by allegiance or law.

Technology amplified this transformation in ways Hobbes and Weber could never have imagined. Cyber warfare, in particular, makes a mockery of geographical monopoly. A hacker in one corner of the world can shut down power grids or steal military secrets in another without crossing a single border or raising a single flag. The digital battlefield has no boundaries, and the actors who operate within it range from state intelligence agencies to freelance collectives to corporate contractors. Legitimacy becomes difficult to establish, accountability harder still. Artificial intelligence compounds the problem, enabling actors to launch disinformation campaigns, deploy autonomous weapons, or analyse intelligence at scales that no traditional bureaucracy can manage. If the state once claimed legitimacy by controlling visible, organised violence, it now confronts a world where invisible, decentralised, and deniable violence undermines its claims.

The breaking point lies in this convergence: globalisation, weakened states, and technological transformation together shatter the idea that violence can be monopolised by sovereign authority. What emerges instead is a pluralisation of force, a marketplace where militias, mercenaries, corporations, hackers, and algorithms operate alongside, and often in competition with, formal state armies. The implications are profound. International law, which presumes the state as the unit of accountability, struggles to regulate actors who operate outside its scope. Political legitimacy, which once depended on the state's ability to provide security, falters when citizens turn to militias or private firms for protection. And strategy, which once revolved around the clash of national armies, must now account for adversaries who may be as diffuse as a cyber collective or as fluid as a network of contractors.

To grasp the end of the state's monopoly on violence, then, is to confront both continuity and rupture. Continuity, because mercenaries, auxiliaries, and proxies have always been part of the story. Rupture, because the scale, scope, and technological underpinning of outsourced violence today represent a structural shift. The state is not disappearing, but its central claim to legitimacy is being challenged as never before. What once appeared as deviation has become the rule. Wars without flags are not exceptions to the international system; they are increasingly its defining feature.

This chapter traces that trajectory, beginning with the philosophical myths that underpinned the idea of monopoly, then exploring the mercenary forces that made empires, the covert armies of the Cold War, and finally the conditions that produced today's pluralised landscape of force. The goal is not to deny the importance of the state but to illuminate how fragile and contested its claim to exclusive violence has always been. By the end, the reader will see that the state's monopoly on force was less a timeless truth than a temporary achievement, one now unravelling under the pressures of a globalised and digitised world.

From Hobbes to Weber: The Myth of Monopolised Force

The notion that states alone possess the legitimate authority to wield violence has long been treated as one of the cornerstones of modern political order, yet history reveals it to be more fragile fiction than immovable fact. What Hobbes and Weber articulated was not so much an enduring reality as an aspiration: a claim to order imposed on a world of competing forces, a framework that lent coherence to the otherwise chaotic and decentralised practice of power. To understand how profoundly this idea shaped the governance of nations—and how precariously it stands today—requires revisiting the intellectual architecture on which it was built and recognising the tensions that were embedded from the very beginning.

Thomas Hobbes wrote *Leviathan* in 1651 amidst the wreckage of the English Civil War, when authority appeared fractured and violence had spilled into every corner of society. His vision of the state was born of desperation: if humans in their natural condition were prone to war of all against all, then only by submitting to a sovereign could peace be secured. Hobbes's sovereign was not constrained by moral principles or democratic procedures; its authority lay in its ability to end anarchy. In handing over the right to violence to a centralised power, individuals secured their lives and, by extension, the possibility of civilisation. The monopoly of violence, in Hobbes's view, was not a technical arrangement but the very foundation of order. Without it, chaos reigned. His was a vision not of perfection but of necessity, forged in an era when the alternative to centralised power was seen in the dismembered body of a nation consumed by civil strife.

Centuries later, Max Weber distilled this notion into a crisp sociological formula. In his 1919 lecture "Politics as a Vocation," delivered in a Germany traumatised by the First World War and revolution, Weber declared that the state is the "human community that successfully claims the monopoly of the legitimate use of physical force within a given territory." It was a radical simplification of complex political realities, but one that carried immense weight. By tying the definition of the state to its monopoly of legitimate violence, Weber set the parameters for how scholars, politicians, and jurists understood sovereignty. What distinguished a state from other organisations was not bureaucracy, territory, or even popular consent—it was its claim, backed by success, to control coercion. Yet Weber's phrasing already hinted at fragility: the state must "successfully claim" legitimacy, which implies that such legitimacy is contested, performed, and constantly in need of reinforcement.

The Hobbesian and Weberian formulations converged in the twentieth century to give the modern state its aura of inevitability. International law, emerging out of the Treaty of Westphalia and solidified in the twentieth century, reinforced this idea by recognising states as the sole legitimate actors in war. Armies wore uniforms, wars were declared, and treaties were signed, all under the assumption that violence had been centralised under sovereign control. This framework provided not just stability but intelligibility: it made war legible, war crimes prosecutable, and peace conceivable. To believe in the monopoly of force was to believe in an international order governed by rational rules rather than arbitrary predation.

But this belief was always more aspirational than descriptive. Even as states professed their monopolies, they routinely outsourced, tolerated, or depended upon non-state violence. The mercenary companies of Renaissance Italy did not vanish with Hobbes's Leviathan; they adapted into auxiliary forces, colonial troops, and later private contractors. Colonial powers in the nineteenth and twentieth centuries extended their empires not with the force of European armies alone but with the labour of local auxiliaries—sepoys in India, askaris in East Africa, or indigenous militias in the Americas. These forces were essential to imperial domination, yet they undermined the very notion of a clean monopoly. The state might claim legitimacy, but it achieved power through networks of force that blurred the lines between sovereign and mercenary, between state violence and private coercion.

The twentieth century further demonstrated the elasticity of the monopoly claim. The Cold War, often depicted as a confrontation between two superstates, was in reality a global web of militias, insurgents, and covert operations. The Central Intelligence Agency funnelled weapons and funds to anti-communist militias in Central America, trained guerrillas in Afghanistan, and supported coups that relied on paramilitary violence. The Soviet Union, in turn, armed and directed revolutionary movements across Africa and Asia, embedding its influence in liberation armies and proxy militias. Neither superpower confronted the other directly, but both relied on a vast outsourcing of violence. Legitimacy was maintained at the rhetorical level—governments insisted they were defending freedom or supporting revolution—while in practice the monopoly of force was dispersed into a thousand battlefields. The myth survived, but its substance had long since been hollowed out.

The fragility of the monopoly is most apparent when states fail. Somalia in the 1990s, Syria after 2011, or Libya after 2011 demonstrate what happens when the state's claim collapses entirely: violence fragments among militias, warlords, and external patrons. Yet even strong states have increasingly discovered that maintaining a monopoly is costly and politically risky. Deploying national armies abroad invites public scrutiny and electoral backlash. Outsourcing to private military companies or covert operatives allows governments to wage war while maintaining plausible deniability. In the twenty-first century, the appearance of monopoly has often mattered more than its reality. Citizens are reassured that the state is in control even as control is subcontracted out of view.

Philosophically, the central tension lies in the difference between *legitimacy* and *effectiveness*. Hobbes grounded legitimacy in effectiveness: the sovereign deserved obedience because it prevented civil war. Weber, by contrast, sought to formalise legitimacy as the defining trait of the state, even if it had to be asserted in the face of contestation. Modern governance has oscillated between these poles. States justify their monopoly by claiming they can protect better than any rival, yet when militias or mercenaries offer superior security—as in parts of Africa or Latin America—the legitimacy of the state is eroded in practice even if preserved in law. *The monopoly of violence has always been a claim to authority rather than a guarantee of reality.*

The digital age intensifies this unravelling. Cyber warfare exposes the geographical fiction of Weber's formula: there are no clear "territories" in which force can be monopolised, and legitimacy is impossible to enforce in spaces where attribution itself is contested. A state can scarcely claim to control violence when anonymous actors on another continent can disable its infrastructure or influence its elections. Artificial intelligence compounds the problem, producing disinformation, automating surveillance, and even directing lethal systems in ways that bypass traditional chains of command. If Hobbes sought to escape the war of all against all by creating a sovereign, cyberspace suggests a return to it—only now with global reach and algorithmic speed.

Some scholars argue that the monopoly of violence was never meant to be read literally, that it was always an ideal type, a way of distinguishing state power from the predations of bandits or warlords. But the normative force of the idea has shaped centuries of governance, law, and international relations. To admit its unravelling is not to say states no longer matter—they remain immensely powerful—but to recognise that their defining claim to legitimacy is now under sustained challenge. Militias provide governance in fragile states; mercenaries secure oil fields; hackers tilt elections; algorithms shape decisions of war and peace. The monopoly has become pluralised, dispersed across a mosaic of actors who wield force without flag or formal sovereignty.

The enduring lesson of Hobbes and Weber is not that states ever truly monopolised violence, but that the *claim* to monopoly served as a stabilising fiction that gave modern politics its coherence. That fiction is now under pressure from realities too obvious to ignore. The more states rely on outsourcing, subcontracting, and deniability, the more tenuous their claim becomes. In its place emerges a world where legitimacy is fractured, accountability diffused, and violence reconfigured as a service to be bought, rented, or deployed by networks of actors who owe allegiance not to nation-states but to contracts, identities, or codes. To recognise the myth of monopolised force is not to abandon the idea of order but to confront the difficult truth that the structures built on that myth are no longer sufficient to contain the forms of violence shaping the twenty-first century.

When Mercenaries Made Empires

The official doctrine of the modern state has long insisted that it alone possesses the right to wage war, yet history repeatedly contradicts this principle. From the battlefields of Renaissance Italy to the far-flung frontiers of European empires, mercenaries were not marginal actors but essential architects of power. States that proclaimed the sanctity of sovereign armies nevertheless built their strength on hired soldiers whose loyalties were secured not by patriotism but by contract. Far from undermining political authority, these men were instrumental in its expansion. They carved borders, secured colonies, and upheld rulers who claimed to embody the monopoly of violence even as they depended on those outside it. The paradox is stark: empires that declared their legitimacy through the language of sovereignty and nationhood were, in practice, assembled by forces whose allegiance was bought and sold.

The Italian condottieri exemplify this paradox in its most vivid form. From the fourteenth to the sixteenth centuries, the wealthy city-states of the Italian peninsula—Florence, Milan, Venice, and others—lacked large standing armies and relied on military entrepreneurs who organised bands of professional soldiers for hire. These condottieri were contracted through detailed agreements, the *condotte*, which specified the size of forces, the length of service, and the price to be paid. They were not patriotic defenders of their city-state but businessmen of violence, calculating risks and profits like merchants. Their services allowed city-states to project power without the burden of maintaining permanent armies, yet their independence often unsettled the very rulers they served. Some condottieri became so powerful that they eclipsed their employers, carving out lordships of their own. Francesco Sforza, originally a mercenary commander, seized control of Milan in 1450 and established a dynasty that ruled for decades. Here was the ultimate inversion: a hired soldier transforming into sovereign, showing how fragile the boundary between legitimate ruler and mercenary contractor truly was.

While the condottieri fought for the wealth of Italian elites, mercenaries were equally central to the ambitions of monarchs who sought to consolidate power beyond the fragmented city-state. The Swiss pikemen became the most renowned mercenary infantry of early modern Europe, their disciplined phalanxes sought after by kings and popes alike. Their reputation for ferocity on the battlefield was such that Machiavelli, no stranger to the dangers of mercenary forces, acknowledged their unmatched effectiveness even as he warned of their faithlessness. Swiss mercenaries served in armies across the continent, their loyalty secured by gold and prestige. Even today, their symbolic legacy endures in the Vatican's Swiss Guard, a ceremonial remnant of a once formidable industry of hired violence. Such examples remind us that the supposed monopoly of force was not a fixed reality but a negotiated arrangement, one in which states borrowed strength from outsiders to shore up their legitimacy.

The reliance on mercenary forces was not limited to Europe. The expansion of European empires depended heavily on the recruitment of local auxiliaries, whose knowledge of terrain, culture, and tactics proved indispensable. The British Empire's dominance in India was secured not by regiments shipped from London but by vast armies of Indian sepoys, trained and commanded by British officers. At the height of the East India Company's rule in the eighteenth century, sepoys made up more than eighty percent of its forces, ensuring that British authority rested on an indigenous backbone. Loyalty was cultivated through a combination of pay, status, and patronage, yet this arrangement revealed its fragility during the Indian Rebellion of 1857, when sepoys turned their guns against their colonial employers. What had been the foundation of imperial strength became the instrument of its near destruction. The episode illustrates the double-edged nature of hired force: mercenaries and auxiliaries could build empires, but they could also unravel them when their interests diverged from those of their patrons.

The French Empire pursued a similar model with its *tirailleurs sénégalais*, African soldiers recruited from colonies across West and Central Africa to fight in European wars. These forces were deployed not only in colonial campaigns but on the battlefields of the First and Second World Wars, where they fought and died in service of a republic that denied them equal rights. Their contribution was vital: without colonial auxiliaries, France could not have sustained its military commitments. Yet the reliance on such forces undermined the claim that the French state embodied the unified will of its citizens. Violence was exercised in the name of France, but much of it was enacted by men whose connection to the nation was mediated by coercion and inequality. The story of the *tirailleurs* is a reminder that mercenaries and auxiliaries were not just tools of conquest; they became symbols of the contradictions that haunted imperial legitimacy.

If colonial auxiliaries demonstrated the indispensability of mercenaries to imperial expansion, the story of the Hessians in the American Revolutionary War highlights their role in sustaining imperial authority. When rebellion broke out in the colonies, the British Crown hired nearly 30,000 troops from German principalities, the largest contingent from Hesse-Cassel. These soldiers fought across North America, reinforcing British lines and garrisoning captured territories. To colonists who already resented taxation without representation, the presence of foreign mercenaries epitomised tyranny, fuelling propaganda that portrayed King George as a despot willing to unleash strangers upon his own subjects. The Hessians fought capably, but their very presence delegitimised British authority in the eyes of many colonists. Here, too, mercenaries both sustained and undermined empires, embodying the tension between effectiveness and legitimacy that defines their place in history.

What unites these examples is not just the recurrent use of mercenaries but the systemic reliance on them as instruments of statecraft. States denounced mercenaries in principle while depending on them in practice. Machiavelli's disdainful warning in *The Prince* that mercenaries were "disunited, ambitious, without discipline, faithless" expressed a fear widely shared among rulers, yet those same rulers repeatedly turned to mercenaries when necessity demanded. The paradox was irresolvable: the state's claim to monopolise violence clashed with the practical advantages of outsourcing it. Mercenaries were cheaper than maintaining large standing armies, they could be disbanded after campaigns, and they offered specialised expertise in particular terrains or tactics. These pragmatic advantages outweighed ideological commitments, ensuring that mercenaries remained integral to empire-building long after official doctrine condemned them.

Critics might argue that by the nineteenth century, the rise of national armies and conscription diminished the importance of mercenaries, replacing them with citizens-in-arms who embodied the state's monopoly of force. Yet even mass conscription did not erase the reliance on hired auxiliaries. Napoleon's armies incorporated foreign contingents drawn from across Europe; Britain continued to deploy colonial troops; and private companies like the East India Company blurred the line between commerce and conquest, maintaining private armies that rivalled those of states. The age of nationalism did not eliminate mercenarism—it merely obscured it beneath the rhetoric of patriotic service. Indeed, the very concept of conscription can be seen as a domesticated form of mercenarism, in which loyalty was compelled through citizenship rather than purchased outright. Both forms revealed the same underlying truth: the state's monopoly of violence was always contingent, always bolstered by borrowed or coerced force.

The legacy of mercenaries in empire-building resonates today, not as an antiquarian curiosity but as a structural feature of global politics. Private military companies, from Executive Outcomes in Africa to Blackwater in Iraq, echo the condottieri and colonial auxiliaries of earlier centuries.

They offer governments and corporations the ability to project power without the political risks of deploying national armies. The rhetoric of legitimacy still privileges the state as the rightful wielder of violence, but the practice of power remains rooted in the marketplace. The mercenaries who once carved out empires have modern counterparts who secure oil fields, guard shipping lanes, and train militias. The lesson of history is not that mercenaries are aberrations but that they are recurring instruments of order and disorder, essential to the making and unmaking of political authority.

To trace the role of mercenaries from Renaissance Italy to colonial auxiliaries is to expose the gap between doctrine and reality. States proclaimed their monopoly of violence, but they relied on hired force to achieve it. Mercenaries made empires not despite the state but through it, embodying the uncomfortable truth that political authority has always been constructed on foundations more fragile and pragmatic than official doctrine admits. The story is not one of deviation from sovereignty but of its very constitution: sovereignty itself has often rested on the shoulders of those who served for coin rather than country.

The Cold War's Hidden Armies

The Cold War is often remembered as a nuclear standoff between the United States and the Soviet Union, with the world held hostage to the balance of terror between two superpowers. Yet the reality of that confrontation was far less static and far more violent than the image of stalemate suggests. Beneath the surface of deterrence doctrines and summit diplomacy, the Cold War unfolded as a global struggle waged by hidden armies—militias, guerrillas, and covert operatives mobilised by Washington and Moscow to fight on battlefields where their own troops dared not appear. Outsourcing violence was not peripheral to the conflict; it was its central mechanism. The very survival of the superpowers' image of monopoly rested on a system of proxies, mercenaries, and clandestine operations that blurred the line between statecraft and deniable warfare.

What made the Cold War unique was not simply its ideological intensity but the way it institutionalised proxy conflict as a governing principle of geopolitics. Both the United States and the Soviet Union understood that direct military confrontation risked escalation to nuclear war, an outcome neither side could afford. This restraint produced a paradox: the superpowers avoided open war with each other, yet they sponsored relentless wars everywhere else. From the jungles of Vietnam to the mountains of Afghanistan, from the savannahs of Angola to the streets of Latin America, hidden armies fought battles that carried the signatures of their patrons but none of their flags. *The Cold War was less a frozen stalemate than a series of outsourced hot wars, fought by others at the bidding of giants who dared not fight directly.*

The United States, through the Central Intelligence Agency, pioneered new methods of covert war that blended paramilitary action, clandestine funding, and psychological operations. In Guatemala in 1954, the CIA orchestrated the overthrow of Jacobo Árbenz, a democratically elected leader whose land reforms threatened American business interests. Rather than deploying U.S. troops, Washington mobilised a small band of exiles and mercenaries, backed by CIA pilots and a psychological campaign that created the illusion of a vast insurgency. The operation was cheap, deniable, and brutally effective—so much so that it became a template for future interventions. Similar methods were deployed in Iran in 1953, in Congo in the early 1960s, and in Chile in 1973, where covert support helped topple Salvador Allende. These were not wars fought by the U.S. Army but wars outsourced to militias, proxies, and intelligence operatives whose existence preserved the fiction that the state retained control while avoiding the political costs of overt intervention.

The Soviet Union adopted its own model of hidden armies, providing weapons, training, and political backing to revolutionary movements across the Global South. In Angola, Moscow supplied the Marxist MPLA with arms and advisers, while Cuban troops, deployed with Soviet support, fought against U.S.-backed forces in one of Africa's most brutal proxy wars. In Afghanistan, the Soviet Union initially intervened directly in 1979, but even here the pattern of hidden armies reasserted itself. The mujahideen resistance, armed and financed by the CIA, Pakistan's ISI, and Saudi Arabia, bled Soviet forces for a decade until Moscow was forced to withdraw. The war demonstrated the potency of proxy mobilisation: relatively small investments in arms and training yielded massive returns in the form of Soviet humiliation and eventual collapse.

What is striking about these conflicts is not only the scale of violence but the degree to which superpowers relied on networks rather than standing armies. The CIA's support for the Contras in Nicaragua illustrates the logic: the Reagan administration funnelled money, weapons, and training to anti-Sandinista militias while maintaining plausible deniability. Congressional restrictions were circumvented through covert funding, most notoriously via the Iran-Contra affair. Violence was privatised, detached from direct democratic oversight, and embedded in secret budgets and clandestine networks. For the Soviets, the reliance on proxies allowed them to project influence in regions where direct intervention was politically or logistically untenable. Supporting insurgencies in Mozambique or Ethiopia offered Moscow leverage without inviting the risks of large-scale deployments. Both sides constructed vast infrastructures of covert support, demonstrating that outsourcing violence was not improvisation but policy.

Hidden armies were not confined to the battlefields of the Global South; they infiltrated Europe itself. NATO's "stay-behind" networks, such as Operation Gladio in Italy, were designed to mobilise resistance in the event of a Soviet invasion but were also implicated in domestic politics, blurring the line between defence and manipulation. These networks, often staffed by former partisans or far-right militants, existed outside conventional military hierarchies yet operated with tacit state blessing. Their exposure in the 1990s revealed how deeply Western democracies had invested in deniable structures of violence, even within their own borders. The Soviet bloc, too, employed clandestine units such as the KGB's spetsnaz and trained insurgents abroad, embedding covert war within the fabric of state security.

The moral and political consequences of these hidden armies were profound. In many cases, the reliance on proxies unleashed cycles of violence that devastated societies long after superpower interests waned. Afghanistan descended into civil war after the Soviet withdrawal, its armed factions later giving rise to the Taliban. In Central America, U.S.-backed militias committed atrocities that scarred generations, while Soviet- and Cuban-supported regimes entrenched authoritarian rule under the guise of revolutionary liberation. Outsourcing violence insulated superpowers from immediate costs but externalised devastation onto weaker states, leaving behind legacies of instability that persist today. *The Cold War's hidden armies were not disposable tools; they became enduring features of fractured political landscapes.*

Yet these practices were not without strategic logic. For Washington, covert interventions were cheaper and politically safer than deploying troops. For Moscow, backing insurgencies offered ideological prestige and geopolitical leverage in regions far from home. Both superpowers rationalised their hidden armies as necessary instruments in a struggle where perception often mattered as much as reality. Victory was measured not in territorial conquest but in the spread or containment of ideology. By that standard, militias and proxies proved effective weapons, their very deniability enhancing their value in a war where open confrontation was too dangerous to contemplate.

The Cold War's hidden armies also highlight a deeper philosophical point: the so-called monopoly of violence was not only breached but actively dismantled by the very states that claimed to embody it. Superpowers that insisted on sovereignty at home willingly eroded it abroad, financing non-state actors to destabilise governments or suppress insurgencies. The contradiction was not accidental but structural: modern states retained the rhetoric of monopoly while constructing systems of warfare that depended on its abandonment. The Cold War institutionalised this paradox, creating a template of deniable conflict that resonates in the twenty-first century, from Russian "little green men" in Crimea to Western reliance on private military companies in Iraq.

To view the Cold War only through the lens of nuclear deterrence is to miss its most pervasive feature: the normalisation of outsourced violence as a tool of global order. CIA-backed militias, Soviet proxies, and covert networks were not aberrations; they were the engines of the conflict. The world of hidden armies shaped not only the outcome of the Cold War but the structure of international politics thereafter. The lesson is sobering: when states find monopoly too costly or risky, they delegate force to others. And once unleashed, these forces rarely disappear with the signing of treaties. They persist, mutate, and resurface, carrying with them the imprint of the hidden wars that created them.

The Breaking Point

The belief that states could monopolise violence has always rested on precarious foundations, but the late twentieth and early twenty-first centuries exposed its fragility more starkly than at any other point since the emergence of the modern state. The combination of globalisation, weakening state structures, and technological innovation did not simply chip away at sovereign control of force—it shattered it, making proxy warfare and outsourced violence the new normal. What Hobbes described as the Leviathan and Weber as the custodian of legitimate violence has entered an era where neither monopoly nor legitimacy can be taken for granted. States remain powerful, yet they now operate in a crowded marketplace of force in which militias, mercenaries, cartels, hackers, and algorithms compete for authority.

Globalisation played a central role in this transformation, not only by expanding markets and connecting economies but by internationalising conflict itself. The same forces that allowed capital, information, and people to flow across borders with unprecedented speed also enabled weapons, insurgent ideologies, and paramilitary networks to spread. The collapse of trade barriers and the proliferation of transport links facilitated a global black market in arms and manpower. Conflict entrepreneurs could recruit across borders, finance themselves through transnational criminal networks, and access technologies once restricted to state militaries. The end of the Cold War accelerated this process. Where once proxy armies were funded through superpower competition, globalisation allowed them to sustain themselves through smuggling, resource extraction, and foreign sponsorship. Civil wars in West Africa during the 1990s, for example, became tied not to ideological struggle but to control over diamonds, timber, and other commodities. Militias could plug directly into global markets, bypassing state structures entirely. *The globalisation of conflict stripped states of their monopoly not only over force but over the economic lifelines that made violence possible.*

At the same time, the internal fragility of states left vast spaces open for non-state actors to operate. Many post-colonial states were weakly institutionalised from the start, their borders drawn more by imperial convenience than by coherent governance. The so-called "failed states" of the late twentieth century—Somalia, Liberia, Afghanistan—became archetypes of this condition. When state institutions collapsed, militias, warlords, and foreign backers filled the vacuum, often providing governance more effectively than the governments they supplanted. In Afghanistan, the Taliban's rise was inseparable from the state's inability to control its territory after decades of proxy warfare. In sub-Saharan Africa, private military companies such as Executive Outcomes secured oil fields and diamond mines for paying clients when state armies were incapable of doing so. Weakness here was not merely absence; it was an opening for alternative authorities to claim sovereignty through violence.

But fragility is not confined to the so-called periphery. Even strong states have chosen to hollow out their monopoly deliberately, finding it more advantageous to subcontract violence than to wield it directly. For democratic states, the political cost of casualties in foreign wars makes proxy forces attractive. By supporting local militias, insurgents, or contractors, governments can project power abroad while maintaining the appearance of restraint. The U.S. reliance on Kurdish fighters against ISIS in Syria illustrates this calculation: Kurdish militias bore the brunt of combat, while the United States provided training, air support, and weapons. For authoritarian states, outsourcing provides plausible deniability. Russia's use of Wagner Group mercenaries in Ukraine, Syria, and Africa allows the Kremlin to pursue strategic goals without formal accountability. In both cases, the monopoly of violence is undermined not by incapacity but by choice. *The very states that claim the monopoly of force strategically abandon it when doing so suits their interests.*

If globalisation and weakened states created the structural conditions for this breaking point, new technologies accelerated and entrenched it. The digital revolution produced a battlefield that transcends borders, rendering Weber's territorial definition of the state increasingly obsolete. Cyberattacks allow relatively small groups to paralyse infrastructure, steal sensitive data, or manipulate political processes in ways once reserved for superpower intelligence agencies. The rise of cyber mercenary firms, offering surveillance tools and offensive hacking capabilities for hire, underscores the commodification of digital violence. States themselves frequently contract these services, blurring the line between public and private force. Unlike traditional mercenaries, cyber operators can be everywhere and nowhere at once, attacking one country's financial system while residing in another, often beyond the reach of international law.

Artificial intelligence deepens this fragmentation by transforming both the scale and the nature of conflict. Autonomous weapons systems, predictive algorithms, and AI-generated disinformation campaigns expand the range of actors who can wield decisive force. Militias and non-state groups, once limited by lack of resources, can now access cheap drones and off-the-shelf AI software to compete with states in surveillance, targeting, and propaganda. States still possess greater resources, but the entry costs of warfare have plummeted. What was once the preserve of superpowers is now within reach of loosely organised networks. The effect is not only military but psychological: information warfare amplified by AI corrodes the legitimacy of governments by undermining trust, destabilising elections, and blurring the boundary between truth and deception. In such conditions, the state's claim to be the guarantor of security sounds increasingly hollow.

This convergence of globalisation, weakened states, and new technologies has made proxy warfare not the exception but the prevailing pattern of conflict. From Yemen, where Saudi Arabia and Iran back rival factions, to Libya, where multiple regional powers fuel competing militias, wars are fought less between states than through networks of clients, proxies, and contractors. These conflicts are not temporary deviations from the norm but reflections of a system in which outsourcing violence is structurally embedded. Proxy warfare offers states flexibility, deniability, and influence at low cost, while giving non-state actors access to resources and legitimacy they would otherwise lack. It is a mutually reinforcing arrangement: states gain reach without responsibility, and proxies gain power without sovereignty. The result is a world where violence circulates through diffuse networks rather than hierarchical chains of command.

The breaking point is therefore not a singular event but an accumulation of pressures that together expose the myth of monopolised force. Globalisation opened the channels, weakened states created the vacuums, and technology supplied the accelerants. The outcome is a system where the state remains one actor among many, its monopoly replaced by a marketplace of force in which authority is constantly contested. What is at stake is not merely the conduct of war but the very definition of sovereignty. If violence can be bought, outsourced, or automated, then the old markers of statehood lose their meaning. Sovereignty becomes less about territorial control and more about networks of influence, less about legitimacy and more about capacity to command and coordinate actors across a fragmented landscape.

The world we now inhabit is one where the breaking point has already been reached. The monopoly of force, once a stabilising fiction, has given way to an ecosystem of violence in which states, corporations, militias, and machines coexist uneasily. Proxy warfare is not a symptom of disorder; it is the organising principle of twenty-first-century conflict. To understand this reality is to grasp that the state no longer stands above the marketplace of violence but competes within it, sometimes as patron, sometimes as client, and often as both. The Leviathan has not disappeared, but it is now one creature among many in a crowded field, its authority fractured, its monopoly broken.

Chapter 2

The Marketplace of Force

War has always been an enterprise of logistics: feeding armies, supplying weapons, and moving men across distances. What distinguishes the twenty-first century is that the provision of war itself—the fighters, the strategy, the force of arms—has increasingly been outsourced to private companies that package violence as a service. Private military companies (PMCs) do not resemble the ragtag mercenary bands of Renaissance Italy, nor the colonial auxiliaries of empire. They are incorporated businesses, registered in capitals from Moscow to Dubai to Washington, operating offices with legal teams, HR departments, and corporate structures. They sell security contracts, but unlike ordinary firms, what they trade in is the ability to kill, protect, and coerce. Violence, once the hallmark of sovereign authority, has been transformed into a line item on a balance sheet. This chapter examines how the commodification of force reshapes the nature of war, politics, and accountability.

The rise of PMCs is often traced to the end of the Cold War, when the downsizing of national militaries coincided with an explosion of conflicts in fragile states. Professional soldiers found themselves without positions, and demand for their expertise surged in places where governments or corporations required armed protection. The result was the birth of companies like Executive Outcomes in South Africa, which in the 1990s offered governments in Angola and Sierra Leone disciplined combat units to fight insurgencies that had overwhelmed national armies. The company secured mining concessions in return, revealing the economic logic of the new model: wars could be fought not just for states but for profit, with companies operating as brokers between political instability and resource extraction. This was not an aberration but the prototype of a global industry. The military contractor was no longer a soldier bound by national service but an employee contracted to deliver results within the terms of an agreement.

If Executive Outcomes marked the beginning, Blackwater signalled the mainstreaming of the PMC model. Founded in the United States in 1997, Blackwater grew rapidly during the Iraq War, becoming synonymous with the privatisation of military force. At its peak, the company employed tens of thousands of personnel, ranging from former special forces operatives to logistical staff, guarding convoys, training local police, and securing U.S. installations. The 2007 Nisour Square massacre, in which Blackwater contractors killed seventeen Iraqi civilians, exposed the darker implications of this outsourcing. The contractors operated in legal grey zones, shielded from Iraqi law and not clearly subject to U.S. military justice. The incident drew international outrage but highlighted a structural issue: when war is conducted by private firms, accountability dissipates into contracts, indemnities, and jurisdictional loopholes. Blackwater later rebranded, but the model endured, embedded into the way modern states conduct war.

Russia's Wagner Group represents the other face of this industry: a PMC deeply entwined with state objectives while retaining the flexibility and deniability of a private entity. Wagner fighters have appeared in conflicts from Ukraine to Syria to several African states, securing strategic objectives while allowing the Kremlin to deny direct involvement. In Libya, Wagner supported Khalifa Haftar's forces; in the Central African Republic, it protected government officials while also extracting mineral concessions. Wagner exemplifies how PMCs can function simultaneously as instruments of foreign policy and as commercial actors. Their presence blurs the line between mercenary and state soldier, between geopolitical strategy and business venture. *The PMC is not simply a replacement for the national army; it is a hybrid form, operating in spaces where the political costs of conventional deployment are deemed too high.*

The logic behind the reliance on PMCs is straightforward: they offer flexibility, speed, and discretion. Governments can deploy them without parliamentary debates, public scrutiny, or formal declarations of war. Corporations can hire them to secure oil installations, shipping routes, or mining concessions in unstable regions where state forces cannot be trusted. Even humanitarian organisations have relied on PMCs for protection in conflict zones, revealing how deeply the model has embedded itself across domains once considered separate from warfare. The marketplace of force is not limited to states and armies; it extends to the private sector, NGOs, and even wealthy individuals. What was once the prerogative of the state has become a service available to clients with sufficient resources.

But commodifying violence has consequences that extend far beyond efficiency. *The profit motive reshapes the incentives of war.* Where national armies are nominally tasked with securing victory, PMCs are tasked with fulfilling contracts, which may involve prolonging conflict rather than resolving it. A company employed to protect an oilfield has little reason to seek political stability beyond the boundaries of its client's interests. A contractor training local forces may find recurring instability more profitable than lasting peace. The commodification of violence introduces perverse incentives into the conduct of war, embedding instability into the very structures designed to manage it. This does not mean that PMCs seek chaos for its own sake, but that the logics of the marketplace rarely align with the pursuit of long-term stability.

Legal and ethical dilemmas follow inevitably. International law struggles to categorise PMCs: they are not formally mercenaries under the strict definitions of the Geneva Conventions, nor are they soldiers subject to military codes of justice. They exist in a liminal space where contracts, insurance policies, and indemnity clauses often carry more weight than international treaties. When a PMC commits an atrocity, who is responsible—the contractor, the client, the host state, or the sponsoring government? The chain of command, once the backbone of military accountability, dissolves into a web of contractual relationships. The Nisour Square massacre was not an isolated incident but a case study in the structural problems of accountability. States use PMCs precisely because they occupy this ambiguous terrain: their deniability is part of their value. Yet this very ambiguity corrodes the idea that violence can ever again be neatly tied to legitimate authority.

Philosophically, the marketplace of force reveals how far we have travelled from Weber's conception of the state. If legitimacy once rested on the state's ability to control coercion, then contracting that coercion to private firms undermines the very basis of sovereignty. Yet states continue to do so, not because they have abandoned sovereignty but because they have redefined it. Sovereignty no longer means monopolising violence; it means managing and outsourcing it to maximise advantage while minimising political cost. This redefinition may be pragmatic, but it carries profound consequences for international order. Wars waged by private firms cannot easily be regulated by treaties designed for national armies. Civilians in conflict zones cannot easily distinguish between combatants and contractors. And accountability—always fragile in war—becomes even more elusive when the actors responsible are corporate entities whose primary duty is to shareholders.

The marketplace of force is not merely a symptom of state weakness; it is also a product of state strategy. Strong states like the United States and Russia have actively nurtured the industry, integrating PMCs into their broader security ecosystems. Weak states, unable to defend themselves, have turned to PMCs for survival. Corporations, eager to protect their assets in unstable environments, have become clients. Together, these dynamics create a feedback loop: as demand for private force increases, so too does its normalisation. Violence is no longer monopolised, nor even exceptional—it is commodified, traded, and managed like any other global industry. The consequences are felt not only on battlefields but in the very idea of what war is, who fights it, and who bears responsibility for its outcomes.

This chapter traces the contours of this transformation, examining how violence has been packaged, sold, and deployed by companies that resemble logistics firms but deliver war. By examining case studies of Blackwater, Wagner, and others, it reveals how PMCs have altered the conduct of conflicts from Iraq to Africa, how profit motives distort the logic of warfare, and how the chain of command itself has dissolved into contracts and deniability. The marketplace of force is not a temporary phenomenon. It is the organising principle of modern conflict, where violence has become a commodity available for hire, and where the lines between state, corporation, and soldier are dissolving into a haze of contracts, interests, and blurred accountability.

Violence for Hire

The most striking feature of contemporary warfare is not only its decentralisation but its commodification. Violence, once monopolised by states and justified in the language of sovereignty, has become a service that can be purchased like logistics or communications support. Private military companies (PMCs) embody this shift, operating as modern corporations that advertise expertise, bid for contracts, and report to boards and investors, yet whose core product is armed force. They provide everything from convoy protection and base security to intelligence analysis and direct combat support. The existence of such firms challenges the long-standing assumption that violence, unlike other commodities, could not be outsourced without destabilising the international order. In practice, states, corporations, and even humanitarian organisations now rely on them as indispensable actors in global security.

The emergence of PMCs is rooted in a confluence of historical trends. The end of the Cold War created a surplus of trained soldiers and officers as militaries downsized. At the same time, conflicts proliferated in fragile states, many of which lacked the institutional capacity to maintain disciplined armies. This mismatch between supply and demand created fertile ground for the growth of private firms offering military expertise. South Africa's Executive Outcomes was among the first, recruiting former apartheid-era soldiers and deploying them in Angola and Sierra Leone during the 1990s. In both cases, the company played decisive roles in halting insurgencies that had overwhelmed national armies. Payment was often secured in the form of mining concessions, revealing how closely tied the provision of force had become to global capital. *The business model was clear: where states could not secure themselves, firms could do so in exchange for access to resources.*

The United States transformed PMCs from peripheral actors into central players in modern conflict. The wars in Iraq and Afghanistan saw an unprecedented reliance on contractors, with firms such as Blackwater, DynCorp, and Triple Canopy deploying tens of thousands of personnel. Their roles extended beyond static security, encompassing convoy protection, interrogation support, and even participation in firefights. At certain points, contractors in Iraq outnumbered uniformed U.S. troops. This reliance was not simply a matter of capacity; it was also political. Contractors allowed Washington to wage war with fewer uniformed personnel, reducing domestic opposition to casualties and bypassing some of the accountability mechanisms attached to state militaries. Yet this convenience carried costs, as illustrated by the 2007 Nisour Square massacre in Baghdad, where Blackwater operatives killed seventeen civilians. The incident underscored the structural problems inherent in privatised force: ambiguous legal frameworks, unclear chains of command, and accountability mechanisms subordinated to contracts rather than public law.

Russia has adopted a different but equally revealing model. The Wagner Group operates in the grey zone between private enterprise and state instrument, providing the Kremlin with a deniable tool for projecting power. Wagner forces have been active in Ukraine, Syria, and across Africa, offering both combat support and political services such as training local armies and securing critical infrastructure. In return, Wagner has often received resource concessions, particularly in mining sectors, cementing the link between violence and commercial extraction. For Moscow, Wagner provides plausible deniability: the state can disavow responsibility for its actions while reaping the benefits of influence and control. Wagner's activities reveal a key feature of PMCs: they do not simply fill security gaps; they enable states to operate outside the constraints of law and diplomacy, pursuing objectives too sensitive or controversial for regular forces.

The expansion of PMCs into corporate and humanitarian sectors further illustrates their normalisation. Multinational corporations operating in volatile regions frequently contract PMCs to secure pipelines, mining facilities, or shipping routes. Humanitarian organisations, despite their commitment to neutrality, have at times hired PMCs to protect aid convoys or refugee camps in war zones. These examples show how violence for hire extends beyond the battlefield, embedding itself in the infrastructures of globalisation. Security, once conceived as a public good provided by the state, has become a private service available to those able to pay. The implications are profound: access to security is stratified by wealth, and the exercise of force becomes aligned with the interests of clients rather than the public at large.

The corporate structure of PMCs reinforces this transformation. Unlike traditional mercenary groups, which were often ad hoc bands of fighters, PMCs present themselves as legitimate businesses. They employ legal teams to draft contracts, compliance officers to navigate regulations, and public relations departments to manage reputations. They lobby governments, participate in international security conferences, and publish reports showcasing their professionalism. This corporate façade distinguishes them from historical mercenaries, granting them access to state contracts worth billions of dollars. Yet behind the legal documents and polished branding, their essential function remains the provision of armed force. *The veneer of corporate respectability masks a deeper continuity: violence as a tradable commodity.*

The growth of PMCs has sparked significant debate over their implications for international law and political accountability. Defenders argue that they bring efficiency, expertise, and flexibility, particularly in environments where national forces are overstretched or ineffective. Critics counter that they erode the principle of state monopoly on violence, create perverse incentives to prolong conflicts, and undermine democratic oversight. The legal status of PMC employees remains contested: they are not traditional combatants, yet they are often armed and involved in hostilities. International conventions on mercenaries are ill-suited to the complexity of modern PMCs, which operate under contracts with states and corporations rather than as free-floating bands of soldiers. As a result, accountability often dissolves in legal grey zones, with abuses investigated only sporadically and prosecutions rare.

Philosophically, PMCs highlight the commodification of security as one of the defining features of the contemporary order. Weber's conception of the state as the sole holder of legitimate violence assumed that coercion was inseparable from sovereignty. The existence of PMCs demonstrates that coercion can now be detached from sovereignty, managed by firms with no direct connection to the populations affected. This shift is not merely a legal or political problem; it is a reconfiguration of the relationship between violence, legitimacy, and profit. Wars can be fought without formal declarations, by actors whose incentives are shaped not by ideology or citizenship but by contractual obligations. The battlefield becomes less about national will and more about client demand.

The rise of PMCs also complicates the moral economy of war. Soldiers in national armies are bound, at least nominally, by notions of service, honour, and sacrifice. Contractors are bound by the terms of their employment. When force is commodified, motivations change: risk is calibrated against pay, loyalty is transactional, and the logic of profit can supersede the pursuit of resolution. This does not mean that contractors lack professionalism—many are highly disciplined former soldiers—but their institutional incentives differ fundamentally from those of state militaries. Conflicts where PMCs are heavily involved often become more fragmented, less accountable, and harder to resolve, as multiple actors with competing interests shape outcomes.

What emerges, then, is not merely the privatisation of violence but its integration into the circuits of global capitalism. PMCs are part of an industry that trades in security services alongside logistics, communications, and infrastructure. They participate in a global market where contracts are awarded, services delivered, and payments secured through financial systems that treat violence as one commodity among many. This does not eliminate the state but reshapes its role. States now function as both regulators and clients, outsourcing force when convenient while still claiming the mantle of monopoly when politically expedient. Sovereignty becomes less about exclusive control and more about strategic management of available providers of violence.

The phenomenon of violence for hire reveals not only the limits of state monopoly but also the new realities of global order. Private military companies operate in the shadows of legality and legitimacy, yet their presence defines modern conflicts as much as conventional armies. They demonstrate how far warfare has shifted from the framework envisioned by Hobbes and Weber: violence is no longer monopolised, nor is it confined to the pursuit of national interest. It has become a tradable service, embedded in contracts, guided by profit, and deployed at the behest of those who can pay. To understand contemporary war is to recognise that it is fought not only by states but by firms, for whom violence is less a matter of sovereignty than of business.

Wagner, Blackwater, and Beyond

Few developments have altered the landscape of modern warfare more dramatically than the rise of private military companies that function not as irregular bands of mercenaries but as organised, legally incorporated businesses. Among them, Blackwater and Wagner have become synonymous with an industry that has reshaped battlefields from Iraq to Ukraine to Africa. They are not anomalies but emblematic of a global shift: the outsourcing of armed force to corporate actors whose loyalties are determined by contracts, profit, and political alignment rather than citizenship or national service. Examining their trajectories reveals how private companies can alter strategic outcomes, destabilise fragile regions, and test the very concept of state sovereignty.

Blackwater emerged during the height of the United States' "war on terror" as the most visible face of privatised force. Founded in 1997 by Erik Prince, a former Navy SEAL, the company initially pitched itself as a training and security provider. The U.S. invasions of Afghanistan and Iraq transformed it into a giant of the industry. The sheer scale of its deployment was unprecedented: by 2007, tens of thousands of contractors operated in Iraq, many employed by Blackwater, guarding convoys, embassies, and installations. They were, in effect, a parallel army, yet one without the public scrutiny or accountability mechanisms applied to regular troops. Contractors were not counted in official troop numbers, allowing policymakers to sustain large-scale operations without triggering the political backlash that might accompany rising military casualties. Blackwater embodied a new form of war—one in which governments could wage extensive campaigns while minimising domestic costs.

Yet Blackwater's prominence also exposed the risks inherent in outsourcing violence. The 2007 Nisour Square massacre in Baghdad, where Blackwater operatives killed seventeen Iraqi civilians, symbolised the dangers of privatised warfare. The contractors were operating under ambiguous legal status: immune from Iraqi jurisdiction and not clearly accountable under U.S. military law. The incident provoked outrage, undermining U.S. legitimacy in Iraq and highlighting how contractors could act with impunity in volatile environments. It forced a reckoning with the central paradox of PMCs: while they provide states with flexibility and deniability, their lack of clear accountability erodes legitimacy, often at critical political moments. Blackwater eventually rebranded as Xe and later Academi, but the structural reliance on contractors within U.S. operations remained intact. The model had proven too useful to abandon, even if its costs were clear.

Where Blackwater epitomised the Western, corporatised model of private military force, Wagner Group represents its more hybrid, state-entwined counterpart. Officially deniable yet deeply connected to the Kremlin, Wagner emerged in the mid-2010s as a key tool of Russian power projection. Unlike Blackwater, which operated under contracts with Western governments and corporations, Wagner functions as an extension of Russian foreign policy. Its fighters first gained prominence in Ukraine, supporting separatists in Donbas, before deploying to Syria to bolster Bashar al-Assad's regime. Wagner operatives provided not just combat power but strategic depth, often engaging in missions too politically sensitive for Russian regular forces. Their role in Syria included securing oil and gas facilities in exchange for a share of revenues, blending geopolitical objectives with commercial interests in a way that blurred the line between state strategy and corporate profit.

In Africa, Wagner has become an entrenched player in conflicts across the Central African Republic, Libya, Mali, and Sudan. It provides military training, secures strategic assets, and offers direct combat support to embattled regimes. In return, it often receives mining concessions, granting it control over gold and diamond revenues that fund its operations and enrich its leadership. This dual role—stabiliser of regimes and extractor of resources—demonstrates how PMCs can entrench dependency in fragile states. Wagner does not simply rent force; it embeds itself within political economies, shaping the trajectories of states long after the fighting ends. For Moscow, Wagner offers the advantages of plausible deniability: it can project power abroad while avoiding the diplomatic and domestic consequences of official military casualties. For client regimes, Wagner offers survival—security against insurgents, rebels, or even popular uprisings that threaten their hold on power.

The trajectories of Blackwater and Wagner illustrate contrasting models of PMCs, yet both reveal common themes about the commodification of force. Both operate at the intersection of profit and politics, their effectiveness derived from their ability to act where states either cannot or will not deploy regular forces. Both demonstrate how accountability fractures in the privatisation of violence. And both have shifted battlefield dynamics in ways that alter not only tactical outcomes but the broader structure of conflict itself. *PMCs make wars longer, messier, and less accountable, embedding commercial interests into the heart of military operations.*

What is striking is that the influence of these companies extends beyond the conflicts where they are directly employed. They shape the norms of war by normalising the presence of private contractors in combat zones. Once the preserve of states, the provision of security and the execution of military operations have become part of the global marketplace. Other firms—DynCorp, Triple Canopy, and a range of smaller actors—have followed similar paths, though often with less visibility. Collectively, they form an industry worth tens of billions of dollars annually, contracting with states, corporations, and international organisations. The distinction between Blackwater's corporate model and Wagner's quasi-state alignment illustrates the diversity of this industry: PMCs can be both neoliberal businesses competing in open markets and clandestine arms of state strategy.

The consequences of this shift are profound. For weak states, PMCs offer survival but at the cost of sovereignty. A government that contracts Wagner or Blackwater is not asserting control over violence but renting it, outsourcing one of the fundamental attributes of statehood. For strong states, PMCs provide flexibility and deniability, but they also corrode democratic oversight, allowing wars to be fought in the shadows of public debate. For conflict zones, PMCs embed new dynamics of exploitation: their presence often ensures that resources flow outwards to contractors and their patrons rather than to local populations. And for international law, PMCs pose challenges that existing frameworks cannot resolve. They do not fit neatly into the categories of mercenaries or lawful combatants, leaving accountability adrift in legal ambiguity.

The phrase "and beyond" is not ornamental but essential, for Wagner and Blackwater are only the most visible manifestations of a broader phenomenon. Smaller firms proliferate in Latin America, Africa, and the Middle East, providing everything from armed escorts for shipping to intelligence analysis for governments. Cyber contractors and surveillance firms extend the logic further, offering digital rather than physical coercion. The industry continues to evolve, expanding the scope of what violence for hire entails. It is not merely about armed men on battlefields but about the infrastructures of war—data, logistics, and information—sold as services to those who can afford them.

Wagner and Blackwater reveal, in different ways, that the line between soldier and contractor, between state and corporation, has become irretrievably blurred. They are not deviations from the international order but its products: mechanisms through which states and corporations navigate a world where the monopoly of violence is no longer feasible or desirable. By studying their operations, we glimpse the future of conflict—fragmented, commercialised, and increasingly shaped by actors who fight not under flags but under contracts.

Profits vs. Principles

War, once justified by appeals to sovereignty, ideology, or survival, has increasingly become subject to the same calculus that governs commercial contracts. When armed force is delivered by private military companies, its logic shifts: the battlefield is no longer only about political objectives but also about revenue streams. *The profit motive does not simply accompany war; it reshapes its conduct.* This fundamental reordering creates conflicts of interest where the extension of violence, rather than its resolution, becomes the more lucrative outcome. The tension between profit and principle has long existed in politics, but when the very instruments of coercion are commercialised, the balance tilts decisively. Wars fought under such arrangements are less accountable, less transparent, and often longer-lasting, for those providing the muscle have incentives that rarely align with peace.

The American experience in Iraq offers a stark illustration of this dynamic. During the height of the U.S. occupation, contractors outnumbered soldiers in certain theatres of operation. Billions of dollars were funnelled to companies like Blackwater, DynCorp, and KBR to provide security, training, and logistical support. These firms were paid not for delivering political stability but for fulfilling specific contractual obligations:

escorting convoys, guarding compounds, training local police. The longer instability persisted, the more contracts were extended, the more lucrative the enterprise became. Unlike a national military, which at least nominally measures success by the achievement of strategic objectives, contractors measure success by the renewal of contracts and the continuation of demand. A quick resolution to conflict, therefore, may undermine their business model. The result is a structural misalignment: while governments might claim to seek stability, the firms they employ are financially rewarded for its absence.

The same logic is visible in the operations of Russian-linked Wagner Group in Africa. In the Central African Republic, Wagner's role is not confined to protecting the government against rebel groups; it also extends to securing lucrative mining concessions in gold and diamonds. Violence, in this case, becomes a tool for ensuring access to resources that sustain both the company and its patrons in Moscow. The presence of Wagner is not geared toward building strong institutions or long-term stability but toward maintaining a level of controlled chaos in which resource flows can be managed and profits extracted. Peace might strengthen the state and reduce Wagner's indispensability, but a fragmented security environment ensures continued reliance on its services. Here again, *profit incentives bend the trajectory of war away from resolution and toward perpetuation.*

This does not mean that PMCs or their personnel deliberately manufacture instability in every instance. Many contractors are professional, disciplined, and effective in fulfilling their roles. Yet the structural incentives remain misaligned. A firm employed to protect oil infrastructure in Nigeria, for example, benefits from recurring threats that justify long-term contracts. A contractor hired to train an army in Afghanistan profits when reforms are partial and require ongoing "capacity-building." Even humanitarian organisations that employ PMCs to secure convoys in conflict zones contribute to this cycle, for their reliance indirectly sustains an industry that thrives on insecurity. Unlike soldiers bound by national service or ideals of duty, private contractors are bound by corporate imperatives that prioritise continuity of revenue.

The profit motive also complicates accountability. When violence is subcontracted, responsibility is diluted. States can disavow responsibility for the actions of PMCs, framing abuses as contractual lapses rather than political failures. PMCs themselves often operate through complex legal structures, with subsidiaries and shell companies that obscure liability. Victims of abuse face formidable barriers in seeking justice, for the chain of command disappears into contracts, indemnities, and jurisdictional ambiguities. The Nisour Square massacre in Baghdad revealed these dilemmas with chilling clarity. Blackwater operatives opened fire in a crowded square, killing civilians. The U.S. government initially shielded them from Iraqi jurisdiction, and accountability took years to pursue, entangled in legal and political manoeuvres. The massacre was not merely an aberration but a symptom of a system where principles of justice are subordinated to the contractual logic of profit.

Supporters of PMCs often argue that profit can enhance efficiency, incentivising firms to deliver high-quality services at lower cost. There is some merit to this claim. Contractors have provided effective security for diplomatic staff, protected vital infrastructure, and supported peacekeeping operations in environments where overstretched national forces would struggle. Yet efficiency in service delivery is not the same as alignment with political or ethical objectives. An efficiently guarded oilfield does not necessarily translate into broader stability for the surrounding society. A well-trained unit of local police may still serve an authoritarian regime that suppresses dissent. In such cases, efficiency in fulfilling contracts masks a deeper erosion of principles, as profit-driven operations reinforce narrow interests rather than public goods.

The most troubling aspect of the profit-principle divide is its effect on the duration of conflict. Historical examples suggest that wars tend to end when the costs outweigh the benefits for those waging them. In the world of PMCs, however, costs are externalised and benefits privatised. Governments can wage wars without the political costs of conscription or mounting casualties, relying on contractors who bear the risks. PMCs profit from prolonged deployments, while host governments or corporate clients treat their services as operating expenses. The longer the war drags on, the more entrenched the contracts become, and the less incentive there is to push for resolution. Afghanistan again provides a vivid example: billions spent on contractors produced layers of dependency without sustainable outcomes. Contractors withdrew when funding ceased, leaving behind fragile institutions that quickly collapsed. *Profit had sustained the war effort, but it had not built peace.*

Philosophically, the collision between profits and principles reveals the fragility of the state's claim to moral authority in war. The monopoly of violence once carried with it a presumption of legitimacy: states fought in the name of sovereignty, defence, or national interest. The involvement of PMCs erodes that presumption, introducing actors whose motivations are explicitly commercial. When war is conducted as a business, legitimacy becomes harder to claim, and accountability harder to enforce. States continue to justify their actions in the language of principles, but the machinery that executes their wars increasingly operates on the logic of profits. This disjunction undermines public trust and corrodes the notion that war is ever fought for collective ends.

The consequences extend beyond the battlefield. By normalising the profit motive in warfare, states create precedents that ripple across the global security landscape. Non-state actors, from cartels to insurgent groups, adopt similar models, financing violence through smuggling, resource extraction, or protection rackets. The boundary between criminal enterprise and military operation blurs, and the commodification of violence accelerates. In this environment, principles—whether humanitarian, legal, or political—struggle to assert themselves against the relentless calculus of profit. Wars linger not because they cannot be resolved but because too many actors benefit from their continuation.

What emerges is a world where violence has become an industry, and war strategies are shaped less by the pursuit of victory than by the pursuit of revenue. Principles remain in the rhetoric of states and the frameworks of international law, but on the ground, profits dictate incentives, strategies, and outcomes. To understand modern conflict is to confront this tension: wars persist not only because of political deadlock or ideological struggle but because they have become profitable to those who wage them. The challenge is not simply to regulate PMCs or curb abuses but to recognise the structural misalignment between profit and principle at the heart of privatised warfare. Without such recognition, the marketplace of force will continue to generate wars that are longer, murkier, and less accountable, sustained not by necessity but by the dividends they deliver.

The Disappearing Chain of Command

The authority to use force has historically depended on clarity of command. In the modern state system, the chain of command was not just a military principle but a political guarantee, ensuring that soldiers acted under orders traceable to a sovereign authority and therefore subject to accountability. When governments subcontract war to private military companies (PMCs), this clarity evaporates. Contractors may follow instructions from corporate managers rather than military officers, report to boards rather than parliaments, and operate in legal grey zones where international conventions have little reach. *The disappearance of the chain of command does not simply complicate battlefield discipline; it undermines the very architecture of accountability in war.*

The Iraq War provides one of the clearest illustrations of this phenomenon. At its peak, there were more contractors than U.S. soldiers deployed in the country, many employed by firms such as Blackwater, DynCorp, and Triple Canopy. Unlike soldiers in uniform, these contractors were not directly integrated into the military hierarchy. They carried weapons, guarded convoys, and engaged in firefights, yet they did so without being subject to the Uniform Code of Military Justice. When Blackwater operatives killed seventeen civilians in Nisour Square in 2007, the world was forced to confront a disturbing reality: those responsible were not soldiers bound by military law, nor were they civilians accountable under Iraqi jurisdiction. They occupied a space in between, where responsibility was blurred and justice delayed. The result was not an isolated tragedy but an indictment of a system in which force is wielded outside the traditional lines of authority.

This erosion of command is not unique to the United States. Russia's Wagner Group demonstrates how governments exploit the opacity of PMCs for strategic gain. Wagner fighters operate with Russian weapons, training, and logistical support, yet Moscow denies formal responsibility for their actions. In Syria, they supported Bashar al-Assad's regime; in Africa, they secured mines and propped up fragile governments. When Wagner personnel committed abuses, Moscow disavowed involvement, claiming they were private actors. This ambiguity is precisely the point. The Kremlin can direct Wagner operatives informally while avoiding the political costs of acknowledging their presence. For host governments and local populations, however, the result is destabilising. When atrocities occur, who is accountable? The company? The state that armed and directed it? The client regime that contracted its services? The chain of command has dissolved into plausible deniability.

The problem is compounded by international law's inability to adapt. Traditional frameworks, such as the Geneva Conventions, assume a binary distinction between combatants and civilians. PMCs disrupt this distinction. They are armed and engaged in hostilities, but they are employees rather than soldiers, and their contracts may place them outside the scope of conventional military jurisdiction. International conventions on mercenaries are largely ineffective, written in an era when mercenary bands were small and unstructured. Modern PMCs, with corporate registration, legal departments, and lobbying offices, evade these definitions. As a result, contractors who commit abuses often fall into legal limbo. They may be tried years later in domestic courts, but such cases are rare and politically fraught. The very essence of the chain of command—that orders are traceable, responsibility assignable, and law applicable—disintegrates when violence is subcontracted.

The ethical dilemmas run even deeper. Military ethics rest on the principle that force is exercised under legitimate authority. Soldiers are taught to balance obedience with responsibility, to recognise unlawful orders, and to operate within codes that trace back to the state's claim to legitimate violence. Contractors, by contrast, are bound by the terms of employment contracts. Their loyalty is transactional, their discipline enforced by corporate managers rather than commanding officers. The decision to fire on a crowd, to interrogate a detainee, or to protect an asset may be shaped less by rules of engagement than by contractual obligations and corporate liability. This shift does not mean contractors lack professionalism, but it means that the ethical frameworks guiding their actions differ fundamentally from those of state soldiers. *When war is waged by employees rather than servicemen, the moral architecture of command collapses.*

Proponents of PMCs often counter that contractors can be tightly regulated through contracts and oversight mechanisms. Governments can, in theory, embed monitoring clauses, impose penalties for misconduct, and require compliance with national laws. Yet the reality on the ground tells a different story. Oversight is often lax, enforcement inconsistent, and political will limited. In Iraq, U.S. government agencies struggled to even track the number of contractors employed, let alone monitor their actions. In Africa, fragile states that contract PMCs often lack the capacity to regulate them. Even when abuses are documented, the complexities of jurisdiction—whether to prosecute in the contractor's home state, the client state, or the theatre of operations—create significant barriers. Unlike soldiers who answer to courts-martial and military codes, contractors are enmeshed in a web of corporate liability, insurance clauses, and diplomatic protections that rarely lead to swift justice.

The disappearance of the chain of command has strategic consequences as well. Military operations rely on coherence, discipline, and predictability. When multiple actors—state militaries, PMCs, local militias—operate side by side, command structures fragment. Lines of communication blur, orders conflict, and accountability becomes diffuse. In Afghanistan, U.S. forces often struggled to coordinate with contractors providing security for convoys or training local forces. Contractors answered not to field commanders but to corporate managers back in Virginia or Dubai. This fragmentation undermined operational effectiveness and eroded trust among both soldiers and local populations. The state's ability to control its own war effort was compromised, not by enemy action but by its reliance on outsourced force.

Philosophically, the disappearing chain of command calls into question the very legitimacy of contemporary warfare. If the monopoly of violence once gave the state moral authority, then subcontracting violence disperses that authority into the market. Responsibility becomes shared, diluted, and often evaded. Governments benefit from plausible deniability, corporations profit from ongoing contracts, and accountability to law or principle becomes secondary. The result is a world in which violence is no longer clearly tied to political decision-making, but floats in a grey space of commercial relationships and strategic ambiguities. For civilians caught in conflict zones, this means less clarity about who wields force, under what authority, and to what end.

The chain of command once symbolised more than military hierarchy; it embodied the principle that violence was subject to political authority and legal responsibility. Its disappearance marks a profound transformation in how war is fought and justified. By subcontracting war to firms beyond international law, governments undermine the very structures that once legitimised their monopoly on force. What remains is not a vacuum but a marketplace, where accountability is elusive, ethics negotiable, and sovereignty compromised. The dilemmas this creates are not peripheral—they strike at the heart of what it means to wage war in the twenty-first century.

Chapter 3

Proxy Armies in Fragile States

The wars of the twenty-first century are not always fought by states defending borders, but by armed groups operating in the murky spaces where sovereignty is weakest and governance is contested. In fragile states, where governments struggle to control territory, provide security, or command legitimacy, militias, mercenaries, and foreign-backed proxies have stepped into the vacuum. They are not simply temporary stopgaps; they are reordering political authority itself. From the deserts of Mali to the forests of Mozambique, from the battlefields of Yemen to the alleyways of Beirut, armed non-state actors have become arbiters of security, patrons of political order, and vehicles for external powers to extend their influence. The phenomenon of proxy armies is not peripheral—it is central to the way global power is mediated through weak states, where the monopoly of violence is less an ideal to aspire to than a fiction sustained by fragile institutions.

What makes proxy armies in fragile states distinctive is that they do not merely contest governments; they substitute for them. In parts of Africa, local populations often rely more on militias or mercenary forces for protection than on official armies, which are underfunded, corrupt, or predatory. The Wagner Group's presence in countries such as the Central African Republic illustrates this starkly. In return for securing mining concessions and political loyalty, Wagner provides security for regimes that could not survive without them. To citizens living under the threat of rebel groups, Wagner fighters appear more capable than national forces. Yet their loyalty is not to the population, nor even to the government they defend, but to the transactional logic of contracts and concessions. This inversion—where the state becomes the client rather than the guarantor of security—reshapes the very meaning of sovereignty. It is not the flag or the constitution that determines authority, but the presence of armed groups able to impose or maintain order.

Militias, too, are not merely destructive insurgents but political actors that govern in their own right. In many contexts, they deliver services, provide justice, and enforce local authority more effectively than weak states. Hezbollah in Lebanon is a paradigmatic example: it operates schools, hospitals, and welfare programmes while maintaining one of the most formidable non-state militaries in the world. Its legitimacy is derived not only from its military capacity but from the governance functions it performs, often outstripping the Lebanese state in effectiveness. Similarly, in Iraq, militias organised under the Popular Mobilisation Forces (PMF) have become integral to the country's political order, holding parliamentary seats while retaining military strength. These examples underscore a critical point: militias are not simply security actors but hybrid institutions that blur the boundary between state and non-state authority. For many citizens, they are more trustworthy than official governments, not because of ideology alone but because of their practical role in delivering stability, however coercive it may be.

Nowhere is the entanglement of proxy armies more evident than in the Middle East, where regional powers project influence through networks of militias. Iran's sponsorship of groups such as Hezbollah, the Houthis in Yemen, and various Iraqi militias allows it to exert influence across borders without deploying conventional forces. Saudi Arabia, for its part, has backed a range of militias in Yemen and Syria, while Turkey has cultivated its own proxies, from Syrian rebel groups to armed factions in Libya. These arrangements turn local conflicts into regional battlegrounds, where fragile states become the chessboards for larger contests of power. For the populations of these states, the result is protracted conflict with little prospect of resolution, as domestic grievances are subsumed into the strategic rivalries of regional powers. *Proxy warfare is not just a symptom of fragility—it is a mechanism through which fragility is perpetuated and exploited.*

The trend raises profound questions about sovereignty. When governments contract foreign fighters to maintain their rule, as seen in Mali's reliance on Wagner or Sudan's engagement with foreign militias, sovereignty is hollowed out. On paper, these states retain their independence; in practice, their survival is contingent on external actors who can withdraw support at any time. This dependency blurs the line between independent governance and client status. It recalls colonial patterns in which local rulers retained nominal authority while real power resided with external patrons. Yet today's arrangement is not colonialism in the classic sense but a more fluid system of dependency, sustained through contracts, resource concessions, and the circulation of armed groups across borders.

The disappearance of clear distinctions between state and non-state force has implications not only for the conduct of war but for the lived experience of ordinary people. In fragile states, the question of who provides security is often more immediate than abstract debates about legitimacy. For a farmer in northern Mozambique, protection against insurgents may come from a militia rather than the national army. For a community in the Central African Republic, justice may be enforced by a mercenary-backed regime rather than by a functioning judiciary. For displaced families in Yemen, their fate may depend on the shifting fortunes of rival militias backed by Iran or Saudi Arabia. These realities make clear that sovereignty, in practice, is negotiated daily between governments, militias, and external patrons, with citizens left navigating a fragmented security order where loyalty and protection are transactional rather than guaranteed.

The importance of examining proxy armies in fragile states lies not only in documenting their proliferation but in recognising how they redefine the architecture of power. They alter the incentives of governments, who come to depend on external patrons rather than domestic legitimacy. They entrench foreign influence, as regional and global powers use militias as cost-effective instruments of policy. They reshape the meaning of citizenship, as individuals pledge loyalty to groups that provide security rather than to distant, ineffective states. And they challenge the international order itself, which remains premised on the fiction of sovereign equality even as many states function more as clients in a marketplace of force than as independent actors.

This chapter situates proxy armies at the centre of twenty-first-century conflict. By examining Africa's shadow wars, the political role of militias, the proxy networks of the Middle East, and the transformation of sovereignty when the state becomes a client, it illuminates how fragile states are not only victims of proxy warfare but active participants in reshaping the terms of global order. For readers seeking to understand why conflicts persist, why states falter, and why external powers wield such influence, proxy armies provide an indispensable lens. They are not aberrations but the organising principle of warfare in fragile states, where sovereignty is less a shield than a commodity, traded and contested by actors with the will and means to wield force.

Africa's Shadow Wars

The collapse of state authority is not always accompanied by the collapse of order. In much of contemporary Africa, order is reconstituted by mercenaries, militias, and foreign-backed forces who step into the vacuums left by fragile governments. These actors do more than fill temporary gaps in security—they redefine the meaning of sovereignty itself. From Mali to Mozambique, conflicts once framed as domestic insurgencies or regional rebellions have been internationalised through the arrival of foreign fighters, especially mercenaries contracted to prop up regimes in exchange for money, resources, or political leverage. *The continent has become a laboratory for outsourced violence, where the outsourcing of sovereignty is not a last resort but a recurring political strategy.*

Mali illustrates this transformation with brutal clarity. After years of French military intervention failed to neutralise jihadist insurgencies, the Malian government turned to the Russian Wagner Group in 2021. Officially, the arrangement was framed as a security partnership; in practice, it marked a reorientation of Malian sovereignty. Wagner fighters provided combat support, training, and protection for the ruling junta, while securing resource concessions as part of their compensation. For Bamako, Wagner offered what France no longer could: a reliable partner unconstrained by Western human rights concerns. For Moscow, Mali became a foothold in West Africa, a platform to project influence and extract resources. For the Malian people, however, the consequences were darker. Reports of massacres, forced disappearances, and indiscriminate violence followed Wagner's deployment, deepening cycles of resentment and radicalisation. The Malian state retained the appearance of sovereignty, but its survival now depended on a foreign private army with priorities distinct from the public interest.

Further south, Mozambique provides a parallel but distinct case. The insurgency in Cabo Delgado, rooted in grievances over exclusion from natural gas wealth, overwhelmed Mozambican security forces. Facing mounting pressure, the government turned not to regional allies or its own institutions but to private contractors. The South African firm Dyck Advisory Group deployed helicopter gunships to support government forces, while later Rwanda sent regular troops as part of a bilateral arrangement. These interventions stabilised parts of the conflict zone, but they also highlighted the incapacity of the Mozambican state to control its own territory. Outsourced violence brought temporary reprieve, but it reinforced a dependency that compromised sovereignty. In effect,

Mozambique's ability to defend its citizens was delegated to external actors whose commitment was tied to contracts and geopolitical interests, not national solidarity.

The Central African Republic (CAR) has become another epicentre of mercenary politics, where Wagner's influence is woven into the very fabric of governance. Facing relentless rebel advances, President Faustin-Archange Touadéra invited Wagner operatives to bolster his government. In exchange, Wagner secured rights to exploit gold and diamond mines, entrenching a relationship where military protection and resource extraction are inseparable. Wagner personnel not only fight rebels but also provide personal security for political elites, manage propaganda campaigns, and embed themselves in the state's decision-making apparatus. This integration transforms the CAR government into a client regime, sustained not by its own legitimacy or strength but by a foreign private force. The dynamic reveals a critical feature of Africa's shadow wars: *mercenaries do not merely fight battles—they reshape the political economies of fragile states, intertwining security with exploitation.*

These examples are not aberrations; they are symptomatic of a broader structural pattern. Fragile states, by definition, lack the capacity to maintain a monopoly on violence. Their militaries are often poorly trained, underfunded, and plagued by corruption. For leaders facing existential threats, mercenaries offer a survival mechanism. They provide rapid capacity without the slow process of reforming state institutions, and they can be dismissed or disavowed when politically expedient. Yet this convenience carries profound costs. Mercenaries are not accountable to domestic publics, parliaments, or international law in the same way state forces are. Their loyalty is tied to payments, concessions, and external patrons. Sovereignty, in this context, becomes transactional: rulers purchase survival, but the state itself becomes hollowed out, its authority mortgaged to private violence.

Critics argue that mercenaries exacerbate instability rather than resolve it. In Mali, Wagner's brutality has fuelled jihadist recruitment, entrenching a conflict that shows no sign of ending. In the CAR, mercenaries have reportedly committed atrocities that deepen cycles of revenge and rebellion. In Mozambique, reliance on contractors has delayed much-needed reform of national forces, leaving the state vulnerable to future insurgencies. In each case, short-term survival strategies undermine long-term stability. The presence of mercenaries may suppress immediate threats, but it corrodes the state's capacity to govern independently, creating dependencies that are difficult to reverse.

Supporters, however, contend that in contexts where states are collapsing, mercenaries provide a pragmatic solution. They bring technical expertise, discipline, and equipment that local militaries lack. They can achieve rapid tactical successes where international peacekeepers or regional forces are constrained by mandates and bureaucracy. For embattled regimes, survival trumps abstract notions of sovereignty. From this perspective, mercenaries are not undermining sovereignty but preserving it—allowing governments to continue functioning when otherwise they would be toppled. Yet this view sidesteps the deeper issue: sovereignty built on rented violence is sovereignty in name only, a fragile façade maintained by external actors with their own interests.

The proliferation of mercenaries across Africa also reflects wider global dynamics. Great powers exploit fragile states as arenas for competition, using private military companies as proxies. Russia leverages Wagner to expand influence, secure resources, and challenge Western dominance. Western states, while publicly condemning mercenaries, continue to employ private contractors in their own interventions, often blurring the line between critique and complicity. Regional powers, too, engage in this marketplace of force, funding militias or contracting foreign security firms to extend their influence. Africa's shadow wars are thus not isolated crises but part of a global trend in which the outsourcing of violence becomes a tool of geopolitics.

The human cost of these shadow wars is borne by ordinary citizens. For communities caught between insurgents, mercenaries, and fragile governments, the question is not abstract debates about sovereignty but the daily reality of survival. Who provides security? Who controls resources? Who dispenses justice? In many cases, it is not the state but the armed actors who have purchased or seized authority. This dynamic reshapes political allegiances, as populations gravitate toward whichever force provides the most stability, even if that stability is coercive and exploitative. For people in Mali, Mozambique, or the CAR, sovereignty is not a principle enshrined in constitutions or treaties; it is experienced through the barrel of a gun, the presence of armed convoys, and the dictates of those who control force.

Africa's shadow wars reveal not only the fragility of states but the transformation of sovereignty in the twenty-first century. Mercenaries are no longer outliers but structural players in the political order of weak states. They demonstrate how violence has been commodified, how governments outsource their most fundamental function, and how global powers manipulate fragility for strategic gain. To understand the future of war in Africa is to recognise that sovereignty is being renegotiated, not in parliaments or international courts, but in contracts signed with foreign fighters and concessions traded for security. What is at stake is not simply the outcome of particular battles but the very meaning of statehood on a continent where power increasingly resides in the shadows.

Militias as Governance

The conventional distinction between state authority and non-state violence presumes that governments govern while militias disrupt. Yet in many fragile states, militias do not simply challenge governments—they replace them, offering security, services, and political representation that weak states are unable or unwilling to provide. These groups operate in the space between rebellion and institution, wielding the gun not merely as a tool of coercion but as an instrument of governance. *When citizens trust militias more than their official governments, it is not because they romanticise armed groups, but because those groups often deliver what the state cannot: protection, justice, and some semblance of order.*

Lebanon's Hezbollah is perhaps the most emblematic example. Emerging in the 1980s as a resistance movement against Israeli occupation, it evolved into a hybrid actor whose influence extends far beyond the battlefield. It runs schools, hospitals, and social welfare programmes, often serving communities neglected by the Lebanese state. Its fighters are formidable, but its legitimacy is equally rooted in its role as a service provider and political party. For many Shi'a communities, Hezbollah has become a surrogate government, more reliable than the fragile and corrupt institutions of Beirut. This dual identity—as both militia and governance structure—allows it to operate with resilience and popular support, embedding itself deeply into Lebanon's political fabric. Its case underscores how militias gain legitimacy not simply through ideology but through practical governance functions that touch daily lives.

In Iraq, the rise of the Popular Mobilisation Forces (PMF) demonstrates how militias can institutionalise themselves within a state without surrendering autonomy. Originally mobilised to combat the Islamic State, the PMF brought together dozens of armed groups under a semi-official umbrella. Over time, these groups gained not only battlefield credibility but also political influence, securing seats in parliament and shaping government policy. For many Iraqis, particularly in Shia-majority regions, the PMF became a more trusted security provider than the national army, which was discredited by corruption and collapse in the face of ISIS. This trust was not unqualified—the PMF has been accused of sectarian violence and abuses—but its governance role, from distributing aid to providing local security, gave it a base of legitimacy that the Iraqi state struggled to match. Here, militias did not merely compete with the state; they became part of it, blurring the line between non-state and state authority in ways that redefine sovereignty.

Across Africa, militias frequently fill governance vacuums created by state fragility. In Somalia, al-Shabaab has combined insurgency with governance, administering justice through its own courts, collecting taxes, and enforcing social order in areas under its control. Its rule is harsh and coercive, but many communities view its justice system as less corrupt and more predictable than that of the Somali government. Similarly, in eastern Democratic Republic of Congo, a patchwork of militias controls territory, regulates commerce, and dispenses justice. For civilians, allegiance is often pragmatic rather than ideological: trust is extended to whichever group provides protection and stability, even if that protection comes with extortion or coercion. *The state's absence does not create anarchy, but a multiplicity of armed authorities that substitute for governance.*

The legitimacy of militias as governance actors is not confined to fragile states alone. In contexts where state institutions exist but lack credibility, militias can become parallel structures of authority. In Mexico, for instance, so-called self-defence militias have arisen in regions plagued by cartel violence. Some of these groups began as genuine community defence organisations, stepping in where state forces were either absent or complicit. Over time, however, many became entangled in the same criminal networks they sought to resist, blurring the distinction between governance, protection, and predation. What begins as a supplement to state authority can easily morph into an alternative—and sometimes rival—form of governance, challenging the monopoly of the state not only in security but in the provision of social order.

The rise of militias as governance providers raises profound philosophical questions. If the state's legitimacy rests on its claim to provide security and justice, what happens when non-state groups fulfil these functions more effectively? Does legitimacy flow from formal sovereignty, or from practical effectiveness in delivering order? In fragile contexts, citizens often answer with their allegiance: legitimacy belongs to those who protect. This pragmatic approach reframes sovereignty as a lived experience rather than an abstract principle. For a family in Baghdad or Mogadishu, the sovereign is not the flag or constitution but the armed group that secures the neighbourhood and resolves disputes. *Trust follows performance, not legal formality.*

Yet reliance on militias as governance comes with costs. Their accountability is limited, their justice arbitrary, and their authority often exclusionary. Hezbollah's services may benefit its supporters, but they reinforce sectarian divides in Lebanon. Al-Shabaab's courts may be more predictable than state ones, but they impose a rigid ideological order. The PMF may protect Shia communities, but often at the expense of Sunni ones. Governance by militias is rarely impartial or inclusive; it is governance shaped by identity, ideology, and the imperatives of armed struggle. While militias may provide security in the short term, they entrench divisions that weaken the prospects of building inclusive and legitimate state institutions.

From the perspective of international law and political theory, militias as governance actors challenge the very foundations of the modern state system. The Westphalian model assumes that sovereignty resides in recognised governments, and that the state alone has the legitimate authority to wield violence. Militias dismantle this assumption by showing that legitimacy can be earned outside formal structures. They reveal a reality in which sovereignty is fragmented, layered, and contested, not monopolised. The proliferation of militias is not merely a symptom of weak states but a reconfiguration of authority itself, where governance is distributed among competing armed actors.

What makes militias particularly resilient is their capacity to weave themselves into the social and political fabric of the communities they serve. They are not temporary stopgaps but enduring features of the political landscape. They adapt, institutionalise, and often outlast the crises that brought them to prominence. Their resilience forces us to reconsider the nature of governance in fragile states: it is not always about rebuilding central institutions but about navigating a mosaic of actors who govern in practice, if not in law. For policymakers, researchers, and citizens alike, the key insight is that militias are not merely disruptors of order—they are creators of alternative orders, often more effective, if more coercive, than those of failing states.

The phenomenon of militias as governance demonstrates that the state's monopoly on violence is not only eroding but being redefined. These groups reveal how authority in fragile states is decentralised, how trust can migrate away from governments toward armed actors, and how governance itself can be delivered by those outside formal sovereignty. They are not anomalies but central players in the twenty-first-century landscape of power, where the boundaries between war and politics, security and governance, citizen and client are dissolving. To understand the future of conflict, one must grasp this paradox: militias, once seen as the antithesis of governance, have become its substitute.

The Middle East's Proxy Web

The modern Middle East is not defined solely by the armies of nation-states but by sprawling networks of militias that act as extensions of regional powers. These groups are not just local insurgents or community defenders; they are instruments of foreign policy, enabling states like Iran, Saudi Arabia, and Turkey to project influence at a fraction of the cost of conventional war. The result is a complex web of proxy relationships where domestic conflicts are internationalised, sovereignty is hollowed out, and local grievances are entangled in regional rivalries. *The Middle East's proxy wars reveal how power is exercised in an environment where open warfare between states is too costly, yet the appetite for influence remains insatiable.*

Iran has mastered the art of building and sustaining proxy networks, developing what analysts describe as the "Axis of Resistance." Hezbollah in Lebanon stands at the centre of this strategy, having evolved from a guerrilla force into a hybrid actor with parliamentary seats, social services, and one of the most sophisticated non-state militaries in the world. Iran's support—financial, military, and ideological—ensures Hezbollah's loyalty while granting Tehran influence across Lebanon and beyond. In Iraq, Iran cultivated militias within the Popular Mobilisation Forces, enabling it to shape politics in Baghdad while maintaining a deterrent against U.S. presence. In Yemen, Tehran's backing of the Houthi movement allows it to pressure Saudi Arabia directly, threatening critical oil infrastructure and shipping routes. These relationships give Iran asymmetric leverage, enabling it to contest rivals without deploying its own troops. *Through proxies, Iran turns local actors into strategic assets, converting insurgent groups into pillars of regional policy.*

Saudi Arabia's approach to proxy warfare is both reactive and expansive. Determined to counter Iranian influence, Riyadh has funnelled resources into militias and armed factions across the region. Nowhere is this clearer than in Yemen, where Saudi Arabia leads a coalition against the Houthis, backing local militias and military units that serve as counterweights to Iranian-supported forces. Yet Saudi Arabia's involvement has often deepened rather than resolved conflicts. Proxies reliant on Saudi funding have splintered into competing factions, creating fragmented battlegrounds where unity of purpose is elusive. In Syria, Saudi support for rebel groups against the Assad regime was designed to weaken Iran's ally in Damascus, but the multiplicity of factions turned the conflict into a proxy maze with shifting allegiances. Riyadh's reliance on proxies has given it reach, but also exposed the limits of influence when local actors pursue their own agendas rather than serving as disciplined extensions of Saudi policy.

Turkey has emerged as the third major player in the Middle East's proxy web, adopting a more pragmatic and transactional approach than Iran or Saudi Arabia. Ankara's use of Syrian rebel groups as proxies has allowed it to project power in northern Syria, counter Kurdish militias, and secure influence over post-war negotiations. Turkish-backed militias have also been deployed beyond Syria, most notably in Libya, where they were instrumental in supporting the Tripoli government against Khalifa Haftar's forces. Unlike Iran's ideologically aligned proxies or Saudi Arabia's heavily financed militias, Turkey's partners often operate within shorter-term arrangements, motivated by material incentives and battlefield calculations. This flexibility has given Ankara an adaptable, if sometimes unstable, network of allies that extends Turkish influence into conflicts once beyond its immediate periphery.

The use of proxies transforms local conflicts into regional battlegrounds. Yemen's civil war, for example, is not merely a struggle between the Houthis and the internationally recognised government but a proxy confrontation between Iran and Saudi Arabia, with the United Arab Emirates pursuing its own agenda through southern militias. Similarly, Syria's war became a magnet for competing proxy strategies: Iran and Hezbollah bolstered Assad, Saudi Arabia and Turkey armed opposition factions, and Russia used private contractors alongside its military to secure its client regime. In Iraq, militias within the PMF are both local powerbrokers and proxies for Iran, complicating Baghdad's efforts to assert sovereignty. Each of these cases demonstrates how local disputes are rarely contained; they are absorbed into wider contests, prolonging wars and complicating pathways to peace.

The entanglement of proxies reshapes sovereignty in profound ways. Governments in fragile states increasingly find themselves dependent on external patrons for survival. The Assad regime remains in power not simply because of its domestic support but because of Hezbollah fighters, Iranian advisers, and Russian airpower. The Yemeni government, exiled and fragmented, exists largely because of Saudi and Emirati backing. Even relatively stable governments, such as Iraq's, are constrained by the power of militias more loyal to Tehran than to Baghdad. *When states become arenas for proxy struggles, sovereignty ceases to be a shield of independence and becomes instead a prize to be contested and bargained over.*

Proxy warfare also raises difficult questions about accountability. Militias backed by external powers operate in grey zones where international law has little reach. When Iranian-backed groups launch missile strikes on Saudi oil facilities, or when Saudi-supported militias in Yemen commit abuses, responsibility is diffuse and deniable. Proxies allow states to wage war indirectly, avoiding the diplomatic and political costs of open confrontation. Yet this deniability comes at the expense of civilians, who endure the consequences of conflicts prolonged by the flow of external resources. For local populations, the distinction between domestic combatants and foreign proxies is often irrelevant; the violence is indistinguishable, the suffering the same.

What makes the Middle East's proxy web particularly enduring is that it aligns with the strategic calculations of both patrons and clients. For regional powers, proxies are cost-effective tools of influence. They allow Iran to stretch its reach across the Levant, Saudi Arabia to contest its rival on multiple fronts, and Turkey to insert itself into conflicts far beyond its borders. For local militias, external patronage offers resources, weapons, and political leverage they could not obtain alone. These mutual benefits ensure that proxy relationships persist even when they produce instability and prolong wars. The very logic of proxy warfare creates self-sustaining cycles of dependency, where neither patrons nor clients have incentives to disengage.

The Middle East's proxy web is not simply a collection of armed groups; it is a structure of power that redefines regional politics. It explains why conflicts in the region are so protracted, why peace agreements often collapse, and why fragile states struggle to reassert authority. Proxies blur the lines between local and regional, between domestic grievances and international rivalries. They entrench foreign influence while undermining state sovereignty, creating a system in which violence is outsourced, deniability institutionalised, and accountability elusive. To understand the geopolitics of the Middle East today is to recognise that militias are not marginal actors but the connective tissue of regional power struggles, weaving together the ambitions of states and the survival strategies of armed groups into one inseparable web.

When the State Becomes a Client

The image of a sovereign state as the ultimate arbiter of violence—self-reliant, independent, and in control of its own destiny—remains one of the most persistent myths of modern political order. Yet in much of the contemporary world, particularly in fragile or conflict-ridden states, sovereignty has become transactional. Governments, far from exercising autonomy, increasingly behave like clients, purchasing protection and survival from foreign actors who provide armed force in exchange for political influence, resource concessions, or strategic footholds. *When the state becomes a client, sovereignty is no longer a shield of independence but a currency traded in a marketplace of violence.*

The Central African Republic offers perhaps the starkest example of this transformation. Besieged by a patchwork of rebel groups and with its national army too weak to secure territory, the government of President Faustin-Archange Touadéra turned to the Russian Wagner Group. Wagner fighters not only provided battlefield support but also took on critical roles in regime protection and resource extraction. In return for defending Bangui, Wagner secured lucrative contracts in gold and diamond mining, embedding itself in the state's political economy. The arrangement preserved the government in the short term but at the cost of sovereignty: decisions about war, peace, and the distribution of national wealth became deeply influenced, if not dictated, by a foreign private military company operating with Moscow's backing. The state retained the outward symbols of independence—its flag, its president, its seat at the United Nations—but its survival was contingent on the power of outsiders.

This pattern is not confined to Africa. In Afghanistan, successive governments relied on an array of international forces and private contractors to maintain their hold on power. From the NATO mission to the tens of thousands of contractors providing logistics, intelligence, and direct combat support, Kabul's ability to function was inseparable from foreign presence. The collapse of the Afghan state in 2021, following the U.S. withdrawal, underscored the fragility of a sovereignty built on dependency. Afghan leaders had long operated less as autonomous sovereigns than as clients of external patrons, their legitimacy underpinned not by effective governance but by the continuation of foreign sponsorship. The state's collapse was not simply military—it was the exposure of sovereignty as a façade, unmasked once the foreign lifeline was cut.

Mozambique provides another case where the boundaries between sovereignty and dependency blur. Facing a growing Islamist insurgency in Cabo Delgado, the government contracted the services of the South African firm Dyck Advisory Group, which deployed helicopter gunships to repel insurgents. Later, Rwanda sent regular troops in a bilateral arrangement. These interventions stabilised parts of the province but left Mozambique dependent on external actors to secure its most strategic resource-rich territory. The dynamic raises a critical question: can a government that cannot defend its territory without foreign soldiers still be considered sovereign, or has it effectively outsourced its most fundamental responsibility? *In these cases, sovereignty becomes less a principle than a performance—projected outward to the world but hollowed within.*

The logic of clientelism is brutally simple. For fragile regimes, survival trumps all else. Leaders faced with existential threats—whether insurgencies, coups, or rebellion—are incentivised to seek immediate protection, even at the cost of long-term autonomy. For external powers, fragile states offer opportunities: strategic positioning, access to resources, or influence over regional affairs. Private military companies and foreign governments alike capitalise on this demand, offering military solutions that are faster and less encumbered by law than building local capacity. The transaction is mutually beneficial in the short term but corrosive in the long term. Governments remain in office, but their authority is diminished; patrons expand their reach, but stability rarely follows.

One of the most revealing aspects of this dynamic is how it reshapes the very concept of legitimacy. Citizens in fragile states often know that their governments survive not because of popular support or effective governance but because of foreign backing. In Libya, rival governments have each relied on foreign fighters—from Turkish-backed militias in Tripoli to Russian-backed contractors in the east. The result is a hollowed legitimacy where governments rule less by consent and more by the coercive capacity of their patrons. This fosters resentment, undermines national unity, and perpetuates cycles of conflict. Sovereignty becomes a mask that covers dependency, and the citizens recognise the masquerade.

Defenders of these arrangements argue that in contexts of acute fragility, external support is indispensable. Without Wagner, the CAR government might have fallen; without NATO, Kabul would have collapsed years earlier; without Rwandan troops, Cabo Delgado's gas projects might have been permanently lost. In this view, contracting foreign fighters or armies is not the abandonment of sovereignty but its preservation by desperate means. Better to retain a weakened sovereignty than to see the state disintegrate altogether. Yet this argument sidesteps the long-term consequences: dependence creates moral hazard. Governments insulated from the costs of their own failings have little incentive to reform, to strengthen their institutions, or to cultivate genuine legitimacy. Why invest in building a professional army or accountable governance when survival can be purchased from abroad?

The proliferation of state-client relationships also reflects a shift in international norms. During the Cold War, foreign-backed regimes were common, but the patronage was largely ideological, aligned with blocs. Today, the logic is increasingly commercial. Contracts, concessions, and transactional deals drive relationships as much as ideology or strategic alignment. Wagner protects in exchange for mining rights; private firms secure oil installations in exchange for payments; regional powers deploy troops in exchange for influence. Sovereignty is commodified, traded on the open market like any other asset. *The government becomes a buyer, the foreign fighter a seller, and the battlefield the marketplace where the transaction is enforced.*

This commodification of sovereignty has global consequences. It creates opportunities for middle powers to expand their influence far beyond their borders. Russia, through Wagner, has entrenched itself in parts of Africa with minimal direct military commitment. Turkey, by deploying Syrian militias in Libya and Azerbaijan, projects influence without overextending its own forces. Even small states, like Rwanda, have leveraged military deployments into international prestige and economic support. In each case, fragile states act as clients, contracting their sovereignty piece by piece in exchange for protection, and reshaping international order into one where power is distributed not solely by borders but by networks of patronage and dependency.

The deeper danger lies in the erosion of accountability. When governments rely on foreign fighters for survival, their accountability shifts away from their own citizens and toward their external patrons. The social contract—security in exchange for legitimacy—breaks down. Citizens are ruled not by governments answerable to them but by governments answerable to outsiders. In the CAR, abuses committed by Wagner fighters are shielded from scrutiny because the government cannot risk alienating its protectors. In Afghanistan, accountability flowed not to the Afghan public but to Western donors and military allies. In Mozambique, security policy increasingly responds to the concerns of foreign investors and partners rather than to local grievances. In each case, the state becomes less a sovereign entity than an intermediary, balancing between citizens and foreign patrons but beholden more to the latter.

When the state becomes a client, the meaning of sovereignty is transformed. It no longer signifies independence or authority but dependency and vulnerability. It exposes the limits of the Westphalian model, showing that in much of the world sovereignty is negotiable, divisible, and for sale. The façade of sovereignty may endure—the flags still fly, the leaders still address the United Nations—but the substance is hollowed out. What remains is a political order where governments survive by renting violence from abroad, citizens live under authorities who serve external patrons, and the distinction between sovereignty and subjugation becomes dangerously blurred. This is not an anomaly but a growing feature of global politics, one that challenges how we understand the very architecture of international order in the twenty-first century.

Chapter 4

Cyber Mercenaries and Digital Battlefields

The battlefield is no longer confined to the geography of trenches, deserts, and city streets. It now extends invisibly through fibre-optic cables, wireless networks, and the screens we carry in our pockets. Conflicts that once demanded tanks and artillery can now be waged with lines of code. This transformation is not theoretical; it is already shaping the distribution of power across the world. From the disruption of hospitals during ransomware attacks to the sabotage of pipelines and the manipulation of elections, cyber operations have demonstrated that societies can be paralysed not by bombs but by keystrokes. *The weaponisation of cyberspace has created a form of warfare without frontlines, where adversaries may never meet face to face, and where power is exercised through disruption, exposure, and invisibility.*

The rise of cyber warfare signals a profound shift in how we understand both war and security. States have always sought to exploit new technologies for strategic advantage, but cyber capabilities are uniquely destabilising because they are asymmetrical. A small group of skilled hackers can inflict damage on infrastructure and economies disproportionate to their size or resources. The attack on Estonia in 2007, which shut down banks, media outlets, and government systems, demonstrated that a NATO member could be incapacitated without a single shot fired. Similarly, the Stuxnet worm that targeted Iran's nuclear programme revealed how code could penetrate high-security environments and sabotage physical infrastructure. These episodes signalled to both states and non-state actors that cyberspace was not only a new frontier but also one in which traditional measures of power—military budgets, troop numbers, territorial reach—mattered far less than ingenuity, stealth, and technical mastery.

This levelling effect has opened the door to a new breed of actors: cyber mercenaries. Just as private military companies emerged to sell armed force on contract, cyber mercenary firms now sell hacking skills, surveillance technologies, and offensive cyber tools to the highest bidder. Companies such as NSO Group, infamous for its Pegasus spyware, have armed governments and intelligence services with the ability to infiltrate smartphones, track individuals, and extract sensitive information. Unlike conventional arms dealers, these firms operate in a legal grey zone. Their products are not bombs or rifles, but software tools that can be deployed for counterterrorism as easily as for suppressing dissent. The commodification of cyber capabilities has created a global marketplace where authoritarian regimes, fragile states, and even corporations can acquire tools once monopolised by intelligence agencies. *The monopoly of advanced cyber operations, once assumed to belong to a handful of great powers, has been shattered by private firms turning expertise into a tradable commodity.*

The consequences of this shift were made vividly clear in Ukraine. When Russia invaded in 2022, the war unfolded not only on the ground but across digital space. Ukraine mobilised an unprecedented coalition of state-backed cyber units, volunteer hackers, and private sector actors in what has been described as the first large-scale digital front in modern warfare. Hacktivist collectives launched denial-of-service attacks on Russian institutions, while international technology companies provided cyber defences and infrastructure resilience. The conflict revealed the potential of distributed, decentralised cyber armies to alter the course of war, blurring the lines between state and civilian combatants. It also demonstrated how war in the twenty-first century is waged simultaneously in physical and digital realms, with each reinforcing the other. The destruction of infrastructure by bombs was compounded by the disruption of networks; the defence of cities was mirrored by the defence of servers. Ukraine's digital front was not an auxiliary to war but a central theatre in its own right.

Cyberspace, however, differs from conventional battlefields in one crucial respect: it lacks enforceable norms and universally accepted rules. While traditional warfare is constrained by treaties, conventions, and at least nominal accountability, cyber conflict operates in a domain where attribution is uncertain and regulation is almost non-existent. A cyberattack can be routed through multiple countries, executed anonymously, and disguised as criminal rather than political activity. This ambiguity benefits aggressors, who can inflict damage while denying responsibility. It also frustrates victims, who may struggle to justify retaliation without definitive proof of attribution. In such a context, *cyberspace becomes the ultimate deniable battlefield—a theatre of war where the aggressor may never be identified, the attack may never be punished, and the cycle of escalation may proceed unchecked.*

The absence of borders further complicates the picture. Unlike conventional war, where geography delineates the combat zone, cyber conflict transcends territorial boundaries. A hacker in one country can strike infrastructure across continents in seconds, while victims may be spread across dozens of nations simultaneously. This creates challenges for traditional notions of sovereignty. When a ransomware attack cripples hospitals in multiple countries, who is responsible for defence? When surveillance software is sold to multiple clients, how do states regulate or restrain its use? The lack of clear frameworks leaves cyberspace as a battlefield where power is exercised but law lags far behind.

What makes cyber mercenaries especially destabilising is that they thrive on this absence of order. In a world where accountability is elusive, their services are in demand not despite the lack of rules but because of it. Governments contract them precisely because they can operate in the shadows, providing plausible deniability. Authoritarian regimes use them to target dissidents abroad, shielded from scrutiny by the complexity of attribution. Even democratic states have been tempted to exploit such services, blurring the line between legitimate intelligence gathering and unlawful intrusion. The result is a proliferation of actors wielding powerful cyber tools without the constraints that traditionally governed warfare.

This chapter delves into this unsettling landscape. It examines how hackers—both state-backed and freelance—have become weapons of war, capable of paralysing economies and destabilising societies. It traces the rise of cyber mercenary firms that have turned hacking into a business model, profiting from the global demand for digital power. It unpacks the lessons of Ukraine's digital front, where cyber operations became inseparable from conventional battles. And it explores why cyberspace, lacking borders and enforceable rules, has become the ultimate battlefield without accountability. By doing so, it reveals how the commodification of cyber power is reshaping not only the nature of conflict but also the architecture of global security.

To understand the twenty-first century battlefield is to recognise that wars are no longer fought only with bullets and bombs but with code and contracts, in an environment where the most decisive blows may come not from armies marching across borders but from invisible adversaries moving through networks. The cyber battlefield is already here, and its mercenaries are rewriting the rules of war.

Hacking as a Weapon of War

When an oil pipeline can be crippled by a ransomware gang, a power grid switched off by remote code, or a financial system shaken by the theft of billions in digital assets, the nature of war takes on a form that no earlier strategist could have fully anticipated. The capacity to project force has moved beyond the battlefield into the circuitry of societies themselves. Hacking, once associated with rogue individuals in basements and universities, has matured into a tool of geopolitics, wielded by states and non-state actors alike with consequences that rival those of conventional armed force. *To understand hacking as a weapon of war is to recognise that the very systems on which modern life depends—energy, finance, healthcare, governance—are now targets every bit as strategic as airfields or ports.*

The first striking feature of cyber warfare is its asymmetry. Unlike conventional armies, which require vast budgets and logistical depth, hackers can achieve disproportionate impact with relatively small teams and modest resources. The 2017 WannaCry ransomware attack, attributed to North Korean actors, infected over 200,000 computers across 150 countries, disrupting hospitals in the United Kingdom's National Health Service, paralysing companies in Asia, and inflicting an estimated $4 billion in damages. No missiles were launched, no soldiers deployed, yet the disruption was global and immediate. This asymmetry empowers not only smaller states but also non-state actors who would otherwise lack the means to challenge major powers. *The asymmetrical leverage of cyber tools is redrawing the balance of power, enabling those without tanks or fleets to strike at societies dependent on code.*

For states, hacking has become an indispensable extension of intelligence and military policy. Russia's incursions into Ukraine offer one of the clearest examples of coordinated hybrid warfare. Even before the physical invasion in 2022, Russian actors were targeting Ukrainian government networks, critical infrastructure, and communications systems. Malware such as NotPetya, initially unleashed against Ukrainian targets in 2017, spiralled into the most destructive cyberattack in history, causing over $10 billion in global damages. For Moscow, these operations were not mere acts of vandalism but deliberate attempts to weaken the opponent's resilience, sow chaos, and prepare the ground for kinetic force. By contrast, Ukraine's digital resistance demonstrated how cyber capabilities can be mobilised defensively, with volunteer hackers, state agencies, and international tech companies collaborating to repel intrusions and restore functionality. The battlefield in Ukraine highlighted a central reality: hacking is no longer ancillary to war but an integrated front, shaping outcomes alongside tanks and artillery.

China, too, has embraced hacking as a strategic tool, though often with different aims. Rather than spectacular disruption, Chinese cyber operations have frequently prioritised espionage and intellectual property theft. From the compromise of the U.S. Office of Personnel Management in 2015, which exposed data on more than 21 million government employees, to campaigns against private corporations, Beijing's approach reflects a long-term strategy of information dominance. The theft of industrial designs, scientific research, and military technologies accelerates China's rise in key sectors without the costs of innovation or development. The scale of these operations underscores that hacking is not only about sabotage but also about strategic enrichment—warfare conducted through the silent acquisition of knowledge rather than the destruction of infrastructure.

Non-state actors, however, complicate this landscape further. Groups such as Anonymous have demonstrated the capacity of loosely organised collectives to disrupt governments and corporations through denial-of-service attacks and data leaks. More dangerous still are ransomware syndicates, often operating with tacit state approval, that extract billions annually from victims worldwide. These groups blur the line between criminality and geopolitics. When North Korean actors deploy ransomware, is it crime or state policy? When Russian cybercriminals launch attacks against Western targets but are shielded by the Kremlin, are they freelancers or informal proxies? The ambiguity itself is strategically useful, providing states with plausible deniability while reaping the benefits of disruption. *Hacking thrives in this grey zone, where the boundaries between war, espionage, and crime collapse into one another.*

The consequences of hacking extend far beyond immediate disruption. Economies can be shaken by sustained campaigns against their financial systems. In 2016, the Central Bank of Bangladesh lost $81 million after hackers breached the SWIFT financial messaging system. The attackers were never definitively identified, though evidence pointed to North Korea. Such intrusions undermine trust in the global financial architecture, where confidence and stability are as critical as liquidity. Healthcare systems, too, have been targeted, as seen in repeated ransomware attacks against hospitals in Europe and North America. During the COVID-19 pandemic, hospitals treating critical patients were forced to divert ambulances and postpone surgeries because their systems were locked. The weaponisation of hacking against healthcare demonstrates the ruthlessness of this form of warfare: unlike conventional weapons, it strikes indiscriminately at civilians, often in their most vulnerable moments.

Perhaps the most insidious application of hacking lies in its capacity to destabilise societies by manipulating information. Cyber operations need not always destroy; they can also distort. The 2016 U.S. presidential election became emblematic of this approach, with Russian actors hacking and leaking emails, amplifying disinformation through social media, and eroding trust in democratic institutions. The target was not infrastructure but perception, not power grids but public confidence. By shaping narratives and amplifying division, hacking becomes a weapon aimed not at physical assets but at the social fabric itself. *The battlefield in this case is the mind of the citizen, where legitimacy and trust are as fragile as any server or network.*

What distinguishes hacking as a weapon of war from traditional forms of conflict is its invisibility and ambiguity. Attribution is notoriously difficult. A cyberattack may be traced to servers in one country, but those servers may themselves have been hijacked. This opacity allows aggressors to strike without fear of immediate retaliation, knowing victims cannot easily assign blame with certainty. It also complicates deterrence: nuclear weapons are deterred by the promise of retaliation, but how does one retaliate against an anonymous cyberattack? States are left to navigate a world where attacks may come from anywhere, anyone, at any time, and where proportional response is uncertain. This creates a climate of permanent insecurity, a low-level war of all against all that never ends and rarely escalates to open confrontation.

Yet hacking is not purely destructive. It also reveals the interconnectedness of modern societies. The very systems that enable efficiency and globalisation—digital networks, centralised infrastructure, cloud platforms—are the same systems that create vulnerabilities. The attack surface of contemporary civilisation expands with every innovation, from smart cities to the Internet of Things. The paradox is unavoidable: the more connected we become, the more exposed we are. For strategists, this means that hacking is not an exotic or supplementary tool but a central theatre of twenty-first-century warfare. For citizens, it means that the next act of war may not be felt on distant battlefields but in the sudden failure of their hospital, bank, or electricity supply.

Hacking as a weapon of war challenges fundamental assumptions about sovereignty, security, and conflict. It empowers small actors against large states, blurs the lines between crime and warfare, and destabilises societies without firing a shot. It demonstrates that the future of conflict is not only about who controls territory but also about who controls information, networks, and code. In this sense, hacking is both a continuation of war by other means and a radical departure from its past forms. The battlefield has shifted from the visible to the invisible, from the tangible to the digital, from the clash of armies to the silent penetration of systems. And in that shift lies one of the greatest challenges of our time: how to defend societies not just against bombs and bullets but against the unseen adversaries who wage war through the very technologies on which we depend.

The Rise of Cyber Mercenary Firms

When Edward Snowden revealed the extent of U.S. surveillance in 2013, the scandal shifted global awareness of digital espionage. Yet hidden in those revelations was a more unsettling truth: the tools of mass intrusion were no longer the exclusive domain of superpowers. A parallel industry was already emerging—one in which private firms, many headquartered in unassuming office parks and start-up hubs, were developing offensive cyber capabilities for sale to the highest bidder. These companies, sometimes cloaked as legitimate security firms, became the cyber equivalent of mercenaries, offering states and clients the ability to surveil, disrupt, and even paralyse adversaries without the oversight or accountability traditionally imposed on national intelligence agencies. *The rise of cyber mercenary firms marks a fundamental transformation in the economy of warfare: digital intrusion and coercion are now commodities traded in the global marketplace.*

Among the most notorious of these companies is NSO Group, an Israeli firm founded in 2010 that came to international prominence for its flagship spyware, Pegasus. Unlike traditional malware, Pegasus did not require victims to click on malicious links or open suspicious files; it could exploit vulnerabilities silently, installing itself on smartphones and granting the operator access to messages, calls, cameras, and microphones. Investigations revealed that Pegasus was used not only against terrorists and criminals—the ostensible justification for its existence—but also against journalists, human rights activists, political opponents, and even heads of state. Reports tied its deployment to authoritarian governments in the Middle East, Africa, and Asia, where it became an instrument for crushing dissent. The scale of Pegasus's penetration, with thousands of phones allegedly compromised across continents, demonstrated how a single private company could sell surveillance power rivalling that of the world's most sophisticated intelligence agencies. NSO Group became the case study par excellence in how *commodified intrusion erodes the distinction between security and repression.*

Yet NSO is far from unique. Around the world, dozens of firms operate in this shadow market. Some, like FinFisher, Gamma Group, and Hacking Team, have developed interception and intrusion software marketed under the guise of "lawful interception." Hacking Team, an Italian firm, once boasted clients across multiple continents, from European police forces to governments with documented human rights abuses. Its tools allowed remote access to devices, bypassing encryption and surveillance safeguards. When the company itself was hacked in 2015, leaked documents exposed a customer list that included regimes accused of torture and political persecution. The irony was glaring: a firm presenting itself as a partner in law enforcement was revealed to be arming authoritarian governments with digital instruments of coercion. *Such firms operate in the grey zone between legality and criminality, selling products that are lawful in narrow contexts yet routinely abused for political control.*

The economic logic of cyber mercenary firms mirrors that of traditional private military companies. Where PMCs like Blackwater offered states the ability to project physical force without formal military engagement, cyber mercenary firms offer digital power without the political costs of deploying intelligence agencies. A government can purchase spyware or intrusion services through contracts, often routed through intermediaries, leaving minimal traces of direct involvement. This outsourcing not only saves resources but also provides plausible deniability. If exposed, governments can claim ignorance or distance themselves from the activities of private vendors. For the firms themselves, the incentive is clear: demand for offensive cyber capabilities is rising exponentially, and the profit margins are vast. *The commodification of surveillance transforms digital warfare into an industry structured by contracts, profit, and customer relationships, rather than national security doctrine.*

Critics argue that this industry has undermined already fragile efforts to regulate cyberspace. International law lags decades behind technological realities, and there are no binding treaties governing the export of spyware or offensive cyber capabilities. While arms sales are subject to treaties and oversight mechanisms, digital weapons often fall into ambiguous regulatory categories. Some countries, such as Israel, nominally control the export of cyber tools developed domestically, but enforcement has been inconsistent, and geopolitical interests often override ethical considerations. In practice, governments see these firms not merely as private businesses but as extensions of soft power. Israel, for instance, has reportedly used NSO's tools as diplomatic levers, offering Pegasus access to allies as part of strategic partnerships. The sale of spyware thus becomes both a business transaction and a form of international bargaining, blurring the lines between commerce and statecraft.

The dangers are not hypothetical. The use of Pegasus and similar tools has been directly linked to arrests, intimidation, and even killings of journalists and dissidents. In Mexico, investigative journalists probing corruption and organised crime discovered they were targets of Pegasus surveillance. In Saudi Arabia, Pegasus is believed to have been used to track associates of Jamal Khashoggi, the journalist murdered in Istanbul in 2018. Such cases underscore that when surveillance power is sold without accountability, the cost is often borne by civil society. Instead of empowering law enforcement to pursue criminals, these tools empower regimes to pursue critics. The consequences extend beyond individual violations: they corrode public trust in technology itself. If any smartphone could be compromised at any moment, the very tools of modern life—communication, organisation, activism—become potential liabilities. *The rise of cyber mercenaries erodes not only sovereignty but also the social contract that underpins digital life.*

Supporters of these firms counter that the threat of terrorism and organised crime requires extraordinary tools. They argue that without spyware capable of bypassing encryption, governments would be unable to monitor networks used by criminals or terrorists. Encryption, after all, shields not only dissidents but also paedophile rings, drug cartels, and extremist groups. To defenders, spyware is a necessary evil in a world where technology empowers malefactors as much as reformers. This argument has weight, but it elides the central issue: once developed, such tools rarely remain confined to their intended use. The logic of the market ensures that capabilities diffuse to actors willing to pay, regardless of their motives. *The tension between security and abuse lies not in the technology itself but in the unregulated marketplace that delivers it.*

The globalisation of the cyber mercenary industry exacerbates these dilemmas. While NSO, Gamma Group, and Hacking Team have drawn headlines, new firms have emerged in Asia, the Middle East, and Eastern Europe, often with fewer constraints and less public scrutiny. Some operate openly, attending trade shows where spyware and surveillance systems are marketed alongside legitimate security products. Others remain hidden, working through shell companies and shadow intermediaries. The result is a fragmented yet interconnected ecosystem where offensive cyber capabilities circulate globally, much as small arms did in earlier decades. Just as AK-47s fuelled countless conflicts by virtue of their ubiquity and affordability, spyware now risks becoming the digital equivalent: a low-cost, high-impact weapon available to a wide array of actors.

This proliferation raises profound philosophical questions about the nature of sovereignty and violence. If surveillance and intrusion can be purchased from private vendors, does the state still hold a monopoly on legitimate coercion? Or has coercion itself become a service industry, subject to the same dynamics of competition and globalisation as logistics or finance? The outsourcing of digital violence suggests that the architecture of global power is shifting not only away from states but also toward networks of private actors whose accountability is minimal and whose motives are primarily financial. *In this sense, cyber mercenary firms are not anomalies but harbingers of a broader transformation: security and coercion as commodities, detached from the authority of law or the legitimacy of the state.*

The rise of cyber mercenary firms forces us to confront a new kind of battlefield, one in which the decisive actors are not generals or presidents but CEOs and engineers. Their code, written in offices far removed from conflict zones, can determine the fate of dissidents, influence elections, or destabilise economies. Yet these actors operate without the ethical and legal constraints imposed on traditional militaries or intelligence services. They are accountable not to citizens or parliaments but to shareholders and clients. The implications are stark: the outsourcing of digital power threatens to dissolve the already thin boundaries between war, crime, and commerce, leaving societies exposed to forces beyond democratic control.

Case Study: Ukraine's Digital Front

When Russian tanks rolled across Ukraine's borders in February 2022, the world expected the battle to be decided by artillery, drones, and infantry. Few anticipated that one of the most decisive theatres of conflict would be invisible: a digital front where hackers, programmers, and cyber units fought to shape the flow of information, cripple infrastructure, and test the future of warfare. For the first time in history, a large-scale interstate war was conducted not only with missiles and battalions but also with code, servers, and networks. The war in Ukraine revealed how cyberspace is no longer an adjunct to traditional combat but a battlefield in its own right, one where civilians, volunteers, and state-backed hackers play roles as consequential as soldiers on the ground. *The Ukraine conflict turned cyberspace from a metaphorical battlefield into a literal one.*

Even before the invasion, Ukraine had been a laboratory for Russian cyber aggression. The attacks on Ukraine's power grid in 2015 and 2016, widely attributed to Russian actors, were the first known instances of hackers shutting down an entire nation's electricity supply. The malware responsible, known as BlackEnergy and later Industroyer, demonstrated the capacity of state-linked hackers to target industrial control systems and disrupt civilian life. These episodes foreshadowed the tactics Russia would employ in 2022: cyber operations aimed not only at gathering intelligence but also at breaking public morale by undermining the very infrastructure on which modern societies depend. The precedent was clear: cyberspace offered a means of coercion without tanks crossing borders. In Ukraine, however, Russia's attempt to replicate this playbook encountered a new and unanticipated force—an international coalition of digital defenders.

At the outbreak of war, Ukrainian officials made a remarkable appeal: they called on civilian hackers around the world to join a volunteer "IT Army." This was not a clandestine initiative but an open mobilisation of coders, penetration testers, and security researchers, organised through public channels like Telegram. Tens of thousands reportedly joined, coordinating distributed denial-of-service (DDoS) attacks against Russian websites, defacing propaganda platforms, and gathering intelligence on troop movements from intercepted communications. While many of these volunteers lacked the sophistication of state-backed units, the sheer volume of activity overwhelmed Russian digital defences. *Ukraine's IT Army blurred the line between civilian activism and military engagement, enlisting global digital labour into a national defence strategy.*

This mobilisation was not one-sided. Russia deployed a range of cyber capabilities, from wiper malware like HermeticWiper designed to destroy data on Ukrainian networks, to phishing campaigns targeting government officials, to the disruption of satellite communications. Perhaps the most striking example came in the early days of the invasion, when Russian actors disabled thousands of Viasat satellite modems across Europe, interrupting communications far beyond Ukraine's borders. This incident underscored how cyber warfare, unlike conventional strikes, rarely respects geographic boundaries. A single attack intended to disable Ukrainian command-and-control networks rippled across multiple NATO countries, disrupting wind farms in Germany and critical services elsewhere. *The Viasat incident revealed the porous nature of cyberspace: an attack on one nation can instantaneously cascade into unintended global consequences.*

Yet what distinguished Ukraine's digital front was not simply the scale of Russian attacks but the resilience of Ukrainian defence. This resilience was the product of years of preparation, international partnerships, and rapid improvisation. Western technology companies, from Microsoft to Google to Amazon, played an unprecedented role, providing cyber threat intelligence, cloud migration support, and defensive infrastructure. Microsoft's security teams, for example, tracked Russian malware campaigns in real time and issued countermeasures to blunt their effects. Amazon Web Services facilitated the migration of Ukrainian government data to the cloud, ensuring that critical records could not be destroyed by missile strikes or cyber sabotage. In effect, multinational corporations became actors in the war, defending Ukraine's digital sovereignty in ways that governments alone could not. *The Ukraine conflict demonstrated that in cyberspace, corporate power is military power.*

Equally significant was the role of open-source intelligence (OSINT) communities. Volunteers around the world mined satellite images, TikTok videos, and intercepted radio chatter to track Russian troop movements, geolocate attacks, and debunk disinformation. These networks of amateurs and semi-professionals created an information ecosystem that rivalled the capabilities of traditional intelligence agencies. Social media became not merely a platform for propaganda but a weapon of verification, where false claims were rapidly scrutinised and corrected by online communities. This phenomenon highlighted a profound shift: information dominance in modern war is no longer the monopoly of states. Civilian networks, harnessing digital tools and platforms, can contest and shape narratives on a global scale.

The information war was as fierce as the technical one. Russia unleashed a torrent of disinformation, seeking to demoralise Ukrainians, fracture Western unity, and present its invasion as defensive rather than imperial. Deepfake videos, including one purporting to show President Zelensky urging Ukrainians to surrender, circulated online. These efforts were largely unsuccessful, in part because Ukrainian officials became adept at rapid, authentic communication. Zelensky himself, through his nightly video addresses recorded in wartime Kyiv, became the face of digital resistance, countering Russian propaganda with raw immediacy. This asymmetry—an authoritarian regime relying on deception and a democratic state leveraging transparency—illustrated how political legitimacy itself is contested in the digital domain. *Authenticity emerged as a weapon, capable of outmanoeuvring even the most sophisticated disinformation campaigns.*

From a strategic perspective, Ukraine's digital front offers three critical lessons. First, cyber warfare is not a substitute for conventional force but a complement to it. Russia's inability to decisively paralyse Ukraine's infrastructure revealed that cyber operations alone cannot secure battlefield victories. Yet their capacity to sow chaos, delay responses, and erode trust makes them indispensable tools in modern conflict. Second, the participation of civilians, corporations, and volunteers has eroded the boundary between combatants and non-combatants. This complicates international law, which assumes clear distinctions between soldiers and civilians. In Ukraine, a software engineer in Canada launching a DDoS attack against a Russian bank is arguably participating in hostilities. Does that make them a lawful target? The law has no clear answers. Finally, the conflict underscores that resilience in cyberspace is as much about adaptability as about firewalls or encryption. Ukraine's success lay not in preventing all intrusions but in rapidly recovering, adapting, and mobilising external support.

Critically, Ukraine's digital front is not an isolated case but a template for future wars. The mobilisation of volunteer hackers, the involvement of private corporations, and the integration of cyber and kinetic operations will likely recur in conflicts where state capacity is uneven. For smaller states, the lesson is that cyber resilience requires not only technical preparation but also the cultivation of networks—diasporas, corporations, and international communities—that can be activated in times of crisis. For major powers, the war raises uncomfortable questions: if cyberspace is open to all actors, what limits, if any, can be imposed on participation? And how does one deter cyber aggression when attribution remains contested and the actors range from state-backed units to teenage volunteers?

The war in Ukraine has shown that the digital front is not ancillary but central to modern conflict. Hackers and volunteers wield influence comparable to artillery brigades, and multinational corporations hold defensive capabilities that rival national cyber commands. Cyberspace has become the new terrain of sovereignty, where legitimacy, resilience, and trust are as decisive as weapons and logistics. *Ukraine's digital front will be remembered not only as the first large-scale cyber war but as the moment when the very definition of warfare expanded to include the vast, borderless domain of the networked world.*

No Borders, No Rules

Few domains of human interaction are as essential yet as lawless as cyberspace. Unlike land, sea, or air—each bound by centuries of treaties, customs, and sovereign claims—the digital world remains an unregulated frontier. There are no universally recognised borders in cyberspace, no neutral zones, no demilitarised areas. Data packets travel across jurisdictions in milliseconds, unimpeded by geography. This makes the internet the ultimate enabler of cross-border activity, but also the perfect terrain for conflict without accountability. When hackers disable a hospital's systems or infiltrate a nation's electoral infrastructure, the question of who is responsible, and under what jurisdiction they fall, often has no clear answer. *Cyberspace has created a condition of permanent strategic ambiguity, where actions can be devastating yet remain unattributed, and where states can plausibly deny their involvement even when the evidence points directly to them.*

The absence of enforceable norms is not for lack of effort. Since the early 2000s, governments and multilateral organisations have attempted to create frameworks for regulating cyber behaviour. The Tallinn Manual, developed under NATO auspices, sought to apply existing international law to cyberspace, outlining principles of sovereignty, proportionality, and neutrality. The United Nations Group of Governmental Experts (UNGGE) worked on voluntary norms, such as refraining from targeting critical infrastructure in peacetime. Yet these initiatives have lacked binding force. They are guidelines rather than enforceable treaties, and states treat them as such—useful when convenient, ignorable when not. *The critical weakness lies in enforcement: cyberspace has no equivalent to the Geneva Conventions backed by courts, inspectors, and sanctions.* Without enforceability, norms in cyberspace are aspirational, not operational.

The logic of sovereignty collapses when applied to a domain designed to route around control. A missile fired across a border is a visible act, traceable to its origin, and attributable to a state. A malware infection, however, may pass through dozens of servers in neutral countries, use compromised machines in third-party networks, and mask its coding signatures to resemble those of another group entirely. Attribution in cyberspace is not only technically challenging but politically contested. For example, the WannaCry ransomware attack of 2017, which crippled systems in more than 150 countries, was attributed by the United States and others to North Korea. But Pyongyang denied responsibility, and many nations declined to join in publicly blaming them. In this ambiguity lies opportunity: states can use hackers as proxies, achieving strategic objectives while preserving deniability. *The fog of war in cyberspace is not the confusion of battle but the deliberate engineering of uncertainty.*

The consequences of this legal vacuum are profound. In the absence of binding rules, states have adopted a doctrine of persistent engagement—intervening in adversaries' networks on a continuous basis, not only for defence but to shape the environment pre-emptively. The United States Cyber Command openly speaks of "defending forward," meaning it seeks to disrupt threats at their source, often inside foreign networks. Russia, meanwhile, views cyber operations as tools of hybrid warfare, integrated with disinformation campaigns and military manoeuvres. China employs cyber espionage on an industrial scale, stealing intellectual property to accelerate its economic and military rise. Each of these approaches reflects a recognition that cyberspace rewards offence over defence. Firewalls can be bypassed, patches delayed, insiders corrupted. Offence, by contrast, requires only one vulnerability. *Without enforceable norms, the advantage tilts decisively toward the attacker, incentivising states to strike rather than restrain themselves.*

Non-state actors thrive in this environment. Criminal syndicates deploy ransomware to extort millions from companies and municipalities, often enjoying implicit protection from host governments. Groups like REvil or Conti operate in the grey zone between crime and geopolitics, at times serving state interests, at times pursuing purely financial gain. Terrorist organisations exploit encrypted platforms for recruitment and fundraising. Hacktivist groups launch politically motivated campaigns that blur the line between activism and sabotage. The proliferation of tools once confined to intelligence agencies—zero-day exploits, spyware, and botnets—has democratised the ability to wage offensive cyber operations. A teenager with the right toolkit can paralyse a small business; a motivated collective can disrupt elections. In cyberspace, *power is cheap, anonymity is abundant, and accountability is almost non-existent.*

The Ukraine conflict has thrown this reality into stark relief. As Russian forces advanced, cyberattacks targeted Ukrainian government websites, financial institutions, and energy grids. At the same time, pro-Ukrainian hacktivists launched attacks against Russian propaganda outlets and state banks. The digital battlefield was global: volunteers from countries far removed from the conflict joined the fray, often coordinating through Telegram channels. No international mechanism existed to regulate their participation, to determine whether such volunteers were legitimate combatants, or to restrain them from targeting civilian infrastructure. The same lack of enforceable rules that allows humanitarian digital volunteers to counter propaganda also allows ransomware groups to attack hospitals. Cyberspace does not distinguish between noble and malicious intent—it merely transmits code.

This lack of regulation contrasts sharply with the long history of arms control in other domains. Nuclear weapons, chemical agents, and landmines are all subject to treaties precisely because their unrestrained use posed catastrophic risks. In cyberspace, however, states have been reluctant to tie their own hands. The incentives point in the opposite direction: every nation wants the freedom to conduct surveillance, gather intelligence, and hold offensive capabilities in reserve. Efforts to impose binding norms have faltered because no great power is willing to submit to inspections or constraints that would limit its digital arsenal. The paradox is evident: all states are vulnerable to cyberattacks, yet none will commit to meaningful restraint for fear of losing the strategic advantages afforded by ambiguity.

The absence of enforceable rules also undermines deterrence. In traditional warfare, deterrence relies on clarity: a strike invites retaliation, a red line defines unacceptable behaviour. In cyberspace, retaliation is difficult because attribution is contested, and red lines are blurry. Does hacking a hospital constitute a war crime? What about interfering in an election through disinformation? The lack of agreed standards means that each incident becomes a case-by-case political decision, filtered through the lenses of plausible deniability and geopolitical interest. This uncertainty emboldens actors: if punishment is inconsistent, the risk of engaging in aggression diminishes. *The digital battlefield thus operates on a principle closer to piracy than to warfare: strikes occur wherever there is opportunity, restrained only by the prospect of retaliation, not by law.*

One might argue that the flexibility of cyberspace makes rigid treaties impractical. Technology evolves too rapidly, vulnerabilities shift too often, and the actors involved are too diverse for static rules to remain effective. Yet this argument risks becoming a self-fulfilling prophecy. By assuming that rules are impossible, states guarantee that none will emerge. The alternative is to pursue incremental norms, akin to the early conventions on maritime conduct that preceded full-fledged naval treaties. Prohibitions on targeting hospitals, electrical grids, or election systems could serve as starting points. Even if imperfectly enforced, they would create expectations of behaviour, against which violations could be judged. *Norms, however fragile, shape conduct over time by establishing the boundaries of legitimacy.*

Cyberspace's defining characteristics—speed, anonymity, borderlessness—ensure that it will remain the most challenging domain for governance. Yet the absence of rules is not a neutral condition. It actively shapes behaviour, rewarding the offensive, emboldening the reckless, and leaving civilians exposed. The more interconnected societies become, the greater the incentives for malicious actors to exploit that interdependence. If no rules are agreed upon, cyberspace will continue to evolve as a domain where the strong prey on the weak, where responsibility is diffused, and where accountability evaporates the moment data crosses a border. *It is not the absence of borders alone that defines cyberspace as the ultimate battlefield, but the absence of rules that give those borders meaning.*

Chapter 5

Algorithms at War

For centuries, the technologies of war have been extensions of human will: the spear, the cannon, the fighter jet, and the missile all magnified the soldier's reach but left the responsibility squarely in human hands. The arrival of artificial intelligence challenges this foundational relationship. What once was an instrument to be wielded is now becoming a decision-maker in its own right, shaping not only how battles are fought but how choices about life and death are made. *Algorithms are no longer confined to machines—they are increasingly the invisible actors that filter intelligence, recommend strategies, and, in some cases, decide when and where to strike.* This transition marks a profound shift in the philosophy and practice of conflict: the move from tools of war to thinking systems at war.

The trajectory began with drones, which redefined surveillance and targeted killing by separating the operator from the battlefield. At first glance, drones seemed merely to extend precision, offering commanders the ability to strike without exposing pilots to risk. But as the volume of data from drone feeds grew, human analysts could not keep pace. Machine vision systems were introduced to identify targets, track movement, and flag anomalies. The handover of tasks from human operators to algorithms was incremental, almost invisible. Yet the implications are dramatic: once machines prove better at recognising patterns, humans inevitably defer to them, not only for efficiency but also for credibility. *When algorithms outperform soldiers in perception and calculation, the question is no longer whether humans should remain in control, but whether they still can.*

The battlefield is not the only theatre where algorithms exert influence. Politics, media, and information warfare have been transformed by artificial intelligence's capacity to manipulate perception. Deepfake technology, for instance, can fabricate speeches, simulate leaders' voices, or create convincing videos of events that never occurred. These tools threaten the foundations of trust on which governance and diplomacy rest. In an age when a fabricated clip can circulate globally within minutes, discrediting evidence or destabilising elections, *the fog of war is no longer confined to combat zones but extends into living rooms, newsfeeds, and parliaments.* The weaponisation of AI-generated deception ensures that information dominance—once about broadcasting power—is now about shaping what can be believed at all.

The debates surrounding lethal autonomous weapons systems, colloquially referred to as "killer robots," expose the tension between technological capability and ethical restraint. Nations such as the United States, China, and Russia invest heavily in research that could allow machines to select and engage targets without human intervention. Proponents argue that such systems could reduce collateral damage by removing human error, fatigue, and emotion from battlefield decisions. Critics counter that delegating the power to kill to machines erodes fundamental principles of humanity in war, undermines accountability, and risks unanticipated escalation. Unlike nuclear weapons, where treaties and deterrence established a fragile balance, autonomous weapons lack a global framework. Discussions at the United Nations have stalled, as states hedge their bets and refuse binding commitments. The absence of consensus leaves the field open to rapid deployment, potentially normalising machine-led killing before society has agreed on its legitimacy.

What is most striking about AI in warfare is that its influence often precedes conscious acknowledgement. Algorithms shape logistics chains, prioritise supply deliveries, and recommend troop deployments. They calculate missile trajectories, anticipate enemy moves, and scan oceans of intercepted communications for patterns invisible to human eyes. These processes are not secondary; they become decisive. *Code operates as an invisible hand guiding outcomes, distributing attention, and framing what commanders perceive as possible.* In this sense, AI is not simply a set of tools but an actor that redefines responsibility. When a recommendation generated by an algorithm leads to a military strike, who bears responsibility if the intelligence was flawed—the programmer, the commander, or the machine itself? The law of armed conflict was not written to contend with responsibility dispersed across human and non-human actors.

This chapter confronts these questions directly, weaving together the progression from drones to decision-making AI, the corrosion of trust by deepfakes, the ethical quagmire of autonomous weapons, and the philosophical transformation brought about by code's invisible governance. It asks what it means for warfare when decision-making itself becomes partially outsourced to algorithms, when perception can no longer be trusted, and when accountability dissolves into lines of code. These are not speculative dilemmas confined to distant futures; they are present realities unfolding on battlefields and in political systems today. *To grasp how warfare is being remade, one must understand not only the machines but the logics that guide them—the algorithms at war that increasingly decide how power is exercised, by whom, and with what consequence.*

From Drones to Decision-Making AI

The first Predator drone strike, carried out by the United States in Afghanistan in late 2001, seemed at the time like a technological marvel: a pilot sitting thousands of miles away in Nevada directed a missile onto a convoy with remarkable accuracy. What was not fully appreciated then was that this event marked the beginning of a transformation in the relationship between humans, machines, and warfare. The drone was more than just another aircraft—it embodied a new kind of distance, not just spatial but cognitive. It separated the soldier from the risks of combat, introduced a different psychology of killing, and produced unprecedented volumes of data that required machines to interpret. Over the following two decades, that data deluge would lay the groundwork for a profound transition: from humans directing machines to algorithms shaping decisions that determine the course of battle.

The drone revolution initially unfolded under the promise of precision. Advocates claimed that unmanned aerial vehicles (UAVs) reduced civilian casualties, eliminated high-value targets, and provided persistent surveillance impossible with manned flights. Yet the reliance on these systems exposed an overlooked reality: the feeds generated by fleets of drones were unmanageable by human operators. Hours of surveillance video, intercepted communications, and metadata from multiple sensors created an analytical bottleneck. Intelligence analysts, overwhelmed by the sheer scale of information, began to rely on machine learning systems to filter, categorise, and prioritise threats. *The transition was gradual but decisive: as the machines proved better at pattern recognition than their human counterparts, the algorithms began to set the tempo of decision-making rather than merely support it.*

One striking example emerged during counterinsurgency campaigns in Iraq and Afghanistan. Algorithms trained on historical insurgent behaviour began to flag suspicious activity—such as repeated visits to known meeting points, sudden changes in traffic patterns, or the clustering of mobile phone signals in areas with prior attacks. Commanders often found themselves relying more on the algorithmic assessment than on human intuition, especially when the systems outperformed soldiers in predicting where improvised explosive devices (IEDs) might be placed. *Trust migrated silently from the human to the machine, reshaping the chain of command from one of human judgement supported by tools to one of human decision ratified by algorithms.*

This migration has far-reaching consequences. First, it accelerates the tempo of warfare. Where human analysis might take hours, algorithms can process terabytes of sensor data in seconds, delivering recommendations that demand immediate action. The danger is not only that humans may defer to machines but that they may be compelled to do so simply to keep pace with adversaries who are also relying on AI-driven systems. Military theorists call this "hyperwar": a battlespace in which decisions unfold at machine speed, too fast for human oversight. If one side hesitates for deliberation, it risks falling fatally behind. The result is an environment in which the imperative to respond eclipses the space for reflection, negotiation, or restraint.

Second, the shift raises difficult questions of responsibility. In traditional warfare, accountability could be traced up the chain of command: soldiers follow orders, officers give commands, and political leaders bear ultimate responsibility. When an algorithm recommends a strike that results in civilian casualties, responsibility becomes diffuse. Did the failure lie with the programmers who trained the model, the commanders who authorised the action, or the machine that identified the target? This ambiguity undermines long-standing principles of international humanitarian law, which presuppose a clear line of accountability from action to actor. *When the actor is a set of lines of code, the entire legal and ethical framework of war begins to fray.*

The evolution from drones to decision-making AI is not uniform across nations, but the trajectory is unmistakable. The United States, for instance, has invested in Project Maven, which applies machine learning to drone footage to accelerate target identification. China, meanwhile, integrates AI across its military doctrine, emphasising what it calls "intelligentised warfare"—an approach that sees AI as central to planning, logistics, and command. Russia has showcased autonomous drones capable of swarming behaviour, where hundreds of small UAVs coordinate without direct human input to overwhelm defences. Even smaller states are experimenting with off-the-shelf AI for reconnaissance and tactical decision support, narrowing the gap between major powers and less resourced militaries. In all cases, the direction of travel is the same: from human-centred control toward machine-centred orchestration.

Critics argue that such reliance risks strategic instability. Algorithms can be brittle, misclassifying objects under novel conditions or misinterpreting benign behaviour as hostile. A pattern-recognition system trained in one environment may falter in another, especially in complex urban settings. A misidentified target in a fast-paced conflict could trigger escalation before humans have time to intervene. During the Cold War, close calls in nuclear command systems were defused by human judgement—operators choosing to question machine warnings. In a future battlefield dominated by AI, the space for such doubt may vanish, replaced by an algorithmic imperative that pushes towards action.

Yet it would be misleading to portray the rise of decision-making AI as an inevitable surrender of human agency. Military institutions are experimenting with "human-in-the-loop" safeguards, requiring human authorisation before lethal actions are carried out. Some argue for "human-on-the-loop" systems, where humans supervise but do not directly control algorithmic decisions. Others fear that in high-pressure combat situations, these safeguards will erode, as commanders prioritise speed over deliberation. The balance between efficiency and accountability, between speed and ethical oversight, remains unsettled. *The dilemma is stark: to slow down is to risk defeat, but to cede control is to risk catastrophe.*

Beyond the battlefield, decision-making AI reshapes geopolitics itself. States that master algorithmic command systems gain a multiplier effect, enabling smaller forces to act with the precision and coordination of larger ones. Non-state actors, meanwhile, gain access to commercial AI tools that allow them to simulate similar capabilities at lower scale. The democratisation of algorithmic warfare blurs the distinction between great powers and insurgents, between the organised military and the enterprising militant group. This diffusion of capability destabilises traditional balances of power and multiplies the number of actors able to influence conflict far beyond their size.

Ultimately, the progression from drones to decision-making AI illustrates a fundamental transformation: warfare is no longer just about machines that extend human force but about systems that reshape human choice. The speed, scale, and autonomy of AI-driven systems alter the rhythm of war, the meaning of command, and the locus of responsibility. These are not theoretical shifts confined to laboratories or future scenarios; they are already evident in military operations across the globe. *To understand the wars of tomorrow, one must grapple with this present reality: algorithms are no longer merely instruments of war but participants in it, accelerating conflict while simultaneously eroding the structures that once ensured human accountability.*

Deepfakes and Disinformation

In 2018, a video of former US President Barack Obama appeared online in which he seemed to call his successor "a total and complete dipshit." It was later revealed to be a deepfake—an AI-generated imitation produced to demonstrate the dangers of synthetic media. While at first glance humorous, the video marked a watershed moment: the threshold had been crossed where anyone, anywhere, could fabricate a convincing piece of political speech that never happened. What once required Hollywood studios and vast resources could now be created on a consumer laptop. The implications were immediate and chilling. Trust in the authenticity of digital information, already eroded by the glut of online misinformation, now faced an existential challenge. *If seeing is no longer believing, then the entire fabric of political communication, electoral integrity, and battlefield intelligence is destabilised.*

The term "deepfake" is shorthand for deep-learning fakes, a technology that harnesses neural networks to generate synthetic but realistic video, audio, or images. Initially confined to niche communities, it rapidly spread across platforms as both a tool for entertainment and a weapon for manipulation. In politics, the potential is devastating. Imagine a fabricated video of a presidential candidate confessing to corruption surfacing days before an election, timed to evade fact-checking before polls close. Or a synthetic audio clip of a military leader issuing a false surrender order broadcast into enemy channels. Both scenarios have moved from theoretical speculation to practical possibility. *The danger lies not only in the successful use of such fabrications but also in their mere plausibility: once people know deepfakes exist, even authentic material can be dismissed as fake, creating what scholars call the "liar's dividend."*

Nowhere is this risk more acute than in elections. In 2020, during municipal elections in India, deepfake videos were circulated showing a prominent politician speaking fluently in dialects he did not know, making it appear as though he was addressing different communities in their native tongues. While this was ostensibly used for campaign outreach rather than slander, it demonstrated the potential for personalised disinformation at scale—messages crafted to manipulate specific audiences with hyper-local precision. By contrast, in the United States and Europe, the greatest fear is less about volume than about timing: a strategically released deepfake could sway a tightly contested race, while the mechanisms of verification—fact-checkers, journalists, independent commissions—struggle to keep pace with the viral speed of digital misinformation.

The battlefield, too, has become a target. During the early stages of Russia's 2022 invasion of Ukraine, a poorly executed deepfake video emerged online showing Ukrainian President Volodymyr Zelenskyy urging his troops to lay down their arms. Though crude and quickly debunked, the attempt revealed how adversaries now view synthetic media as a component of psychological warfare. The mere appearance of such a video, even if implausible, can plant seeds of doubt, sow confusion, and force governments to divert resources to rapid response and clarification. As technology improves, future iterations will be more convincing, and the line between digital sabotage and traditional propaganda will blur to invisibility.

What distinguishes deepfakes from earlier forms of propaganda is their *granularity*. Classic disinformation often relied on distortion of facts or selective framing; deepfakes go further by fabricating sensory evidence itself. This makes them extraordinarily persuasive, as they bypass rational scrutiny and exploit the brain's innate tendency to trust what it sees and hears. Cognitive scientists note that humans evolved to rely on visual and auditory cues as reliable anchors of reality. Deepfakes weaponise this trust, creating a cognitive dissonance that is difficult to resolve even when one knows intellectually that the material is fake. *It is not merely about convincing the public of falsehoods but about destabilising their confidence in the very possibility of truth.*

This corrosion of trust carries strategic implications beyond elections and propaganda campaigns. In international diplomacy, where much depends on credibility, the risk of synthetic fabrications is immense. Imagine a deepfake video showing a government official making inflammatory remarks about a rival nation, released just before sensitive negotiations. Even if later debunked, the damage could already be done, hardening positions and fuelling escalation. Similarly, in conflict zones, deepfakes could be deployed to undermine alliances, discredit local leaders, or provoke reprisals. In such contexts, the problem is not only the falsehood itself but the collapse of confidence in any information channel. When no source can be trusted, the battlefield becomes not only physical but epistemological.

The technology is evolving at alarming speed. Early deepfakes were detectable by digital artefacts—unnatural blinking, mismatched lighting, distorted voices. Today's models, trained on massive datasets and refined through adversarial learning, can produce outputs virtually indistinguishable from reality. Detection methods exist, but they are locked in a perpetual arms race: as soon as one forensic technique is developed, new generation models circumvent it. Governments and tech companies invest heavily in detection tools, yet their effectiveness remains limited, especially given the speed and virality of online distribution. A fake needs only hours to do irreparable damage; verification often lags days behind. *The asymmetry favours the attacker: generating doubt is easier, faster, and cheaper than restoring trust.*

The ethical dilemmas posed by deepfakes extend to the role of private firms. Companies like Meta, Google, and Microsoft have announced initiatives to label or watermark synthetic media, but these efforts face pushback from free speech advocates and from regimes that may use detection tools selectively to suppress dissent. Meanwhile, the technology itself is widely accessible: open-source frameworks allow almost anyone with modest technical skills to create convincing deepfakes. Unlike nuclear weapons or advanced drones, synthetic media requires no centralised infrastructure, making regulation exceptionally difficult. As with cyber weapons, the diffusion of capability ensures that deepfakes will be wielded not only by states but also by activist groups, criminal syndicates, and lone actors.

The deeper issue, however, lies not only in the technology but in its social environment. Disinformation succeeds not simply because falsehoods exist but because audiences are predisposed to believe them. Deepfakes exploit polarisation, distrust of institutions, and the fragmentation of media ecosystems. A fake video of a politician will spread most virulently among those already inclined to distrust them. Thus, the solution cannot be purely technical; it must also address the social and political vulnerabilities that make societies fertile ground for manipulation. Without rebuilding trust in institutions, journalism, and civic discourse, detection tools alone will be insufficient.

On the battlefield of ideas and politics, deepfakes represent both a continuation and an escalation of disinformation campaigns. They build upon centuries-old practices of deception but supercharge them with realism and scale. *Their true power lies not in creating a single lie that convinces everyone but in creating a flood of plausible fakes that convinces no one of anything.* In this sense, they are less about persuasion than about paralysis. If every video can be fake and every recording fabricated, then every truth can be denied. In democracies, this undermines the very possibility of informed citizenship. In authoritarian states, it provides regimes with new tools to discredit dissent. In conflict zones, it strips combatants and civilians alike of confidence in what is real.

The age of deepfakes thus forces a new reckoning with one of the most basic assumptions of modern life: that evidence can be trusted. From politics to war, the erosion of this assumption carries profound consequences. The challenge is not only to develop better detection or regulation but to adapt to a world where *the burden of proof has shifted.* Once, it was enough to present an image or video as evidence; now, the default posture must be scepticism, demanding corroboration, context, and transparency. This shift is uncomfortable, but it may be the only way to navigate a digital environment where deception is cheap, pervasive, and untraceable. In this way, deepfakes represent not only a technological problem but a societal one, reshaping how individuals, institutions, and states construct and contest the meaning of truth itself.

Autonomous Weapons and Killer Robots

In 2020, a United Nations report suggested that a Turkish-made drone operating in Libya may have independently targeted human combatants without direct human oversight. Whether the incident was fully autonomous or semi-automated remains debated, but the claim alone marked a turning point: the prospect of machines deciding, without human intervention, who should live and who should die had shifted from speculation to battlefield reality. For decades, science fiction portrayed "killer robots" as dystopian fantasies; today, the development of lethal autonomous weapons systems (LAWS) suggests those fantasies are converging with policy debates, military procurement strategies, and the practical dilemmas of twenty-first-century warfare. *The stakes could not be higher, for once the decision to kill is ceded to algorithms, humanity must confront profound ethical, legal, and strategic questions about the role of machines in conflict.*

The current debates about autonomous weapons revolve around degrees of control. Militaries already employ automated systems, from missile defence batteries like Israel's Iron Dome to the US Navy's Aegis combat system, capable of detecting and intercepting threats faster than human operators could respond. These defensive systems are broadly accepted as legitimate, precisely because they operate under tightly defined parameters against incoming projectiles rather than human beings. What troubles policymakers and ethicists is the gradual expansion from automated defence to autonomous offence: machines capable of identifying, selecting, and engaging human targets on their own. Advocates argue that such systems could reduce collateral damage by making faster, more precise decisions than fallible human soldiers under stress. Critics counter that delegating lethal authority to machines undermines fundamental principles of international humanitarian law, which require human judgement in the application of force. *The essential question is whether morality can ever be meaningfully encoded in lines of code.*

Supporters of lethal autonomy often frame the issue in pragmatic terms. Human soldiers are vulnerable to fatigue, fear, prejudice, and revenge, whereas autonomous systems could in principle operate without such flaws. Proponents claim this could make warfare not only more efficient but paradoxically more humane, minimising civilian casualties through precision. For instance, algorithms trained on vast datasets of battlefield imagery might theoretically distinguish combatants from non-combatants more reliably than a frightened conscript under fire. Military planners also note that in high-speed domains like cyber conflict or missile interception, human reaction time is already inadequate. If adversaries deploy autonomous systems, refusing to develop them could put one's own forces at a disadvantage. *From this perspective, the debate is not whether killer robots will be built, but how quickly states can harness them while retaining a strategic edge.*

Opponents, however, warn that the allure of efficiency obscures deeper dangers. International humanitarian law rests on concepts like distinction, proportionality, and accountability—principles developed over centuries to restrain the savagery of war. Autonomous systems, no matter how sophisticated, lack genuine understanding of human context, cultural nuance, or moral consequence. An algorithm might identify a target with high probability but cannot grasp what it means to kill a father in front of his children, or to weigh the proportionality of striking a military leader inside a crowded marketplace. Responsibility becomes diffuse: if an autonomous drone commits a war crime, who is accountable—the programmer, the commander who deployed it, or the machine itself? The absence of a clear chain of accountability threatens to hollow out the very notion of justice in war. *Machines may be efficient instruments of violence, but they are incapable of bearing responsibility for it.*

The geopolitical dynamics further complicate the debate. Major powers such as the United States, China, and Russia are investing heavily in AI-driven weapons research, often shrouded in secrecy. Smaller states, lacking the resources to develop indigenous systems, may buy off-the-shelf autonomous drones from defence exporters. Non-state actors, too, are entering the field. The same machine vision algorithms that power consumer products can be adapted to create autonomous loitering munitions, sometimes referred to as "suicide drones," which hover until a target presents itself. The democratisation of such technology raises the prospect that warlords, militias, or terrorist organisations could one day wield swarms of autonomous weapons against state militaries or civilian populations. *Unlike nuclear weapons, which require scarce materials and complex infrastructure, autonomous weapons draw on dual-use technologies already embedded in the civilian economy, making their proliferation almost impossible to control.*

Attempts to regulate lethal autonomous weapons through international treaties have so far faltered. The UN's Convention on Certain Conventional Weapons (CCW) has hosted years of discussions, but consensus remains elusive. Some states, including Austria and Brazil, have called for a pre-emptive ban, arguing that once widespread deployment begins, control will be lost forever. Others, notably the United States and Russia, resist binding restrictions, preferring voluntary guidelines. Their rationale is clear: a ban would be unverifiable, unenforceable, and strategically disadvantageous in a world where adversaries may ignore it. Civil society groups, under banners such as the Campaign to Stop Killer Robots, argue that ethical imperatives demand restraint even in the absence of universal compliance. The stalemate highlights the broader difficulty of regulating emerging technologies in an international system fractured by mistrust and great power rivalry. *In effect, humanity faces a collective action problem where inaction may lead to a future everyone fears but no one can prevent.*

The philosophical implications run deeper than legal debates. War has always been a human affair, however mechanised. From ancient warriors to modern soldiers, the act of killing has been bound up with human agency, responsibility, and sacrifice. The introduction of autonomous lethal systems severs that link. It raises the possibility of conflicts fought entirely between machines, with humans relegated to spectators or collateral damage. Some analysts argue this could lower the threshold for war: if politicians can deploy robotic armies without risking the lives of their citizens, the political costs of military adventurism may shrink. Others counter that autonomous wars could be more devastating, as swarms of machines fight at machine speed, escalating beyond human comprehension or control. *When machines decide, the tempo of war accelerates to a pace where human deliberation is excluded, leaving politics behind.*

Nor are the risks confined to battlefields. Autonomous weapons embody a broader shift in how societies understand responsibility in an age of algorithmic governance. Already, AI systems make decisions in finance, policing, and healthcare. The military application simply extends the logic: if algorithms can optimise hospital resource allocation, why not battlefield tactics? Yet the moral distinction is profound. In civilian life, errors can be corrected and lives saved; in war, errors kill. The delegation of lethal authority thus represents the ultimate test of whether society is willing to treat algorithms not merely as tools but as actors in their own right. *The risk is not just technical malfunction but the erosion of the human moral compass in decisions about life and death.*

What emerges from these debates is not a binary question of "yes or no" to killer robots, but a complex spectrum of technological possibility, ethical constraint, and strategic necessity. Autonomy is not absolute but incremental: from systems that merely assist humans in decision-making, to those that execute pre-programmed missions, to those capable of adaptive, unsupervised action. Each step forces a re-examination of legal categories, military doctrine, and ethical boundaries. What unites the critics and supporters alike is recognition that the technology is advancing faster than the frameworks meant to govern it. The challenge is less about whether killer robots will exist—they already do in rudimentary form—and more about how humanity will live with the consequences of machines that kill without conscience.

The debate over autonomous weapons thus encapsulates the paradox of technological progress in warfare. On one hand, they promise greater precision, reduced human risk, and tactical superiority. On the other, they threaten to erode accountability, destabilise geopolitics, and sever the link between violence and human responsibility. *The question is not simply technical or legal but profoundly moral: should machines ever be permitted to decide who lives and who dies?* How the world answers will shape not only the future of war but the very meaning of human agency in the face of advancing technology.

The Invisible Hand of Code

When algorithms enter the battlefield, they do more than assist in decision-making; they begin to redefine what it means to hold responsibility for violence. For centuries, responsibility in war has been tied to human agency—commanders issuing orders, soldiers carrying them out, courts weighing accountability when crimes occur. Yet as artificial intelligence systems take on roles once reserved for human judgement—target selection, threat analysis, even the timing of strikes—the architecture of accountability begins to dissolve. *The invisible hand of code now mediates between intention and action, raising a question that military traditions have never had to face: can a line of code be considered an actor in war?*

The common defence of algorithmic systems in conflict is that they are simply tools, like rifles or aircraft, neutral instruments of human will. But the analogy is increasingly strained. Unlike a rifle, which is inert until used, AI systems shape outcomes in dynamic and sometimes unexpected ways. A predictive targeting algorithm may highlight suspicious activity based on patterns too complex for a human analyst to see, thereby framing which lives are considered potential threats. A defensive system trained to intercept missiles may fire autonomously in response to what it classifies as an attack, even if the input data was ambiguous or manipulated. *At that point, the algorithm is no longer a passive instrument but a participant in the decision loop, influencing when and how force is applied.*

This shift becomes especially visible when things go wrong. Consider the 2003 Patriot missile incidents during the Iraq War, where automated defence systems mistakenly shot down allied aircraft. Though not powered by modern AI, these systems revealed a precursor to today's dilemmas: once machine logic drives lethal action, responsibility becomes contested. Was it the operator who trusted the system? The commander who authorised its use? Or the engineers who designed it? In practice, blame was dispersed, absorbed into the fog of technological complexity. With machine learning systems, this problem deepens, as the rationale behind an algorithm's decision may be inscrutable even to its creators. *War crimes traditionally demand identifiable perpetrators; autonomous systems risk creating crimes without criminals.*

Proponents of AI in warfare argue that these technologies, while disruptive, still operate within human-defined frameworks. Humans build, train, and deploy them; therefore ultimate accountability must remain with human overseers. Yet this reassurance conceals the extent to which machine decision-making alters human behaviour. Commanders under pressure may defer to algorithmic recommendations, treating them as objective or impartial, even when they encode hidden biases. Political leaders may order strikes with greater ease if they believe machines can ensure precision, lowering their own sense of moral burden. Over time, reliance on AI can erode human responsibility not by replacing it outright, but by diluting it through systems that appear authoritative and detached. *Responsibility is not lost in a single stroke; it erodes through deference to code that feels wiser than human fallibility.*

The implications are not only ethical but philosophical. For centuries, war has been governed by the principle that violence must be a human choice, bound by conscience and accountable to law. AI challenges this by introducing actors that are neither moral agents nor fully controllable tools. A machine cannot be punished, deterred, or rehabilitated. Its "decisions" lack intent in the human sense, yet they produce real-world consequences indistinguishable from those of a human soldier. In this light, AI systems become a new category of participant: non-human actors whose actions shape war but evade traditional frameworks of moral or legal accountability. *They are not soldiers, not commanders, and not states—but something in between, destabilising our categories of responsibility.*

The geopolitical stakes amplify these dilemmas. States deploying AI-driven systems are not only grappling with ethics but also with strategy. If adversaries use autonomous systems to accelerate decision-making, a state may feel compelled to do the same or risk falling behind. This logic mirrors the nuclear arms race, but with one crucial difference: whereas nuclear weapons' destructive potential made deterrence central, AI systems thrive on use. Their value lies precisely in acting, in shaping battlefield events in real time. Thus, even as states debate regulation, they are drawn into deploying systems that shift responsibility away from human hands. The paradox is stark: to remain competitive, militaries must adopt technologies that erode the very human control they claim to preserve. *The invisible hand of code is not only shaping wars but compelling states into patterns of dependency on it.*

Civil society advocates and international lawyers have sought to restore clarity by demanding "meaningful human control" over all autonomous weapons. Yet what counts as meaningful? Is a commander approving a mission days in advance sufficient, or must a human intervene at the very moment of engagement? Technical complexity blurs these distinctions. A human may be "in the loop" formally but unable to grasp the rapid calculations driving the system's actions. Conversely, systems designed to act independently may still be programmed with human-derived rules of engagement. The ambiguity is fertile ground for both denial and abuse. Governments may claim oversight while hiding behind the opacity of algorithms, deflecting responsibility for civilian deaths or mistakes. *What emerges is a new landscape of plausible deniability, where accountability can always be shifted into the black box of code.*

Historical analogies offer limited guidance. The industrialisation of war once raised similar fears: machine guns, chemical weapons, and aerial bombardment all forced societies to reframe laws and ethics. Yet those technologies, however devastating, did not displace human agency in the same way. A bomber crew could still be held responsible; a gas attack still traced back to commanders. By contrast, algorithmic systems operate in a realm of partial autonomy, where responsibility is distributed across designers, operators, and machines. This diffusion resembles not industrialisation but financial markets, where algorithmic trading can trigger crises without a single identifiable culprit. In war, such diffusion is more dangerous, for the currency is not money but human life. *When responsibility becomes fragmented, justice becomes unreachable.*

Perhaps the most unsettling dimension is how AI reshapes our cultural understanding of agency itself. Societies already speak of algorithms as if they have will: "the system flagged this individual," "the model predicted that outcome." In war, this anthropomorphising tendency magnifies. If a drone selects a target, commanders may describe it as if the machine "chose," blurring the line between metaphor and reality. The more we speak of code as an actor, the more it becomes one in practice, influencing human decisions by commanding attention and trust. *The invisible hand of code is not mystical; it is the cultural consequence of treating algorithms as authoritative participants rather than silent tools.*

The challenge, then, is not merely technical regulation but a rethinking of the human relationship to machines in contexts of ultimate consequence. If AI is treated as just another instrument, responsibility will slip through the cracks of complexity. If AI is recognised as a new kind of actor, societies must confront whether they are prepared to extend the language of responsibility, law, and ethics to non-human systems. Neither option is comfortable, but the choice cannot be evaded. Code already shapes who is killed, when wars escalate, and how leaders rationalise their decisions. *It is no longer accurate to say that AI is only a tool; it has become an agent in its own right, silently redrawing the boundaries of human responsibility in war.*

Chapter 6

The Business of Violence

Violence has always had an economic dimension, but today it increasingly resembles a commercial product—packaged, priced, and delivered to clients as if it were cloud storage or outsourced logistics. The battlefield is no longer the exclusive theatre of states; it has become a marketplace where armies, security firms, and criminal syndicates sell their services with contractual precision. *War, once tied to questions of sovereignty and ideology, is now embedded in the grammar of commerce.* Its supply chains, business models, and financial incentives shape not only who fights, but also why conflicts endure and how they evolve.

The rise of "war as a service" is one of the most striking features of modern conflict. Governments that once monopolised organised violence now contract it out like any other public function, purchasing security packages from private military companies or surveillance capabilities from cyber mercenary firms. But the clientele extends well beyond fragile states. Multinational corporations seek protection for oil rigs off the Nigerian coast or lithium mines in South America. Shipping consortia quietly hire private navies to guard container vessels transiting the Gulf of Aden. Even drug cartels and insurgent groups acquire outsourced expertise—training, weapons procurement, and intelligence—through networks that blur the lines between criminality and military professionalism. The commodification of war means that violence has become scalable, adaptable to budgets and business models, detached from the formal structures of statehood. *When conflict becomes transactional, the logic of the marketplace begins to dictate the rhythms of war.*

This transformation is particularly visible where the global economy's arteries run. Oil fields in the Niger Delta, once theatres of insurgency, are now guarded by private contractors who strike deals with both governments and corporations, ensuring the steady flow of crude regardless of local grievances. In Somalia, security firms patrol shipping lanes against piracy, turning protection into a billable service that makes maritime insurance viable for global trade. In Silicon Valley and Dubai alike, tech companies quietly contract digital mercenaries to shield servers, platforms, and data flows, treating cyber defence not as a sovereign guarantee but as a service procured from the open market. These examples reveal a striking reality: violence is no longer confined to traditional conflict zones but integrated into the infrastructure of global business. *The distinction between the marketplace and the battlefield is collapsing.*

At the same time, the boundaries between organised crime and militarised force are dissolving. Cartels in Mexico command arsenals that rival national militaries, but their capacity is amplified through connections to arms dealers, ex-special forces trainers, and security consultants who shift fluidly between legal and illicit spheres. In parts of West Africa, smuggling networks double as armed groups, protecting trade routes that carry narcotics, weapons, and migrants alike. The overlap between crime and war is not incidental but structural: the same actors, logistics, and financial systems sustain both. Private military companies may secure pipelines in one context and provide muscle for criminal networks in another. *The convergence of crime and war signals a world in which violence is not an exception to business but a sector of it.*

Perhaps the most unsettling development is the financialisation of conflict. Investors and capital markets, often at a remove from the battlefield, profit from the spread of privatised violence. Shares in private security firms rise with instability, creating perverse incentives where war sustains returns. Hedge funds and insurance companies trade on risk assessments of conflict zones, turning instability into a commodity. In some cases, resource extraction firms backed by Western capital hire mercenaries to secure mining concessions, effectively linking Wall Street portfolios to the suppression of local dissent. This is not the shadowy conspiracy of fiction but the logical extension of a global system that treats violence as another field of investment. *Conflict becomes not only a tool of politics but an asset class in itself.*

The implications extend beyond economics into the moral and political order. When violence is purchased like a subscription service, accountability is diluted. A government that contracts a private force to quell unrest can deny direct responsibility for atrocities committed. A corporation that outsources security to protect its supply chain can claim plausible deniability when local communities are displaced or brutalised. Investors profiting from the business of violence can remain insulated from the consequences of the wars that sustain their dividends. *The further violence is integrated into the market, the more its human costs are obscured by the language of contracts, portfolios, and quarterly returns.*

This chapter examines these dynamics in detail: how violence is commodified, how business and security are entangled, how criminal and military spheres converge, and how finance capital profits from instability. It argues that the transformation of war into business is not a peripheral trend but a defining feature of twenty-first-century geopolitics. The reader will see how the logics of profit and risk have reshaped the organisation of violence, making war both more diffuse and more enduring. If the previous chapters traced the outsourcing of conflict to mercenaries, militias, and cyber actors, this chapter situates that trend within its wider economic architecture. *To understand today's wars, one must follow not only the guns but the money—and see how the business of violence has become a central pillar of global power.*

War as a Service

Violence, once the most unyielding expression of state power, has become modular, flexible, and astonishingly transactional. The outsourcing of military force is no longer an emergency measure for overstretched governments but a fully fledged industry, offering war as if it were a subscription service. Clients now include not only fragile states but corporations protecting global supply chains and cartels competing for dominance in illicit markets. The commodification of violence has shifted conflict from the exceptional to the routine, embedding war into the logic of markets, procurement contracts, and service agreements. *What was once the prerogative of sovereigns is now accessible to anyone with the resources to pay.*

The subscription model of violence mirrors trends across the wider economy. Just as businesses shifted from owning servers to renting cloud computing power, so too have states and non-state actors discovered the advantages of outsourcing combat. Instead of maintaining standing armies with all the burdens of training, equipment, and long-term political accountability, clients can now contract discrete units of force for specific tasks—protection of oil fields, suppression of insurgencies, or cyber intrusions against rivals. The flexibility is seductive: costs are predictable, services are scalable, and failures can be disowned. Violence is delivered not as ideology or duty but as a package tailored to demand, with contracts specifying scope, duration, and deliverables. *This transformation represents a profound break with the centuries-old notion that force is tied to sovereignty rather than subscription.*

Consider the oil companies operating in Nigeria's Niger Delta. Decades of unrest, sabotage, and kidnapping threatened one of the world's most critical energy arteries. Governments struggled to protect installations, and local security forces were often compromised or collusive. Enter private military contractors, hired directly by corporations to secure pipelines, offshore platforms, and staff. These contractors provided not only muscle but intelligence, logistics, and crisis response—often with more professionalism than local militaries. The relationship resembled a corporate service agreement rather than a military alliance. Contracts could be renewed or terminated depending on performance, while the corporations paid for stability without the political obligations of state-to-state diplomacy. *The commodification of security meant that oil flowed, investors were reassured, and the Niger Delta's communities remained trapped in cycles of violence in which they had no contractual stake.*

The same model extends to maritime security. At the height of Somali piracy in the late 2000s, commercial shipping faced staggering insurance premiums and the real risk of hijackings that disrupted global trade. Navies from the United States, Europe, and Asia patrolled the Gulf of Aden, but they could not cover every route. Shipping companies began hiring private armed guards who boarded vessels before entering high-risk waters. Some firms even deployed privately owned patrol boats to escort convoys. The service was billed per journey, often bundled into comprehensive maritime insurance packages. The subscription-based provision of force transformed piracy from an existential crisis for shipping into a calculable cost of doing business. The model proved so effective that piracy declined sharply, but its success also normalised the idea that global trade routes could be secured through private violence, financed collectively by insurers and shippers rather than guaranteed by states. *Security became a commodity circulating through markets, not a sovereign assurance embedded in global governance.*

Perhaps the most striking shift is visible in cyber conflict. Here, the service model is almost indistinguishable from the broader tech industry. Firms such as the NSO Group sell surveillance and intrusion tools to governments, corporations, and sometimes shadowy intermediaries. The contracts resemble those for enterprise software: licences, upgrades, technical support, and compliance clauses. What is being purchased, however, is not productivity software but the ability to penetrate encrypted communications, track dissidents, or disable critical infrastructure.

Cyber mercenary firms pitch themselves as service providers rather than combatants, yet their products alter balances of power within and between states. Their clients can be authoritarian regimes seeking to suppress opposition, democratic governments eager to keep pace with adversaries, or even corporate actors protecting trade secrets. *The subscription logic is clearest here: offensive capability, like cloud storage, is bought, billed, and upgraded as needed.*

Cartels and criminal organisations have not been slow to adapt this model. Mexican cartels, flush with cash from narcotics, hire ex-special forces operators as trainers and tacticians. The arrangement is transactional: former soldiers or contractors provide expertise in exchange for generous salaries and relative impunity. These services can include instruction in small-unit tactics, urban warfare, or explosives, effectively professionalising groups that were once ragtag bands. Cartels do not need to invest in a standing military infrastructure; they rent the skills of professionals who cycle between legitimate and illegitimate employers. In Colombia, smuggling groups have hired private security firms to defend clandestine airstrips or secure smuggling routes, often using the same networks that service legitimate businesses. *The fusion of crime and commerce demonstrates that the subscription model of violence is not confined to the formal economy but permeates illicit markets as well.*

The philosophical implications of "war as a service" are profound. When violence is commodified, its moral weight is transformed. Wars are no longer fought in the name of sovereignty, ideology, or national identity but as contractual transactions. The chain of accountability is blurred: who bears responsibility when a contracted force commits abuses—the client who paid for the service, the company that delivered it, or the individuals who carried it out? Unlike state militaries, which are at least nominally constrained by laws of war and democratic oversight, private providers operate in a grey zone of regulation. Contracts may stipulate rules of engagement, but these are subject to market pressures rather than international norms. *The very act of commodifying war corrodes traditional frameworks of responsibility and legitimisation.*

Supporters argue that outsourcing violence increases efficiency and reduces costs. Governments avoid the expense of large standing armies. Corporations secure their operations without relying on fragile host states. Even humanitarian organisations sometimes rely on private security firms to protect staff in conflict zones. In this view, war as a service is not a distortion of global order but an adaptation to its realities—a pragmatic solution to the inadequacies of state power. Yet critics counter that the service model extends conflicts by making violence more sustainable. If clients can simply pay to maintain security without addressing underlying grievances, wars are prolonged rather than resolved. Moreover, the profit motive creates incentives for instability: firms and individuals make money not from peace but from the continuation of violence. *When war becomes business, stability ceases to be the overriding goal.*

The subscription model also fragments sovereignty. States that rely on outsourced violence concede slices of their authority to private actors, undermining the very idea of a monopoly on legitimate force. In fragile states, this reliance often becomes dependency: governments cannot survive without the services of contractors, making sovereignty contingent on financial capacity rather than political legitimacy. At the global level, corporations and wealthy non-state actors gain access to tools of violence once restricted to states, flattening hierarchies of power and eroding the state-centric order. *War as a service destabilises the very architecture of international politics, replacing sovereignty with solvency as the determinant of who wields force.*

What emerges is a world in which violence is available on demand, tailored to budgets and objectives, unmoored from ideology, and increasingly divorced from accountability. From oil companies in Nigeria to shipping firms in the Gulf of Aden, from cartels in Mexico to cyber mercenaries selling intrusion tools, the logic is consistent: war has become a service industry. This shift does not merely alter the mechanics of conflict; it redefines its meaning. When violence is packaged as a commodity, conflicts are shaped not only by political goals but by market transactions. *The subscription model of war signals a profound transformation: conflict is no longer simply waged—it is purchased, renewed, and scaled like any other global service.*

Insurance, Security, and Extraction

At first glance, an insurance underwriter in London or New York might appear far removed from a convoy of armed guards patrolling the oil fields of Nigeria, the private vessels escorting tankers through the Strait of Malacca, or the biometric scanners securing a data centre in Dubai. Yet these worlds are intimately linked. *Insurance markets, private security contractors, and resource extraction industries form an interlocking system in which risk, violence, and profit are mutually reinforcing.* Violence is not only contained within battlefields but embedded in the global flows of oil, data, and capital. The decision of whether to insure a shipment, safeguard a pipeline, or harden a tech hub against sabotage dictates the deployment of private force. Security has become both a financial calculation and a commodity in its own right.

The modern oil economy illustrates this relationship most starkly. Resource-rich states such as Nigeria, Iraq, or Libya are both indispensable to global energy markets and deeply fragile in terms of governance. Oil companies operating there do not merely drill wells; they build miniature security states. In Nigeria's Niger Delta, private contractors man checkpoints, monitor river traffic, and patrol perimeters with helicopters. Their salaries, equipment, and even casualty costs are embedded in the operating budgets of multinational energy firms. Insurers demand such measures as conditions for underwriting, while financial markets evaluate companies' security arrangements when assessing risk exposure. *In effect, the cost of private armies is folded invisibly into the price of fuel paid at the pump.* The intertwining of insurance and security transforms warlike activity into a financial instrument, bundled into commodities futures and shareholder returns.

This securitisation of extraction is not limited to oil. Mining operations in regions such as the Democratic Republic of Congo or Mozambique operate under a similar logic. Vast deposits of cobalt, tantalum, and rare earth minerals—critical for smartphones, electric vehicles, and military hardware—exist in areas plagued by armed groups and weak governance. Extraction companies turn to private military and security firms to secure their sites and transport corridors. Insurers, in turn, will only provide coverage if credible security measures are in place. The result is a triangular arrangement: extraction generates wealth, insurance stabilises the investment, and private security provides the muscle to ensure both proceed uninterrupted. *The cycle is self-reinforcing: the more valuable the resource, the more intense the security, and the more entrenched the market in private violence becomes.*

Maritime trade, the lifeblood of global commerce, underscores the same dynamic in a different domain. When Somali piracy surged in the late 2000s, shipping companies faced exorbitant insurance premiums. Underwriters made clear that vessels without armed protection would pay punitive rates or struggle to obtain coverage at all. This forced the industry into contracting private maritime security companies, whose personnel boarded ships before entering high-risk waters. Some insurers even partnered directly with these security providers, effectively creating a bundled product of protection plus insurance. *The logic was brutally pragmatic: violence, or at least the credible threat of violence, became an actuarial necessity.* What began as an emergency response to piracy hardened into a permanent service model, and the integration of insurance with private security fundamentally reshaped maritime trade economics.

The same principles now extend to the digital economy. Data centres, fibre optic cables, and undersea infrastructure form the backbone of twenty-first century commerce and communication. They are not immune to sabotage, cyber intrusion, or even physical assault. As geopolitical rivalry intensifies, the security of these assets has become an urgent priority for technology giants and governments alike. In places such as Dubai's Internet City or Kenya's burgeoning tech hubs, private security companies manage access control, biometric identification, and real-time monitoring of personnel and equipment. Insurance firms factor these arrangements into their willingness to underwrite operations, particularly against cyberattack or terrorism. The extraction here is not of oil or minerals but of data—a resource just as valuable and contested as hydrocarbons. *The commodification of digital security echoes the logic of oil fields and shipping lanes: private protection becomes the price of access to global flows.*

Critics argue that this intertwining of insurance, security, and extraction entrenches inequality. The benefits of protection flow to corporations and investors, while local communities often endure displacement, surveillance, or outright violence. In Nigeria, the same contractors hired to protect pipelines have been accused of harassing or killing residents who protest against environmental degradation. In the Congo, mine security forces have clashed with artisanal miners whose livelihoods depend on small-scale extraction. Even in cyberspace, the emphasis on securing corporate assets often comes at the expense of individual privacy or local sovereignty. *When violence is priced into business operations, accountability shifts from democratic oversight to contractual liability—a profound reordering of political responsibility.*

Yet from another perspective, this system reflects the realities of globalisation. States, especially fragile ones, often lack the capacity to guarantee security for critical infrastructure. Without private contractors and insurance mechanisms, extraction and trade might grind to a halt, depriving both global markets and local economies of vital resources. Supporters contend that private security provides stability in zones where states have failed, and insurance mechanisms discipline the process by pricing risk accurately. In this view, the fusion of finance and force is not a pathology but a rational adaptation to global disorder. *Security, like logistics or supply chains, has simply been marketised and integrated into the infrastructure of global capitalism.*

What is clear is that the lines between war, business, and finance are dissolving. Oil companies hire security firms that answer not to voters but to shareholders. Insurers effectively dictate the presence and scope of armed guards in shipping lanes. Technology giants build fortified digital fortresses policed by private contractors, their costs amortised through subscription fees and advertising revenue. Each of these arrangements embeds violence within the structures of global commerce, rendering it invisible to most consumers but decisive in shaping the world economy. *Every litre of petrol, every cargo container, every cloud-stored file carries within it the hidden premium of private force.*

The convergence of insurance, security, and extraction represents more than a technical or financial arrangement—it is a profound shift in the architecture of global order. Sovereignty is increasingly irrelevant to the question of who provides protection; what matters is solvency, credibility, and contractual compliance. In this model, violence is not an aberration but a line item, priced and packaged alongside transportation and logistics. The result is a world where force is no longer monopolised by states but distributed across markets, insurers, and corporate clients. *The battlefield has expanded to boardrooms, underwriting offices, and data centres, where decisions about premiums and protection shape the geography of violence itself.*

The Criminal-Military Nexus

The boundary between organised crime and organised warfare has never been as porous as it is today. Cartels, militias, gangs, and private military companies increasingly inhabit the same ecosystem, trading tactics, technology, and personnel with little regard for the distinctions that once defined them. *When war becomes profitable and crime becomes militarised, the two converge into a single continuum of violence governed less by ideology than by economics and control.* This merger destabilises states, corrodes sovereignty, and forces policymakers to confront adversaries that are neither conventional armies nor mere criminal networks, but something far more adaptable and dangerous.

Latin America provides some of the clearest evidence of this convergence. Mexican cartels such as the Zetas emerged not just from the drug trade but from the professionalisation of violence. The Zetas were originally composed of defectors from Mexico's elite special forces, trained in counterinsurgency by the United States. Their military background allowed them to transform drug trafficking from a clandestine business into a territorial enterprise defined by checkpoints, patrols, and zones of control. They were no longer simply smuggling narcotics; they were running parallel military campaigns against both rivals and the state. The cartels' firepower, tactical sophistication, and capacity for intimidation forced the Mexican government to deploy the army in response, blurring the distinction between counter-crime and counterinsurgency. *The cartel had effectively become a paramilitary force, indistinguishable in structure from insurgent movements but motivated by profit rather than ideology.*

A similar blending of crime and war is visible in West Africa. Smuggling networks that once trafficked cigarettes and contraband across the Sahel evolved into armed groups financing themselves through narcotics, human trafficking, and kidnapping. Groups like al-Qaeda in the Islamic Maghreb (AQIM) derived funding from illicit trade while simultaneously pursuing political agendas, intertwining jihad with organised crime. These groups forged alliances with local bandits and militias, creating hybrid structures that confounded traditional security responses. The question for governments became whether they were fighting terrorists, warlords, or traffickers. In reality, they were fighting all three at once. *When illicit profit streams sustain armed campaigns, violence ceases to fit neatly into categories of crime or war; it becomes both simultaneously.*

The role of private military companies (PMCs) adds yet another dimension to this nexus. Groups like Wagner in Africa have been contracted by states to provide security, but their operations often overlap with resource extraction and illicit trade. In the Central African Republic, Wagner contractors guard diamond mines whose revenues help fund both local elites and foreign patrons. The company blurs the line between a state-sanctioned security actor and a criminal enterprise, its activities protected by political contracts but fuelled by the exploitation of natural resources. From one perspective, Wagner is a paramilitary arm of Russian foreign policy; from another, it resembles a cartel that controls territory and extracts profit through violence. *The PMC model illustrates how state and non-state actors can merge military and criminal functions under the cover of legality.*

Urban gangs also illustrate the criminal-military continuum on a micro scale. In cities from Rio de Janeiro to Port-au-Prince, gangs act as both criminal organisations and de facto security providers. They levy taxes, resolve disputes, and control access to territory. Their arsenals increasingly include military-grade weapons sourced from black markets or corrupt supply chains. In Haiti, gangs have evolved into quasi-political actors capable of paralysing the state itself, while in Brazil, favelas are patrolled by heavily armed groups that function less like street gangs and more like occupying armies. These groups, although lacking the international connections of PMCs or cartels, embody the same principle: crime and war fuse when armed groups exert governance functions.

This convergence is further accelerated by globalisation and technology. The same weapons trafficked to insurgent groups in the Middle East often find their way into the hands of Latin American cartels. Cybercrime provides new revenue streams for both gangs and armed groups, with ransomware funding terrorist organisations and narcotics networks alike. Mercenaries who once fought in conflicts in Africa or the Middle East now sell their expertise to cartels seeking to train gunmen in urban combat. The result is a transnational web in which criminal, political, and military actors draw on the same tactics, markets, and personnel. *Violence has become a fungible commodity, exchanged across domains of war and crime without distinction.*

The consequences for governance are profound. States confronted with these hybrid actors often lack the legal or strategic frameworks to respond. Treating them as criminals underestimates their military capacity, while treating them as insurgents obscures their economic motivations. This confusion plays into the hands of the groups themselves, who thrive in ambiguity. Governments attempting to dismantle them frequently discover that official security forces are compromised, infiltrated, or even colluding with criminal-military networks. In Mexico, entire police departments have been found on cartel payrolls. In parts of West Africa, military officers have profited from smuggling operations. The very institutions meant to combat these groups become part of the nexus.

From a philosophical perspective, the criminal-military nexus challenges one of the foundational ideas of modern political order: that the state holds a monopoly on legitimate violence. When non-state actors can field armies, control territory, and integrate themselves into global economic systems, the distinction between legitimate and illegitimate force collapses. Insurance firms, investors, and consumers often become complicit, knowingly or unknowingly, in sustaining these hybrid structures. Oil purchased from fields secured by PMCs, minerals mined under the protection of militias, or drugs trafficked by militarised cartels all flow into global markets. *The merging of crime and war is not confined to the peripheries of weak states; it is woven into the very fabric of global capitalism.*

The challenge is not only material but conceptual. Traditional international law is ill-equipped to categorise or prosecute groups that operate simultaneously as gangs, businesses, militias, and armies. Efforts to apply counterinsurgency doctrine to cartels, or anti-crime measures to insurgents, often misfire because they fail to grasp the hybrid nature of these entities. Similarly, attempts to regulate PMCs stumble over their dual role as legitimate contractors and extractive enterprises. The criminal-military nexus defies neat definitions, demanding new frameworks that recognise the continuum of violence rather than forcing it into outdated categories.

Ultimately, the merging of crime and war reflects the erosion of the neat boundaries that once defined conflict. Cartels act like armies, PMCs operate like cartels, and gangs assume the functions of governments. Each feeds into the other, creating a feedback loop in which violence becomes a tool of profit, power, and governance simultaneously. *Understanding this continuum is essential, because strategies built on false distinctions will always fail against adversaries that thrive in ambiguity.* States that continue to treat crime and war as separate domains risk fighting the wrong battles while hybrid actors consolidate control.

The criminal-military nexus is not an anomaly; it is fast becoming the dominant form of conflict in the twenty-first century. Whether in the jungles of Colombia, the deserts of Mali, or the streets of Port-au-Prince, the same pattern emerges: armed groups that straddle the line between organised crime and organised war. Their rise signals not only a crisis of security but a transformation of the political order itself. In this new world, *violence is no longer a question of legality or illegality, but of market access and operational capacity.* The state must contend not just with rivals in war or crime, but with adversaries who have made those categories obsolete.

Investors in Conflict

Wars are no longer only fought by states, and profits no longer flow only to generals or arms manufacturers. In today's financialised world, *conflict itself has become an asset class.* Pension funds, hedge funds, and private equity firms often benefit indirectly—and sometimes directly—from privatised warfare, with dividends, insurance products, and extractive concessions linking Wall Street to battlefields in Africa, the Middle East, and beyond. The fact that investors thousands of miles away can profit from violence without ever seeing bloodshed raises uncomfortable questions about responsibility, accountability, and the invisible architecture that sustains modern conflict.

Private military companies (PMCs) and private security contractors sit at the core of this convergence between finance and force. While images of mercenaries on the ground dominate headlines, the capital that sustains them is often raised in boardrooms. When a government hires a firm like DynCorp or GardaWorld, the contract is underwritten by investors whose portfolios span everything from airports to oil fields. In this sense, conflict is securitised: shares in companies that provide war services can be traded, bundled, and valued like any other commodity. For financiers, war becomes predictable risk, not tragedy. *The commodification of violence allows investors to profit from instability while remaining insulated from its consequences.*

The war in Iraq illustrates how this model matured. Halliburton subsidiary KBR became synonymous with outsourcing the logistics of occupation, from building bases to feeding troops. Its contracts, worth billions, were funded by taxpayers but translated into shareholder returns. Mutual funds and pension funds that invested in Halliburton benefited from a war fought thousands of miles away. This was not incidental profit but structural: the business of violence was integrated into the global financial system. For ordinary citizens holding retirement accounts, the paradox was stark—they might simultaneously oppose the war politically while profiting from it financially. *Conflict had become embedded in everyday economic life through the machinery of capital markets.*

Africa reveals a different but equally telling dynamic. In resource-rich fragile states, PMCs are often compensated not just with cash but with concessions to exploit oil, gas, or mineral wealth. Investors then buy shares in these companies or in the extractive firms tied to their operations. The Central African Republic provides a striking example, where Wagner Group's security contracts were linked to diamond and gold mines. The revenues from these ventures flowed into networks of shell companies, often routed through financial centres, and ultimately tied into global markets. Investors with no direct intention of financing mercenaries could unknowingly benefit from the minerals extracted under their protection. *Here, violence is not simply protected by finance; it is transformed into finance itself.*

The insurance industry represents another underexamined pillar of investor entanglement. Shipping firms transiting high-risk zones such as the Gulf of Aden must purchase war risk insurance. Premiums fluctuate with conflict intensity, creating speculative opportunities. The more volatile the region, the higher the insurance revenues—profits that are distributed to shareholders of global insurers. This creates a perverse symmetry: while piracy or armed conflict raises costs for shippers, it can boost earnings for financial institutions invested in insurers. Similarly, political risk insurance—covering corporations against losses from coups, expropriations, or insurgencies—turns instability into a managed financial product. For investors, chaos becomes just another market signal.

Critics argue this financialisation of conflict creates structural incentives for wars to persist. If investors profit from long-term instability—whether through insurance premiums, security contracts, or resource exploitation—then peace can threaten revenue streams. This does not mean that investors consciously lobby for perpetual war, but it highlights the uncomfortable reality that *markets can price violence into their models in ways that make it profitable to endure rather than resolve*. The logic of capital, indifferent to human suffering, transforms conflict from an aberration into a business model.

Defenders of the system counter that investment does not necessarily prolong conflict but merely reflects economic realities. They argue that without private capital underwriting PMCs, many fragile states would collapse into deeper anarchy. By securitising conflict, investors allow governments to stabilise oil fields, protect infrastructure, or guarantee trade routes. In this telling, profit is not parasitic but necessary for global order. Critics, however, point out that such stability often benefits investors and elites more than citizens, entrenching dependency rather than building sovereignty. *The financialisation of war thus exposes the tension between stability for capital and justice for people.*

The role of sovereign wealth funds further complicates the picture. Wealth generated from oil in the Gulf or manufacturing in Asia is often reinvested in Western defence firms and security contractors. This globalises the investor base, making it difficult to disentangle who benefits from conflict. A war fought in Mali may generate returns not just for private equity in London but for sovereign funds in Singapore or pension funds in Norway. This dispersal of responsibility dilutes accountability: when so many are financially tied to the machinery of violence, no single actor feels compelled to challenge it. *The diffusion of profit across borders ensures that war remains a viable and lucrative business proposition in the global economy.*

Technology firms are also increasingly drawn into this investor-conflict nexus. Surveillance companies like Palantir, which design software used by intelligence agencies and militaries, rely heavily on venture capital and public investment. When their shares rise after signing contracts with defence ministries, investors celebrate growth without interrogating the human rights implications. The NSO Group, infamous for its Pegasus spyware, was funded in part by private equity. Investors were not merely passive; they structured, guided, and scaled a business model built on surveillance and control. *The financial backing of cyber-mercenary firms shows how markets now underwrite not only physical violence but digital repression.*

The philosophical question that emerges is whether financial markets can ever be neutral in the context of war. Capital seeks returns, not morality, and yet those returns often depend on human suffering. Investors may rationalise their role by claiming ignorance or distance, but ignorance itself is a choice in a world where information is accessible. Moreover, the abstraction of finance—the way war becomes reduced to earnings-per-share or risk-adjusted return—creates ethical anaesthesia. A drone strike or the seizure of a mine is transformed into a quarterly dividend, detached from the lives it destroyed. *Finance, in this sense, does not just fund war; it sanitises it, making violence legible only in terms of profit and loss.*

At the same time, it is possible to imagine a different trajectory: investor pressure has historically shaped corporate behaviour in areas like environmental, social, and governance (ESG) compliance. If investors can demand decarbonisation, why not demilitarisation? Some funds have begun excluding arms manufacturers from their portfolios, though few extend this logic to PMCs or insurers of conflict. The challenge is that unlike fossil fuels, war is not universally stigmatised—states rely on it, industries depend on it, and global markets absorb it. The question for the future is whether investors will remain passive beneficiaries of violence or whether they can be mobilised as actors for restraint.

What is clear is that privatised warfare cannot be understood solely by looking at battlefields or boardrooms in isolation. The true engine lies in the capital that links them. Investors in New York, London, or Zurich may never meet the mercenaries guarding an oil field in Libya or the hackers disrupting an election, but their money sustains those operations. In turn, those operations generate profits that flow back into global financial systems, feeding retirement accounts, sovereign funds, and private wealth. *The circuit is complete: war is financialised, and finance is weaponised.*

By tracing these flows of capital, one sees that modern conflict is not only fought with guns or drones but also with spreadsheets, contracts, and trading screens. The investors in conflict are not the men on the frontlines but the institutions and individuals who view violence as a risk-adjusted return. To recognise this reality is to confront an unsettling truth: the marketplace is as central to contemporary warfare as the battlefield itself. And until that reality is acknowledged, the business of violence will continue to thrive, legitimised not just by governments but by global capital itself.

Chapter 7

Psychological Warfare in a Stateless Age

The most potent weapon in today's conflicts is not always a missile, a drone, or a line of code. It is belief—shaped, manipulated, and projected until it commands obedience, fear, or loyalty stronger than any uniform. In an age where wars are increasingly fought without the banners of nation-states, the battlefield has shifted inward, targeting minds, identities, and the fragile social fabric that determines how communities live and die together. Psychological warfare, once considered a tactical supplement to physical conflict, now stands at its core.

The absence of a state flag creates both vulnerability and opportunity. For fighters in proxy wars or non-state militias, allegiance rarely stems from patriotism in the traditional sense. Instead, it emerges from three overlapping impulses: greed, identity, and belonging. In Libya's fragmented battlefields, young men have joined militias less out of nationalist fervour than because a gun and a salary provide survival in a collapsing economy. In Syria, sectarian affiliations, not the Syrian flag, determined lines of loyalty. In the Donbas, volunteers were mobilised by narratives of defending "Russian civilisation" or resisting "Western imperialism" rather than by abstract notions of Ukrainian sovereignty. The lesson is stark: *where the state loses monopoly over loyalty, alternative bonds fill the void, and psychological warfare thrives by manipulating them.*

Legitimacy becomes the most contested currency. Groups without recognised sovereignty must justify their existence, not only to themselves but also to potential recruits and sympathetic audiences abroad. They manufacture narratives that portray them as defenders, liberators, or custodians of faith and identity. Hezbollah frames itself as a resistance movement against occupation, not merely a militia. The Taliban, even before reclaiming Kabul, cast themselves as authentic rulers who upheld Islamic tradition against foreign corruption. The Islamic State went further, presenting itself as a state-in-waiting, with propaganda videos that mimicked the trappings of governance—courts, police, and even welfare distribution—while simultaneously projecting horrific spectacles of violence. These were not contradictions; they were a calculated dual strategy of reassurance for insiders and terror for outsiders. *The ability to define legitimacy without a flag is not rhetorical ornament—it is survival strategy in a stateless age.*

Theatre, rather than brute force, often becomes the decisive act. A single beheading broadcast on global networks can achieve what weeks of skirmishes cannot: demoralisation, polarisation, and a global ripple of fear. Terrorist groups have long understood this, but cyber armies now exploit similar logics. A hack that shuts down hospitals, banks, or critical infrastructure can paralyse a society psychologically even if physical casualties are minimal. Russia's cyber-attacks on Ukraine were as much about instilling doubt and helplessness as about material disruption. In this respect, *terror has evolved from battlefield spectacle to digital performance, with audiences targeted as deliberately as enemies.*

For civilians, this psychological dimension reshapes daily life in ways far more invasive than conventional warfare. In Mexico, communities living under the dual shadow of cartels and corrupt security forces must decide who to trust when both sides claim authority. In Iraq or Afghanistan, villagers navigate overlapping allegiances—cooperating with international forces by day while paying "taxes" to insurgents at night. In cyberspace, ordinary citizens become pawns in battles of disinformation: during elections in Europe and North America, fabricated stories circulate faster than corrections, corroding trust in institutions. The result is a pervasive uncertainty that outlives battles. *When violence is outsourced, the civilian's new reality is not merely insecurity but the impossibility of distinguishing protector from predator.*

Philosophically, this stateless psychological warfare marks a profound shift in how humans conceive of conflict. The twentieth century's wars were often justified through the language of sovereignty, ideology, or liberation; today's conflicts are narrated through identity and perception. A militia that holds no territory can still dominate headlines, elections, and even policy debates by controlling narratives. Likewise, a cyber collective with no flag can disrupt economies more effectively than a conventional army. The tools have changed, but so too has the essence of warfare: *power now lies less in controlling land than in shaping minds.*

This chapter examines these dynamics through four interlocking perspectives. First, the reconstitution of loyalty in environments where state authority has collapsed, highlighting the roles of greed, identity, and belonging. Second, the crafting of narratives by militias and non-state actors as a substitute for sovereignty and legitimacy. Third, the strategic use of spectacle—whether through terrorism, media, or cyber-disruption—as a form of psychological domination. Finally, the lived experience of civilians who must navigate shifting allegiances, disinformation, and fear in order to survive. Each strand reveals not only how psychological warfare functions, but how it erodes the very categories—nation, citizen, enemy—that once anchored global order.

To understand psychological warfare in a stateless age is to confront an uncomfortable reality: the battleground is no longer defined by geography but by perception, trust, and belonging. The wars without flags are waged inside minds, and their outcomes are measured not in captured territory but in captured loyalties. This chapter argues that until we grasp this shift, we will misunderstand both the causes of modern conflicts and the reasons why they prove so difficult to resolve. The war of ideas, identities, and fears is not an accessory to conflict—it is its foundation.

Loyalty Without Nations

The soldier of the twenty-first century is no longer defined by a flag, a uniform, or even a clearly identifiable chain of command. Across fractured states and shadowy conflicts, men and women take up arms for causes that are less about national sovereignty and more about survival, identity, and belonging. The collapse of traditional state authority and the proliferation of proxy wars have forced a reckoning with the question of why individuals fight when the traditional markers of patriotism and citizenship have lost their meaning. The answer lies in a complex intersection of greed, identity, and community—forces that, in many cases, prove more compelling than nationalism ever was.

Greed is the most obvious and frequently cited motivator, yet it is also the least understood. In fragile states from the Central African Republic to Syria, militias recruit not by appealing to ideology but by offering immediate material incentives. Fighters are promised salaries, food, or looted spoils. For young men in collapsing economies, the opportunity to earn $300 a month by joining a militia can be more persuasive than abstract political rhetoric. The Wagner Group's recruitment in Africa is emblematic of this dynamic: fighters are often drawn not from ideological sympathisers but from those desperate for wages, with the prospect of plunder or resource control acting as additional enticement. Greed in these contexts is not simply opportunism; it is a rational calculation in environments where poverty and unemployment leave few alternatives. *The marketplace of loyalty in such contexts is transactional, with allegiance auctioned to the highest bidder or the most reliable patron.*

Yet to reduce fighters' motivations solely to economic calculus is to miss the deeper, less tangible forces at play. Identity exerts a powerful gravitational pull, often eclipsing material gain. When militias invoke religious, ethnic, or sectarian narratives, they offer recruits something far more enduring than pay: a sense of purpose and recognition. In Iraq, Shia militias recruited by framing their struggle as defence of community against existential threats. In Bosnia during the 1990s, men took up arms less for money than for the survival of ethnic kin. Such identities do not merely mobilise fighters; they legitimise violence by casting it as a sacred duty or an act of protection. In this way, *identity transforms killing from a mercenary act into a moral enterprise, offering combatants not just incentives but justification.*

Belonging—subtler but equally potent—explains why many continue fighting even when material rewards diminish or ideological clarity wanes. Militias provide more than weapons and wages; they offer camaraderie, status, and a substitute for the absent state. In Somalia, al-Shabaab has been able to sustain recruitment not only through coercion or religious appeal but also by providing young men with a sense of brotherhood and structure otherwise unavailable in fragmented societies. Similarly, in Colombia, generations of guerrilla fighters remained within insurgent movements because those groups had become their social universe, providing community, hierarchy, and even family life. Belonging ensures that even when states regain ground or economic alternatives emerge, many fighters are unwilling—or unable—to reintegrate, as their very identity has fused with the militia structure. *The gun becomes not just a tool but a passport to community and meaning.*

These motivations rarely exist in isolation. Greed, identity, and belonging often intertwine, creating layered forms of loyalty that resist simplistic categorisation. A fighter in Mali may join initially for wages but remain because of ethnic solidarity with Tuareg rebels. A young man in Gaza might pick up arms for a stipend but find enduring purpose in the narrative of resistance against occupation. These overlaps complicate both analysis and intervention: development aid alone cannot dismantle militias if identity grievances remain unresolved, nor can counter-propaganda campaigns succeed if militias also deliver economic benefits. *The durability of militias lies precisely in their ability to combine material incentives, ideological legitimacy, and social belonging into a single package of loyalty.*

The implications for sovereignty are profound. States historically claimed a monopoly on the legitimate use of violence, with loyalty anchored in citizenship and the defence of territory. But in environments where states are weak, corrupt, or absent, this monopoly dissolves. Militias and non-state actors emerge as alternative authorities, commanding loyalty through non-national mechanisms. In some cases, they provide more reliable governance than states themselves, collecting taxes, administering justice, or delivering basic services. Hezbollah in Lebanon, for instance, has long operated as both militia and welfare provider, blurring the line between armed group and state institution. This dual function strengthens loyalty not because fighters believe in abstract nationalism, but because their immediate needs are met and their identities affirmed.

Critics may argue that loyalty without nations is inherently fragile, that mercenaries will desert once payments falter or ideological groups fracture under pressure. Yet history shows otherwise. Many proxy forces outlast their sponsors, evolving into entrenched political or military actors. The Afghan Mujahideen, once funded as proxies during the Cold War, transformed into movements that continued long after foreign support waned. In this sense, loyalty forged through greed, identity, and belonging can prove remarkably resilient, capable of sustaining wars beyond their initial geopolitical logic. *The disappearance of national flags does not diminish loyalty; it reconfigures it into forms that are more flexible, adaptive, and difficult to dismantle.*

The moral consequences of this shift cannot be ignored. When fighters are motivated by greed, identity, or belonging rather than national duty, the traditional frameworks of accountability weaken. International law assumes combatants are tied to states, making it possible to assign responsibility and enforce norms. But when loyalty resides in a militia or proxy force without formal sovereignty, accountability becomes murky. Who is responsible when a group of fighters loyal to a cartel commits atrocities in Mexico? Who answers for cyber militias loyal to identity narratives rather than states? *The erosion of national loyalty undermines not just political order but the ethical architecture of war itself.*

At its core, loyalty without nations is both a symptom and a cause of the fragmentation of the international system. As state authority wanes, militias step into the vacuum, offering wages, identity, and belonging where governments cannot. Yet by doing so, they further weaken the very states they replace, perpetuating cycles of dependency and instability. For policymakers and analysts, understanding these motivations is not an academic exercise but a practical necessity. Counter-insurgency strategies that ignore the pull of identity or belonging will fail, as will economic programmes that neglect the political and social dimensions of loyalty.

Ultimately, the story of loyalty without nations is one of human adaptation to statelessness. When the traditional bonds of citizenship break down, individuals seek alternative structures of meaning, protection, and community. Militias, cartels, and proxy forces have learned to provide these in ways that modern states often cannot or will not. The challenge for the international community is not merely to dismantle these groups but to address the deeper voids—economic, social, and psychological—that make them viable. For as long as those voids persist, fighters will continue to find in militias what they no longer find in nations: security, purpose, and a place to belong.

Narratives That Justify Violence

When a group lacks the trappings of sovereignty—no seat at the United Nations, no recognised borders, no formal army—it cannot draw on the traditional markers of legitimacy that states have long relied upon to frame their wars as just. Instead, non-state actors manufacture legitimacy through narrative. They weave stories that transform their violence from criminality into struggle, from atrocity into sacrifice. These narratives are not decorative propaganda; they are the operating systems of stateless warfare. They determine who counts as a hero, who as an enemy, and why bloodshed is not only permissible but righteous. In an international order that privileges the nation-state, narrative becomes the surrogate flag under which militias, insurgents, and cyber armies march.

The first strategy of justification is often to invoke *history*. Groups construct genealogies of grievance, tracing present violence back to real or imagined wrongs. Palestinian armed factions, for example, frame their struggle in the language of historical dispossession, locating legitimacy in narratives of land loss and occupation. Kurdish militias across Iraq and Syria present their campaigns not as isolated insurgencies but as chapters in a centuries-long story of statelessness and betrayal by global powers. By embedding their violence in such histories, these actors portray themselves as inheritors of unfinished struggles rather than initiators of fresh conflict. This sense of historical continuity creates a moral alibi, transforming otherwise brutal tactics into expressions of justice delayed.

Religion provides another potent source of narrative legitimacy. Groups such as al-Qaeda and Islamic State do not simply cloak violence in theological terms; they redefine the very act of violence as worship. Suicide bombings are rebranded as martyrdom operations, acts of destruction reframed as steps toward divine justice. The rhetorical shift is critical. It dislocates responsibility from the individual fighter and relocates it within a transcendent moral order. What would otherwise be indefensible acts of terror are recast as fulfilments of sacred duty. *By elevating violence into the realm of the sacred, these groups inoculate themselves against charges of illegitimacy: to oppose them becomes not only political dissent but apostasy.*

In contexts where neither history nor religion resonates universally, actors often lean on *identity*. Ethnic militias from South Sudan to Myanmar build their legitimacy on the language of survival, arguing that violence is necessary to protect their people from annihilation. Here, violence is not presented as choice but as compulsion: kill, or be exterminated. The logic of identity-driven narratives is circular yet persuasive. Any attack against the militia is depicted as an attack against the entire community; any atrocity committed by the militia is justified as pre-emptive defence. The story told is simple and powerful: without us, you would not exist. *In this way, militias elevate themselves from optional actors to existential necessities.*

Even groups motivated largely by profit or power grasp the necessity of narrative. Cartels in Mexico, for example, are not content to be seen as organised criminals; they construct mythologies of social banditry, portraying themselves as protectors of communities against corrupt states or rival gangs. Through narco-ballads, graffiti, and social media, cartels tell stories of themselves as Robin Hood figures, redistributing wealth and defending dignity in areas where the state has failed. While these narratives bear little resemblance to reality, their repetition creates a cultural environment in which violence can be rationalised as order-making rather than simple predation. *Without such stories, their killings would be seen only as murder; with them, they become justice in the absence of law.*

Perhaps the most striking development in recent years is the rise of *digital narratives of legitimacy*. Cyber militias, hacktivist groups, and state-backed information warriors operate in an environment where physical sovereignty is irrelevant. Their legitimacy derives from narrative battles fought on social media, forums, and encrypted channels. Anonymous, for instance, has historically justified its operations through appeals to collective morality, claiming to be defenders of freedom against censorship and authoritarianism. Russian disinformation networks justify digital sabotage not by invoking nationalism but by sowing confusion about truth itself, making it impossible to draw clear lines between victim and aggressor. In cyberspace, narrative legitimacy is not about who has the right to fight, but about who can control perception long enough to make accountability impossible.

It is worth noting that these narratives are not always manufactured top-down by leaders; they often emerge organically from the communities that sustain armed groups. Families of fighters retell stories of martyrdom, local media circulate tales of resistance, and cultural symbols reinforce the moral framework in which violence is embedded. Over time, narratives acquire the weight of common sense, no longer needing to be argued because they are assumed. The danger here is that such embedded stories can outlive the conflicts themselves, preparing the ground for future cycles of violence. A child raised on tales of betrayal and sacrifice may be more willing to fight than one presented only with the memory of violence. *Narratives not only justify violence; they reproduce it across generations.*

The power of these narratives lies not only in what they include but in what they erase. Groups rarely frame their actions in terms of the atrocities they commit. Civilian deaths are reclassified as collateral damage, defections as treachery, rival factions as puppets of foreign powers. What remains visible is only the moral arc of the group's chosen story. This selective storytelling explains why groups facing overwhelming evidence of brutality can still command loyalty. If the story makes sense within the community's worldview, then facts become irrelevant. *Narrative provides not truth but coherence, and in war, coherence is often more compelling than accuracy.*

For policymakers, this poses a dilemma. If violence is justified through stories rather than law, then countering militias cannot rely solely on military strength or legal condemnation. Bombing a group that frames itself as a victim often validates its narrative; sanctioning a cyber army may only prove to its recruits that the enemy fears their influence. Effective responses require dismantling the stories themselves—offering alternative narratives of belonging, justice, and identity that compete with those used to rationalise violence. Yet this is far easier said than done. Stories rooted in history, faith, and survival are not easily displaced by external messaging campaigns. *The contest over legitimacy is therefore not only fought with weapons but with words, and it is a contest in which the most persuasive story often wins.*

At its core, the reliance on narratives to justify violence reveals the fragility of international norms. The Westphalian state order assumes that wars are legitimate only when waged by sovereign entities, yet the prevalence of narrative legitimacy demonstrates how hollow that assumption has become. For countless fighters, legitimacy does not flow from treaties or recognition but from the stories that tell them why they fight and why their struggle is just. Whether framed as sacred duty, historical correction, ethnic survival, or digital rebellion, these narratives provide the scaffolding upon which stateless violence is built. Without them, militias would be mere gangs; with them, they become movements capable of commanding sacrifice, sustaining loyalty, and reshaping entire regions.

Terror as Theatre

Terrorism, insurgency, and cyber aggression are not merely contests of violence; they are contests of visibility. The act of violence itself often kills fewer than the fear it generates, and the fear derives less from the action than from its staging. Militias and cyber armies understand this with extraordinary clarity: the battlefield is only partly physical; the true arena is psychological. *Terror is most effective when it is performed, repeated, and amplified—when the act is designed not just to harm, but to be witnessed.*

The most visceral examples are those of extremist militias that have weaponised spectacle. The Islamic State's decision to broadcast beheadings in high-definition video was not an incidental act of cruelty but a carefully calculated performance. The staging—the orange jumpsuits evoking Guantanamo, the choreographed speeches, the cinematic editing—was designed to shock, provoke, and dominate the global information space. These videos achieved multiple aims simultaneously: they terrified opponents, galvanised recruits, and provoked Western governments into military action that could then be reframed as proof of the group's narrative of persecution. The act of killing was only half the point; the other half was ensuring that the image of the killing would reverberate across borders. *In this sense, the violence was less about the victim than about the audience.*

Cyber warfare, though less bloody, follows the same theatrical logic. A data breach is not valuable to hackers unless it becomes known, unless the exposure itself destabilises confidence. When the WannaCry ransomware crippled hospitals, logistics firms, and government offices across dozens of countries in 2017, the disruption of daily life communicated vulnerability more powerfully than any physical attack. Similarly, Russian-linked hackers targeting power grids in Ukraine sought not only to disable infrastructure but to instil a deep sense of insecurity: if the lights can go out at Moscow's choosing, then sovereignty itself becomes a fragile illusion. These attacks rely on the choreography of chaos, staging small acts of disruption in ways that imply much greater power. The effectiveness lies less in the code and more in the psychological aftershock.

Disinformation operates in much the same theatrical mode. Campaigns of fake news and manipulated content are less concerned with persuading than with unsettling. The use of deepfakes—convincing synthetic media of politicians saying or doing things they never did—illustrates the theatricality of digital deception. A false video does not need to be believed universally; it needs only to spread doubt, to circulate widely enough that trust erodes. In this way, cyber armies weaponise the spectacle of information itself, turning the very act of public debate into an arena of uncertainty. The goal is not victory in the conventional sense, but the destabilisation of collective confidence: if nothing can be trusted, then nothing can be resisted with certainty. *The spectacle is not the lie itself but the collapse of trust it produces.*

Spectacle also functions internally, shaping the morale and cohesion of the groups themselves. Militias that broadcast their brutality do so not only to intimidate outsiders but to harden insiders. Participating in or even witnessing acts of spectacular violence binds recruits into a shared moral universe, where brutality is no longer an aberration but a ritual. The performance of violence is thus both external propaganda and internal initiation. The same is true in cyberspace: hacker collectives that announce large-scale breaches or defacements strengthen their internal bonds by dramatising their capabilities to one another. The performance of power sustains loyalty in groups that might otherwise fragment.

The strategic use of spectacle creates difficult dilemmas for governments and media alike. To cover an atrocity risks amplifying its psychological effect; to ignore it risks minimising the suffering of victims or leaving propaganda unchallenged. When IS beheading videos surfaced, many news outlets debated whether to show stills, blurred frames, or nothing at all. Each choice carried consequences. Similarly, when cyberattacks unfold, the timing and framing of government announcements determine whether the public perceives resilience or vulnerability. The theatre of terror forces its adversaries into the role of audience, compelled to respond even when silence might be preferable.

The effectiveness of theatrical violence also exposes an uncomfortable truth: *terror works because people watch.* Spectacle relies on the infrastructure of media and communication. Without satellite channels, social media platforms, and instant news cycles, the capacity of militias and cyber armies to amplify their acts would be severely constrained. Yet in liberal societies committed to freedom of speech and information, curtailing the circulation of such spectacles raises profound ethical challenges. Restricting images of violence risks censorship; permitting them risks psychological manipulation. Terror thus exploits the very openness of modern communication systems.

Beyond immediate fear, the theatre of violence has long-term political consequences. Spectacular acts often provoke disproportionate responses that serve the perpetrators' strategic aims. The September 11 attacks, for instance, killed thousands, but their theatrical impact reshaped global politics for decades. By staging the most visually striking terrorist act in modern history, al-Qaeda succeeded in drawing the United States into costly wars that destabilised entire regions. Similarly, when small militias commit brutal acts that receive outsized attention, they gain influence far beyond their actual military strength. In this way, spectacle distorts the calculus of power: the ability to shock becomes as valuable as the ability to win battles.

What distinguishes today's environment is the blurring of physical and digital theatres. A beheading video and a hacked power grid are both performances, designed for maximum psychological effect. Militias that once relied on spectacle in the physical domain now amplify it digitally, while cyber armies adapt techniques of theatre from insurgent groups. The merging of these spheres means that modern warfare is increasingly fought in the mind of the observer. The battlefield may be a street in Raqqa or a server farm in Kiev, but the decisive terrain is public perception. *Terror as theatre collapses geography, making every screen a front line.*

Ultimately, the concept of terror as theatre underscores the asymmetry of modern conflict. Groups that cannot match states in conventional military power instead turn to performance, where impact is not measured in casualties or territory but in the scale of psychological disruption. They understand that fear spreads faster than bullets, that perception can outweigh reality, and that the image of power can sometimes be more effective than power itself. In this way, militias and cyber armies exploit one of the oldest truths of conflict: that wars are won not only on battlefields, but in the minds of those who watch them unfold.

The Civilian's New Reality

For most of human history, the primary danger to civilians in war came from invading armies and occupying forces. Today, the experience of ordinary people caught in conflict is shaped by something far more fragmented and unpredictable: the outsourcing of violence. The rise of private military contractors, proxy militias, cyber armies, and corporate security forces means that civilians increasingly live in landscapes where power is exercised not by a single authority but by overlapping actors with competing agendas. *This shift has altered not only the physical dangers people face but also the very texture of daily life—how they assess risk, who they trust, and what they fear.*

In fragile states from Libya to Afghanistan, it is no longer unusual for civilians to interact with several different armed providers of security in a single week. One day a private military contractor might be escorting a humanitarian convoy; the next, a local militia controls the checkpoint on the road to market; and in the evenings, rumours circulate online of cyber intrusions or surveillance that suggest foreign intelligence services are watching. The citizen does not ask who holds legitimate sovereignty—they ask who has the power that day, who controls the streets, who can guarantee safe passage. This constant recalibration breeds a survivalist pragmatism: loyalty is transactional, trust is provisional, and fear is ambient rather than episodic.

The phenomenon is stark in oil-rich states and conflict zones where multinational corporations hire private security firms to protect pipelines, refineries, or mining sites. For the workers who live in nearby communities, the company's guards may be the most visible armed presence. They enforce order, deter attacks, and sometimes mediate disputes—but they answer not to the public but to the firm that pays them. Civilians thus experience security as a commodity: something that exists not as a public good but as a service purchased by those with resources. *This commodification of protection corrodes the traditional expectation that the state's monopoly on violence is linked to responsibility for its citizens.* Instead, violence becomes part of an outsourced ecosystem, where protection is unevenly distributed and contingent on financial or political leverage.

At the same time, civilians must navigate the unpredictable psychological impact of cyber conflict. Unlike bombs or bullets, cyberattacks create uncertainty without clear boundaries. When ransomware disables a hospital's IT systems, patients waiting for surgery are as much casualties of war as soldiers on the front line. When a state-sponsored cyber unit hacks mobile phone networks, ordinary users cannot distinguish between espionage, propaganda, or criminality. Fear becomes ambient, intangible, and often more corrosive than visible threats. *In digital battlefields, the civilian's new reality is one of blurred lines between everyday life and acts of war: a shopping transaction, a news headline, or a text message may carry hidden risks.*

This environment demands new coping strategies. Communities living under such conditions often develop sophisticated, if informal, systems of intelligence. Families track rumours of which roads are safe, neighbourhoods share knowledge of militia commanders' shifting allegiances, and young people develop keen instincts for detecting disinformation online. Trust, however, becomes hyper-localised: people may trust neighbours or kin, but rarely institutions. The state—too weak or too compromised to deliver consistent protection—is sidelined as a reference point. Instead, legitimacy is derived from actors who demonstrate capacity, however coercively, to enforce some semblance of order.

The effects on civic identity are profound. In a world where violence is outsourced, civilians no longer relate to the state as guarantor of safety; they relate to multiple actors as negotiators of survival. This fractures the social contract. In Somalia, for instance, residents in Mogadishu may rely on clan militias for immediate protection, private security for commercial transactions, and international peacekeepers for strategic stability. Each provides a piece of the puzzle, but none provides the whole. *The result is not anarchy, but a patchwork of overlapping sovereignties that redefine what it means to be a citizen.*

For wealthier civilians—particularly expatriates, contractors, and business elites—the new reality often involves access to layers of private security that insulate them from many of the dangers faced by local populations. Armoured convoys, fortified compounds, and insurance packages create parallel worlds of safety. Yet this stratification deepens inequality: those who cannot afford such measures are left exposed. The globalisation of private violence thus not only fragments authority but exacerbates divides between protected and unprotected, insiders and outsiders, those who can purchase security and those who must navigate without it.

The psychological toll should not be underestimated. Living under constant, fragmented threat erodes the ability to plan for the future. Families delay investment in businesses, parents hesitate to send children to school if the routes are unsafe, and entire communities internalise uncertainty as the baseline condition of life. In cyberspace, a comparable anxiety arises: if digital infrastructure is perpetually vulnerable to attack, how can citizens trust banks, governments, or even social connections? This chronic insecurity reshapes what it means to live in conflict zones, creating an enduring sense of fragility even in moments of calm.

Outsourced violence also complicates accountability. When civilians are harmed by militias, private contractors, or cyber units, the chain of responsibility is often opaque. Was the contractor acting under direct state orders or in pursuit of corporate interests? Was the disinformation campaign orchestrated by a government, or by a proxy group working with tacit approval? For the civilian, the distinction is irrelevant: harm is harm. But for justice, the distinction matters deeply—and too often, it remains unresolved. *This accountability vacuum leaves civilians not only vulnerable to harm but also deprived of recourse.*

Yet civilians are not passive victims. In many contexts, they adapt creatively to these conditions. In Latin America, communities in cartel-dominated regions have developed their own systems of local defence, sometimes arming themselves, sometimes negotiating truces, sometimes appealing to international attention. In Ukraine, civilians became active participants in the digital war, flagging disinformation, contributing to cyber defence, and creating grassroots intelligence networks. The civilian's new reality is not one of helplessness, but of constant negotiation—between fear and resilience, between dependence and agency, between vulnerability and adaptation.

The outsourcing of violence does not mean the disappearance of order; it means that order is plural, contested, and conditional. For civilians, this reality is disorienting but not entirely novel. In many parts of the world, the state was never the sole provider of security. What is different today is the scale and complexity of the actors involved—global corporations, foreign militaries, transnational criminal networks, and anonymous cyber collectives. Civilians must now navigate not only local power brokers but global ones, whose decisions in distant capitals or boardrooms shape the risks they face on the ground.

This new reality is a stark reminder that war is no longer something that happens *to* civilians in moments of declared conflict; it is something woven into the fabric of daily life through diffuse and outsourced mechanisms of violence. To live under such conditions is to live with a constant recalibration of trust, an ever-present awareness of risk, and the knowledge that protection is not a right but a privilege. *The modern civilian's battlefield is everywhere and nowhere at once, defined less by front lines than by shifting networks of power.*

Chapter 8

The Collapse of Accountability

Modern conflict is not defined solely by the weapons used or the actors who wield them, but by the growing absence of responsibility for the harm inflicted. When a drone piloted by an artificial intelligence system misidentifies a target, or when a mercenary company massacres civilians while under opaque contractual arrangements, the central question becomes not *what happened* but *who, if anyone, can be held to account.* This is not a peripheral issue of legal semantics; it strikes at the heart of the moral and political architecture that underpins international order. *Accountability was once the fragile thread linking violence to justice, war to law, and power to legitimacy. Its collapse is among the most defining transformations of contemporary conflict.*

Consider the aftermath of a battlefield atrocity: a village reduced to rubble, unarmed civilians left dead, evidence of deliberate targeting. In earlier decades, international law provided at least a formal route toward redress. Perpetrators might be tried in national courts, commanders could face tribunals, and states could be sanctioned for breaches of the Geneva Conventions. Today, the path is often obscured or blocked entirely. If the actors responsible are private military contractors hired through shell companies, jurisdiction is muddled: are they subject to the laws of the hiring state, the host state, or none at all? If the attack was carried out by autonomous drones operating under machine-learning algorithms, who bears culpability—the programmer, the commander who deployed the system, or the machine itself? *The battlefield, once tethered to chains of command, is now littered with broken lines of accountability.*

This legal disarray is not accidental. States benefit from it. The outsourcing of violence to proxies, mercenaries, or cyber militias offers strategic deniability: actions can be disowned, responsibility deferred, and blame redirected. Russia's use of the Wagner Group in Ukraine, Syria, and Africa exemplifies this tactic: the Kremlin reaped the benefits of projection without formally acknowledging the costs or admitting liability. Likewise, states that deploy offensive cyber operations can deny involvement by pointing to the difficulty of attribution in digital domains. In this sense, *the collapse of accountability is not merely a side effect of new forms of warfare; it is a feature deliberately cultivated to preserve strategic flexibility while minimising political risk.*

International law, designed for an earlier age, is proving ill-suited to these challenges. The Geneva Conventions and subsequent treaties presupposed clear categories: combatant and civilian, war and peace, state and non-state actor. Private military companies blur those distinctions, operating simultaneously as businesses, armies, and political tools. Cyber warfare escapes territorial definitions altogether: a malware attack launched in one country, routed through dozens of servers, and executed by a mix of state and non-state actors defies conventional models of jurisdiction. The principle of sovereignty—once the anchor of accountability—is becoming porous in the face of transnational, deniable violence. *The fog of law now parallels the fog of war, leaving gaps that those with power are adept at exploiting.*

The implications are profound. Without enforceable norms, war becomes less constrained not only in practice but also in perception. If atrocities are committed without consequence, they risk becoming normalised, folded into the background noise of conflict rather than condemned as violations of human dignity. Civilians learn quickly that appeals to international justice are hollow; communities devastated by contractors or cyberattacks rarely see perpetrators face trial. This breeds cynicism, eroding the legitimacy of international institutions and weakening the fragile trust that underpins the possibility of cooperation between states. *When accountability collapses, it is not only victims who lose; the entire architecture of international order begins to corrode.*

Yet the story is not solely one of absence. New frameworks are emerging, tentative and uneven, but important nonetheless. Some propose treating private military companies not as anomalies but as regulated actors akin to corporations, subject to binding international law and transparent oversight. Others advocate for a Geneva Convention for cyberspace, establishing norms around acceptable targets, attribution mechanisms, and bans on particular classes of cyberweapons. There are also efforts to embed responsibility directly into the design of autonomous systems, requiring human-in-the-loop decision-making or clear audit trails for algorithmic choices. While none of these initiatives has yet stabilised into binding global norms, they signal a recognition that the collapse of accountability cannot go unaddressed. *The task is not to return to an imagined past of absolute state monopoly on violence, but to adapt principles of responsibility to a plural and technologically complex battlefield.*

The challenge, however, is that accountability requires not only legal codification but political will. States that benefit from deniability have little incentive to constrain themselves. Powerful actors often resist rules that might limit their freedom of manoeuvre. Even when treaties are negotiated, enforcement is weak: international courts depend on state cooperation, and sanctions can be circumvented. This asymmetry creates a world in which accountability is most likely to be enforced against weaker actors, while stronger ones evade scrutiny. The collapse of accountability thus deepens global inequality, insulating great powers while exposing fragile states and non-state actors to disproportionate scrutiny.

Still, there is a deeper philosophical dimension that must be confronted. Responsibility in war has traditionally been understood as human and hierarchical: leaders command, soldiers execute, courts adjudicate. But in an age of autonomous systems and distributed networks, the chain of causation fractures. Algorithms make decisions based on data sets opaque even to their designers, mercenaries act in shifting contractual arrangements that diffuse intent, and cyber militias emerge spontaneously from online communities with only loose connections to states. *The problem is not only that accountability has collapsed, but that our very conception of accountability may need to be reimagined.*

The collapse of accountability in modern warfare is not just a legal or political dilemma—it is an existential one. To live in a world where violence is unmoored from responsibility is to accept a future where justice is perpetually deferred, where victims are left in silence, and where power operates without checks. This chapter interrogates that collapse: how it emerged, why it persists, and what faint signs of renewal might yet point the way toward new norms. If the battlefield has become ungoverned space, the pressing question is not whether accountability can be restored to what it once was, but whether it can be reinvented for the conflicts of today and tomorrow.

Who Owns the Battlefield?

When a war crime is committed by a state army, the framework of responsibility is difficult enough to enforce, but at least the contours are familiar: commanders may be tried, soldiers prosecuted, governments sanctioned. Yet when the perpetrator is a private military contractor in the employ of multiple intermediaries, or when the action is executed by an artificial intelligence system that operates beyond clear human oversight, the question of *who owns the battlefield* becomes not merely practical but existential. The contemporary battlefield is crowded with actors who are neither clearly accountable to international law nor confined within the jurisdiction of any one state. This erosion of clarity raises the most fundamental of questions: when violence occurs outside the traditional chain of command, whose law governs, and whose justice applies?

The example of Nisour Square in Baghdad in 2007 illustrates the point with brutal clarity. Blackwater contractors, hired by the United States government to protect diplomatic personnel, opened fire in a crowded traffic roundabout, killing 17 Iraqi civilians. For years, legal proceedings floundered, caught in a tangle of overlapping jurisdictions and political pressure. Were the contractors accountable under Iraqi law, where the killings occurred? Under American military law, though they were not soldiers? Or under civilian criminal statutes, despite operating in a war zone? The eventual convictions and later presidential pardons underscored not resolution but fragility: accountability was possible only through political will, and reversible at a stroke. *The battlefield had no clear owner, and the law proved malleable in the hands of power.*

Artificial intelligence magnifies this dilemma. Imagine an autonomous drone misidentifying a wedding procession as an insurgent convoy, launching a strike that kills dozens. Does culpability rest with the military commander who deployed the system, the engineers who coded its targeting algorithms, the manufacturer that built its sensors, or the state that authorised its use? Traditional doctrines of command responsibility falter in the face of distributed agency, where intent is diffuse and decision-making opaque. Legal systems grounded in human culpability struggle to ascribe responsibility to code, and yet *to leave such acts unpunished risks normalising a violence unmoored from human accountability altogether.*

The problem is compounded by the geography of modern conflict. Warfare today is not confined to state borders or neatly defined battle zones. Cyberattacks launched from one jurisdiction ripple across global financial systems and power grids; mercenary groups based in one state carry out missions in another, often financed by a third. In Mali, Wagner Group operatives have been accused of massacres, but trials are elusive: Russian domestic law shields its nationals, Mali's fragile judiciary lacks power, and international courts move slowly if at all. In cyberspace, attribution itself is contested—was a given attack the work of a state military unit, a patriotic hacker collective, or a for-hire cyber mercenary? *Without attribution, jurisdiction collapses; without jurisdiction, accountability dissolves.*

International law has tried, haltingly, to adapt. The Geneva Conventions and Additional Protocols sought to protect civilians and codify the responsibilities of combatants, but they presupposed identifiable state actors and uniformed soldiers. The Montreux Document of 2008 attempted to establish best practices for private military and security companies, but it is non-binding, unenforceable, and often ignored. Efforts to draft international treaties on lethal autonomous weapons—often dubbed "killer robots"—have stalled at the United Nations, blocked by states that view regulation as a strategic constraint. Cyber norms, too, are debated endlessly but rarely agreed upon. *The legal architecture remains rooted in twentieth-century assumptions of state control, even as the twenty-first century battlefield is populated by actors untethered from state sovereignty.*

The question of ownership is therefore not merely about jurisdiction but about legitimacy. Who has the authority to decide when and how law applies in spaces where traditional sovereignty is fractured? For communities on the receiving end of violence, the absence of legal recourse reinforces perceptions of abandonment. Civilians killed by contractors in Iraq, targeted by drones in Afghanistan, or harmed by cyberattacks on hospitals during the COVID-19 pandemic often have no viable route to justice. They live in a world where the perpetrators of harm operate under multiple shields—contractual, technological, political—none of which align with their lived experience of loss. *To ask who owns the battlefield is also to ask who owns the responsibility for human suffering in war.*

There are competing philosophical perspectives on this impasse. Some argue that sovereignty must be reasserted: states must be held accountable for the actions of contractors and machines they employ, regardless of outsourcing or technological mediation. This view treats private or autonomous actors as extensions of state power, closing loopholes by reattaching accountability to its source. Others contend that new categories of responsibility must be invented: corporations, programmers, and even algorithms themselves must be recognised as actors in international law. A third, more sceptical position suggests that war has always been about impunity for the powerful, and what we are witnessing today is less a collapse of accountability than its logical continuation under new guises. *Each perspective frames ownership differently—state-centric, distributed, or nihilistic—but none resolves the core dilemma in practice.*

Pragmatic attempts to address the gap often collapse under the weight of politics. International Criminal Court prosecutions depend on cooperation from states least inclined to subject themselves to scrutiny. National courts may lack extraterritorial jurisdiction or political will. Civil lawsuits against contractors are lengthy, expensive, and often dismissed on grounds of immunity. Meanwhile, the victims of algorithmic or privatised violence are left in limbo, their suffering acknowledged in reports but rarely adjudicated in courts. *The disjuncture between harm and justice grows wider, eroding faith in the very idea that war can be governed by law.*

The battlefield, then, is not simply a physical space of conflict; it is a contested legal and moral terrain. Ownership is dispersed, overlapping, and often deliberately obfuscated. States, corporations, militias, and algorithms all shape the outcomes of violence, but none are reliably held to account when atrocities occur. To interrogate who owns the battlefield is to confront the uncomfortable reality that, at present, it may belong to no one—or worse, it may belong only to those powerful enough to shape its outcomes while evading its consequences. The urgency lies in recognising that unless ownership is clarified, violence risks becoming a domain of unchecked impunity, where the victims are many, the perpetrators diffuse, and justice perpetually deferred.

The Fog of Law

The laws of war, once drafted in the shadow of battlefields dominated by nation-states and uniformed armies, were never designed to cope with the fractured, outsourced, and digitised nature of violence in the twenty-first century. The Geneva Conventions of 1949, hailed as the bedrock of humanitarian law, make sense when combatants are soldiers identifiable by insignia, accountable to a sovereign chain of command, and confined to territorially defined wars. They falter when those who carry weapons are contractors working for a foreign government, militias fighting for ideology or profit, or algorithms executing decisions without human oversight. International treaties have not so much failed outright as been outpaced, caught in a fog where the actors of modern conflict cannot be neatly classified and the norms that might regulate them remain contested or absent. *The battlefield has transformed faster than the law has evolved, leaving states, corporations, and civilians navigating legal ambiguity as dangerous as the conflicts themselves.*

Private military companies (PMCs) exemplify this problem. By the late twentieth century, their rise blurred the line between soldier and contractor, public interest and private profit. Yet the legal architecture governing their activities remains skeletal. The Montreux Document of 2008 was an attempt to establish guiding principles on PMCs, endorsed by dozens of states. It was not a treaty but a voluntary framework, offering best practices rather than binding law. The absence of enforceability means that contractors implicated in atrocities—from the Sierra Leone civil war to Iraq's Nisour Square massacre—often escape meaningful accountability. States that hire PMCs can deny direct responsibility, while contractors argue they were acting under orders. *The result is a zone of impunity: everyone is partially accountable, but no one is fully responsible.*

Cyberspace has only deepened the legal vacuum. The Tallinn Manual, drafted by international legal scholars, sought to apply existing laws of armed conflict to cyber warfare. But its authority is interpretive, not legal; it reflects consensus among experts, not binding commitments among states. Nations pick and choose when to invoke its principles, often subordinating them to strategic convenience. Cyber operations rarely trigger the thresholds of "armed attack" that would justify self-defence under the UN Charter, yet their consequences can be devastating: paralysing hospitals, disrupting elections, or crippling critical infrastructure. *The law struggles to recognise war without bombs, damage without craters, and enemies without uniforms.*

The fog is not accidental. States exploit ambiguity to pursue military aims while avoiding the costs of formal war. Plausible deniability thrives in legal grey zones. Russia has relied on Wagner Group contractors and "little green men" to intervene in Ukraine and Africa while denying official involvement. The United States has employed drone strikes and private contractors in ways that stretch the definitions of combat and combatant. China and Iran maintain cyber units whose operations blur espionage, sabotage, and warfare. By operating in spaces where international law is either unclear or unenforceable, powerful actors reap strategic gains while insulating themselves from legal repercussions. *Ambiguity becomes a weapon, as useful as guns or malware, precisely because it shields perpetrators from accountability.*

The philosophical tension lies in whether international law must adapt to new forms of conflict or whether it should constrain them by reaffirming traditional boundaries. Advocates of adaptation argue that PMCs, hackers, and autonomous systems must be integrated into legal frameworks as legitimate actors, each with defined responsibilities and liabilities. Critics fear that such recognition would normalise their existence, eroding the principle that states alone should hold a monopoly on legitimate violence. In cyber law, some scholars insist that only a wholesale rewriting of treaties can address the realities of digital conflict, while others argue that stretching existing principles is sufficient. *At stake is not merely regulation but the very definition of war and who has the authority to wage it.*

Real-world consequences of this legal fog are profound. In Iraq and Afghanistan, civilians harmed by contractors often had no recourse to either local courts or international tribunals. Victims of cyberattacks struggle to attribute responsibility, let alone demand justice, when perpetrators hide behind layers of anonymity and state denial. Even where trials occur, such as the belated prosecution of Blackwater guards in the United States, outcomes are shaped as much by political calculation as by law. In the cyber domain, attribution disputes allow states to deny involvement and stall international condemnation. The absence of enforceable norms leaves the victims of twenty-first-century conflicts in a legal no-man's-land, their suffering acknowledged in reports but rarely redressed in courts.

Attempts to pierce the fog have repeatedly faltered. The UN's efforts to regulate lethal autonomous weapons have been deadlocked by geopolitical rivalry. Proposals to strengthen regulation of PMCs through binding treaties face resistance from states that rely on them for strategic flexibility. In cyberspace, repeated attempts to establish global agreements on behaviour—such as prohibiting attacks on critical infrastructure—collapse under mistrust between great powers. Even when norms are declared, enforcement mechanisms are weak or non-existent. *Lawmakers remain reactive, struggling to patch outdated frameworks rather than proactively designing institutions for a transformed battlefield.*

The fog of law thus serves not only as a metaphor for confusion but as a description of deliberate opacity. States and corporations benefit from a landscape where accountability is uncertain, responsibility dispersed, and enforcement rare. Yet the longer this fog persists, the more it corrodes the legitimacy of international law itself. If treaties fail to regulate those who wage war in practice, their authority withers, and the idea that war can be bounded by law risks becoming obsolete. What is left is a global security environment where violence is outsourced, digitalised, and automated, but justice is neither local nor global—merely absent.

To understand the fog of law is to confront the uncomfortable truth that the rules governing war are no longer universal. They are contingent, selective, and often performative. States invoke them when convenient and ignore them when strategic. PMCs operate in gaps between jurisdictions, while cyber armies exploit the borderless nature of networks. Emerging technologies only widen the gap between law's intent and law's reach. The challenge ahead is not only to clarify these laws but to ask whether international society can summon the political will to create binding norms for a battlefield that is increasingly stateless, digital, and privatised. Until then, *law remains more an aspiration than a shield, a fog through which violence passes largely unimpeded.*

The Deniability Dilemma

Few strategies have proved as useful to modern states as plausible deniability. It enables them to act with force while pretending restraint, to reap the benefits of aggression without paying the costs of accountability. In an age where warfare is no longer the exclusive domain of national armies but increasingly outsourced to contractors, militias, hackers, and autonomous systems, deniability has become not merely a tactic but a governing logic of conflict. *By creating distance between action and attribution, states weaponise ambiguity itself, making accountability not just difficult but structurally unattainable.*

The appeal of deniability rests on the shifting standards of proof in international politics. Unlike a courtroom, where evidence can establish guilt beyond reasonable doubt, the arena of geopolitics is built on perception, suspicion, and narrative. States accused of sponsoring cyberattacks or deploying mercenaries can exploit the absence of definitive attribution to deny involvement, knowing that opponents rarely risk escalation based on uncertain evidence. This gap between what is suspected and what can be proven creates the space in which states manoeuvre. The result is a paradox: the more sophisticated intelligence becomes, the more sophisticated denials also become, and the cycle of ambiguity deepens.

Private military companies illustrate the phenomenon with clarity. Russia's Wagner Group, deployed from Ukraine to Syria to the Sahel, has repeatedly acted in ways indistinguishable from official military operations: securing territory, suppressing opposition, and advancing Moscow's foreign policy goals. Yet the Kremlin insists Wagner is a private venture, unaffiliated with the Russian state. This denial is thin—Wagner depends on Russian military logistics, intelligence, and political cover—but effective. It allows Moscow to project power without formally committing its armed forces, thus avoiding direct legal or diplomatic consequences. When atrocities occur, the state's hands remain ostensibly clean, while Wagner's opaque corporate structure obscures accountability further. *The denial is not meant to be believed in a literal sense; it is meant to be irrefutable in a legal one.*

Cyber warfare takes deniability to another level. Unlike mercenaries on the ground, hackers leave trails of code, server logs, and digital artefacts—but these traces are endlessly malleable. A cyberattack can be routed through servers in multiple countries, mimicking the signatures of other groups, or concealed within ordinary network traffic. Attribution requires months of forensic analysis, during which the political moment may pass and retaliation may be deemed impractical. The Stuxnet attack on Iran's nuclear facilities in 2010—widely attributed to the United States and Israel—was never officially acknowledged by either country. Even when evidence mounts, silence persists, because denying involvement allows states to enjoy the benefits of sabotage without admitting to setting precedents that others might later exploit. In cyberspace, *the threshold for definitive proof is almost unattainably high, ensuring that deniability is not an occasional refuge but the default condition of conflict.*

The deniability dilemma is not merely a product of technological complexity but also of political calculation. States have discovered that operating through proxies is not only less costly in terms of blood and treasure but also diplomatically safer. Sponsoring militias, insurgents, or cartel-linked actors allows governments to destabilise rivals while disclaiming direct involvement. Iran's use of Hezbollah, the United States' reliance on Kurdish militias in Syria, and Pakistan's longstanding ties to militant groups in Afghanistan all reveal the same logic: the state can shape outcomes while avoiding the risks of open war. The denials may be unconvincing to analysts, but they provide cover for domestic audiences and a fig leaf of legitimacy in international forums.

Yet deniability corrodes the very idea of accountability in war. Traditional frameworks of humanitarian law presuppose identifiable actors who can be held responsible—states, militaries, commanders. But if responsibility can be outsourced, fragmented, or hidden behind corporate structures, the chain of accountability breaks. When a drone strike is carried out by contractors rather than soldiers, who is liable for civilian deaths: the company, the contractor, or the state that hired them? When an algorithm selects a target in milliseconds, can a commander truly claim authorship of the decision? The diffusion of responsibility creates an environment in which harm is abundant but blame is scarce. *The violence is real, but the perpetrator is perpetually elusive.*

The philosophical implications are stark. Deniability erodes not only accountability but also the norms of deterrence. Classical deterrence theory relies on clear attribution: adversaries refrain from aggression because they fear punishment. But when attribution is obscured, deterrence collapses. If a hospital's network is paralysed by ransomware, but the attack could plausibly have originated from criminals, activists, or state-backed hackers, retaliation becomes uncertain. States may hesitate to strike back, fearing miscalculation. This uncertainty incentivises further covert operations, as aggressors learn that ambiguity shields them more effectively than armour. In this sense, *deniability has become the currency of modern conflict: it buys room for manoeuvre, lowers the cost of aggression, and raises the threshold for accountability.*

There is, however, a tension worth examining: deniability is most effective when audiences remain credulous, yet in many cases the denial is so implausible that no one truly believes it. Russia's denials of involvement in Crimea in 2014 were met with near-universal scepticism, yet they succeeded strategically because they created just enough doubt to prevent decisive international action. Similarly, China's disavowal of state-sponsored cyber theft is met with widespread disbelief, but absent definitive legal proof, sanctions are piecemeal and accountability diffused. The paradox is that denials need not convince; they need only confuse. The audience is not expected to accept the lie, merely to acknowledge that the truth cannot be proven.

Attempts to close this loophole face formidable obstacles. Strengthening attribution mechanisms in cyber warfare has proven technically difficult and politically divisive. Regulating PMCs through binding international treaties is resisted by the very states that benefit from their deniability. Emerging discussions on autonomous weapons systems reveal the same tension: delegating lethal decisions to algorithms allows states to disown responsibility when things go wrong, attributing errors to technical malfunction rather than political intent. As the tools of war become more distributed, automated, and outsourced, deniability is not retreating but expanding. *It is not a symptom of disorder but an intentional strategy, a way of waging war that thrives in the seams of law and technology.*

The deniability dilemma leaves civilians in the most precarious position. When violence is inflicted, whether through mercenaries on the ground or hackers in the cloud, victims struggle to identify a perpetrator against whom they can seek justice. International courts are hamstrung by questions of jurisdiction, while domestic courts often lack the evidence or authority to prosecute. The moral calculus is inverted: the weaker the victim, the stronger the protection enjoyed by the perpetrator through the cloak of deniability. The result is a battlefield where accountability is not absent but deliberately untraceable.

Ultimately, plausible deniability reshapes the ethics and politics of war itself. It transforms accountability from a principle into a bargaining chip, deployed when convenient and denied when costly. States, contractors, and cyber units all benefit from this ambiguity, but its cumulative effect is corrosive. Law is weakened, deterrence is undermined, and victims are silenced. Deniability was once a tactical device, used sparingly in the shadows. Today it is the architecture of conflict, a pervasive strategy that defines the twenty-first century battlefield more than firepower or territory. *The dilemma is that while everyone knows who is responsible, no one can ever be held responsible—and that is precisely the point.*

Toward New Norms

The collapse of accountability in modern conflict is often described as a crisis of law, yet it may be more accurately understood as a crisis of imagination. International legal frameworks that once appeared robust—the Geneva Conventions, conventions on mercenaries, treaties banning chemical and biological weapons—were built for a world in which states were the primary actors and armies were the primary instruments of violence. That world has receded. Today's conflicts are fought with drones piloted by contractors, cyber units hidden behind screens, and militias that blur into criminal networks. Traditional mechanisms of accountability falter not because they are forgotten, but because they no longer map onto the reality of warfare. *The question is not whether accountability is necessary, but whether it can be reconstituted in forms that match the distributed, deniable, and digital nature of contemporary violence.*

Emerging efforts point toward frameworks that diverge from the old state monopoly on violence without abandoning the demand for responsibility. These attempts are fragmented and tentative, but they suggest directions in which accountability might evolve. One approach emphasises corporate responsibility. Private military companies, cyber security firms, and arms manufacturers operate in legal grey zones, profiting from conflict while insulated from liability. Extending principles of corporate due diligence—already applied in areas such as human rights and environmental protection—into the security sector would create obligations not just for states but for firms. If a PMC commits atrocities in a conflict zone, the company's investors and executives could be held legally and financially accountable, much as corporations today face litigation for complicity in forced labour or environmental destruction. *The battlefield would no longer be shielded from corporate law; it would be enfolded within it.*

Another pathway lies in technological attribution. For decades, the problem of cyber warfare has been framed by its anonymity—attacks are easy to launch, hard to trace. Yet advances in digital forensics, blockchain-based verification, and artificial intelligence are beginning to make attribution more reliable. While no system can eliminate uncertainty entirely, a shared international architecture for cyber incident verification could establish thresholds of evidence sufficient to trigger accountability mechanisms. This would require cooperation among states, tech companies, and independent watchdogs, but it would also create a new norm: that denial in the face of overwhelming forensic evidence carries political cost. *Accountability in cyberspace may not depend on eliminating doubt, but on redefining how much doubt is tolerable.*

There are also experiments in extending jurisdiction beyond borders. The International Criminal Court, though limited, has asserted authority over crimes committed by non-state actors where state courts fail. Universal jurisdiction—the principle that some crimes are so grave they can be prosecuted anywhere—offers another tool. Applied selectively to mercenary abuses, war profiteering, or algorithmic warfare gone awry, it could close loopholes exploited by states hiding behind contractors or code. The obstacles are immense: political resistance, selective enforcement, accusations of neo-colonial bias. But precedents matter. Each prosecution, however imperfect, chips away at the expectation of impunity. *Even partial enforcement can signal that deniability is not an impenetrable shield but a temporary refuge.*

Civil society is also becoming a locus of accountability. Non-governmental organisations, investigative journalists, and open-source intelligence communities now document war crimes in near-real time, often with greater accuracy than official bodies. From satellite imagery of bombed hospitals to geolocated videos of militia executions, the evidence collected by citizens has already shaped international opinion and policy. What is emerging is not simply transparency but a form of distributed accountability, where states and corporations are judged in the court of global public opinion, amplified by digital networks. While such judgments lack the force of law, they wield political and reputational power. Governments and firms increasingly recognise that denial is less effective in an age when evidence circulates instantly and globally. *The new norm may be that accountability is not imposed from above, but demanded from below.*

A further innovation lies in the regulation of algorithms themselves. As artificial intelligence assumes roles in targeting, surveillance, and battlefield decision-making, the line between human agency and machine action blurs. Traditional legal doctrines rely on the idea of a responsible human actor—a commander, a soldier, a policymaker. But when an autonomous system selects and engages a target, responsibility is diffused across engineers, operators, and political leaders. To address this, some propose "explainability standards" requiring AI systems used in warfare to generate audit trails that can be examined post-action. Others argue for codifying a principle of "meaningful human control," ensuring that lethal decisions cannot be fully delegated to machines. These frameworks do not restore the old model of accountability but create new ones, in which responsibility attaches to the design, deployment, and oversight of code as much as to the pulling of a trigger. *In the age of autonomous weapons, accountability may reside in systems architecture as much as in human intent.*

Crucially, emerging norms need not come only from states. Cities, corporations, and international organisations increasingly shape global security practices. Municipalities that adopt sanctuary policies, tech firms that refuse contracts for lethal AI, or financial institutions that blacklist mercenary-linked companies all contribute to a patchwork of accountability mechanisms. These actions are often uneven and politically contested, yet they demonstrate that power to define norms is no longer monopolised by sovereign governments. *The diffusion of authority mirrors the diffusion of violence; both create instability, but both also open new spaces for innovation.*

Of course, there are dangers. Norms that emerge from decentralised processes risk being selective, biased, or easily manipulated. Public shaming may substitute for legal due process; forensic attribution may be politicised; corporate responsibility regimes may be more symbolic than substantive. Yet the alternative—clinging to outdated state-centric models while impunity flourishes—is worse. Norms do not need to be perfect to be valuable; they need only to shift expectations, gradually recalibrating what is tolerated and what is condemned.

What becomes evident is that accountability in the twenty-first century cannot be about restoring a lost monopoly of state violence. The battlefield is too fragmented, the actors too numerous, the technologies too autonomous. Instead, new norms must recognise this plurality and build responsibility into it. They must hold firms as well as states, engineers as well as generals, networks as well as hierarchies. Accountability will not be a return to the past but a reinvention for the future. *The task is not to close the spaces where deniability thrives, but to illuminate them with frameworks that make denial costly, and responsibility inescapable.*

Chapter 9

Democracy Under Siege

Democracy has always been fragile, but the threats it faces today are of a distinctly new order. Its vulnerabilities no longer lie solely in tanks at the border or coups within parliaments; they are embedded in invisible algorithms, covert networks, and platforms that shape what citizens see, hear, and believe. The democratic process, once thought secure behind constitutions and institutions, has become an exposed frontier in the shifting landscape of hybrid conflict. *What is striking is not simply that democracies are under attack, but that their greatest strengths—openness, pluralism, and the free circulation of ideas—have been re-engineered into weapons against them.*

Elections have become the most visible battlegrounds in this struggle. Where armies once sought to conquer territory, hostile actors now seek to conquer perception. The 2016 United States presidential election, with Russian disinformation campaigns and data-driven targeting of voters, demonstrated that interference no longer requires the deployment of troops or the occupation of land. It requires the strategic seeding of narratives, micro-targeted advertising, and the manipulation of social networks. In countries from Brazil to India, electoral integrity is now contested not only at ballot boxes but in the torrents of disinformation circulating on WhatsApp, Twitter, and Facebook. *The act of voting still takes place in polling stations, but the decision of how to vote is increasingly shaped in the opaque corners of cyberspace.*

The corrosion, however, extends beyond election cycles. The weaponisation of trust undermines the very institutions that sustain democratic life. Disinformation campaigns rarely aim to persuade everyone of a single lie; more often, they seek to erode confidence altogether—confidence in the press, in judges, in scientific expertise, even in the possibility of shared truth. This is a form of political entropy: by injecting doubt and confusion, attackers weaken the ability of citizens to distinguish between fact and fabrication. Democracies survive on the presumption that arguments can be resolved through evidence, debate, and majority decision. But when truth itself is destabilised, those mechanisms falter. *An electorate that cannot agree on what is real cannot sustain the idea of legitimate governance.*

Into this vacuum step the private platforms that mediate almost all contemporary public discourse. Facebook's content moderation policies, Twitter's suspension of accounts, and YouTube's algorithmic demotions are not simply business decisions; they are exercises of quasi-sovereign power. For billions of people, these companies—not governments—decide which speech circulates and which is silenced. This is the privatisation of censorship: decisions about the boundaries of free expression, once made through parliaments, courts, and public deliberation, are now made by corporate trust and safety teams, guided by opaque rules and commercial incentives. While states once guarded the line between permissible dissent and dangerous propaganda, that line is now drawn by platforms headquartered in Silicon Valley, Shenzhen, or Dublin. *The architecture of free speech is being rebuilt by engineers and executives, not legislators or citizens.*

The paradox is that democracies are attacked precisely because of their openness. Authoritarian regimes, with centralised media control and restricted speech, present far fewer avenues for subversion. Democracies, by contrast, rely on the free flow of information and the assumption that debate—even heated, even divisive—can coexist with stability. That openness becomes a vector of attack. Cyber armies, troll farms, and algorithmic amplification exploit the very liberties that distinguish open societies. Yet the answer cannot be simply to abandon those liberties; to do so would hollow democracy from within. *The challenge is how to safeguard openness without letting it become a suicide pact.*

This chapter examines democracy under siege not as a metaphor but as a literal description of contemporary conflict. Elections are treated as theatres of psychological operations, social media platforms as contested terrain, and citizens as both targets and vectors of influence. The focus is not only on how democracies are attacked, but on the deeper questions these attacks raise: What happens when the marketplace of ideas becomes a battlefield? Can democratic institutions survive when trust itself is the object of assault? Who should arbitrate truth in societies committed to freedom of speech? And can open systems defend themselves without succumbing to the logic of authoritarian control?

The reader will find here a mapping of the critical fault lines: how digital interference reshapes elections, how disinformation corrodes trust, how corporations assume roles once reserved for the state, and how the paradox of democratic openness creates vulnerabilities that cannot be sealed without compromising core values. The purpose is not to lament democracy's weakness but to clarify the stakes, illuminate the mechanics of its subversion, and grapple with the possibilities of renewal. *For the future of democracy may depend not on whether it can eliminate its vulnerabilities, but on whether it can adapt to survive them without ceasing to be itself.*

Elections as Battlefields

When citizens cast their ballots, they imagine themselves participating in one of the most sacred rituals of democracy. Yet in the twenty-first century, the ballot box is less a sanctuary of sovereignty than a target within a sprawling theatre of conflict. Elections are no longer shielded by geography or by tradition; they have become *front lines in hybrid wars waged with code, networks, and narratives rather than tanks and artillery.* The act of voting, once defended primarily against fraud at the local level, is now contested by foreign intelligence services, cyber militias, private contractors, and algorithmic tools designed to manipulate hearts and minds at scale.

The strategic value of elections lies not only in determining who governs but in shaping the legitimacy of governance itself. A compromised election is a compromised regime, and adversaries understand that eroding confidence in electoral integrity can be as destabilising as altering results outright. Russia's interference in the 2016 United States presidential election is now the most cited case study, but it was neither the first nor the last. Similar patterns have surfaced in the French presidential election of 2017, when Emmanuel Macron's campaign was hacked and leaked materials timed to damage his credibility, and in the Brexit referendum, where targeted misinformation campaigns spread across social media platforms sowed confusion about immigration, trade, and sovereignty. These operations rarely change vast swathes of votes directly. Instead, they seek to narrow margins, intensify polarisation, and above all leave citizens doubting whether the process was truly fair. *Suspicion itself becomes the weapon.*

Cyber armies approach elections as complex systems rather than single events. Attacks can occur at multiple layers: direct assaults on voting infrastructure; disinformation campaigns designed to shape public opinion; micro-targeted advertisements that weaponise personal data; and coordinated networks of bots that distort the visibility of narratives online.

Each layer requires different tools, but all exploit the interconnectedness of the digital environment. For instance, a well-placed story on a fringe website, amplified by fake accounts on Twitter, can migrate into mainstream media coverage within hours. By the time fact-checkers debunk it, the emotional impact has already taken hold. The battlefield is not just the count of votes but the contest of perceptions before, during, and after election day.

What distinguishes these campaigns is their asymmetry. States or organisations with limited conventional power can punch far above their weight by targeting elections abroad. The cost of running a troll farm in St Petersburg or a disinformation campaign outsourced to a marketing firm in Manila is negligible compared to deploying military forces, yet the political dividends can be immense. In Ukraine, Russia deployed not only soldiers and mercenaries but also waves of digital propaganda aimed at undermining faith in Kyiv's government and bolstering narratives of Russian legitimacy. Similarly, Iranian and Chinese operations have been traced to influence campaigns in the United States, Europe, and parts of Africa, each tailored to local grievances. *The ease of entry means that the defence of elections is no longer a matter of policing borders but of protecting cognitive sovereignty.*

There is also a growing role for private actors. Companies offering "reputation management" or "political consulting" services operate in a grey zone between marketing and psychological warfare. Cambridge Analytica's work during the 2016 election cycle exposed how commercial data collection could be transformed into electoral manipulation, with psychographic profiling used to micro-target individuals with messages calibrated to their fears and desires. While framed as marketing, these tactics function as a form of battlefield reconnaissance: mapping vulnerabilities in the electorate and exploiting them with precision-guided narratives. Unlike traditional propaganda, which broadcast the same message to millions, digital operations personalise the attack, turning every voter into a bespoke target. *Elections cease to be mass events and become millions of parallel battles, each fought in the private screens of individuals.*

The vulnerabilities extend beyond disinformation. Hard infrastructure—the machines and networks that register voters, tally results, and transmit outcomes—remains alarmingly insecure in many jurisdictions. In 2017, the US Department of Homeland Security revealed that election systems in at least 21 states had been targeted by foreign hackers. Although there is little evidence of votes being directly changed, even the mere perception of vulnerability undermines public trust. In countries with weaker technical safeguards, the risks are greater. Reports from Africa and Latin America have documented attempts by both domestic elites and external actors to manipulate voter rolls, crash servers, or delay results in ways that delegitimise opposition victories. The message is clear: technical security is inseparable from political legitimacy.

What makes elections uniquely attractive targets is their predictability. Unlike other events in political life, elections occur on known dates, with enormous media attention and guaranteed stakes. Adversaries can plan years in advance, testing narratives, building networks, and rehearsing tactics. The predictability gives attackers time to refine their methods and defenders less room for surprise. Moreover, the international community has yet to establish robust deterrents. Whereas an armed attack on a nation's territory invites collective defence under existing treaties, interference in elections rarely triggers the same unified response. The norms are blurred, the responses inconsistent, and the penalties often negligible. *This legal and diplomatic grey zone has emboldened attackers while leaving democracies scrambling for adequate defences.*

The philosophical dimension is equally troubling. Elections are not just technical procedures; they are rituals of legitimacy that embody the social contract. When citizens believe those rituals have been tainted, the foundational trust upon which democracy rests begins to erode. Even without altering outcomes, disinformation campaigns can achieve their aims by convincing losing sides that they were cheated, thereby paralysing governance and fuelling unrest. This phenomenon has been starkly visible in the United States after 2020, where unfounded claims of electoral fraud catalysed an assault on the Capitol and left millions of citizens convinced that democracy itself had failed them. The battlefield is thus not only external but internal: the struggle for the narrative legitimacy of the system itself.

Some argue that election interference is merely an updated form of what great powers have always done—propaganda, covert funding, manipulation of foreign media. What is different today, however, is the speed, scale, and intimacy. Propaganda in the Cold War era required leaflets, broadcasts, or planted stories. Today it requires a tweetstorm, a viral video, or a targeted advertisement, all delivered instantaneously to a global audience. The personalisation of digital platforms means that interference penetrates the private sphere of voters with unprecedented precision. It is no longer a matter of hearing rumours in a café or reading slanted articles in a newspaper; it is a matter of receiving a tailored message on one's phone, crafted from harvested personal data, and designed to press psychological buttons invisible to others. *The manipulation becomes invisible, making resistance far more difficult.*

Defending against these incursions is not merely a technical problem. It raises deeper questions about the resilience of democratic culture itself. Can democracies foster critical media literacy, civic education, and institutional transparency robust enough to resist manipulation? Or will the logic of the digital battlefield force democracies into defensive measures that themselves erode openness, such as greater censorship or surveillance? The paradox is stark: to defend free elections may require restricting some aspects of the information environment that make them possible. The answers are far from clear, but the stakes could not be higher.

What emerges is a portrait of elections as battlefields where the weapons are narratives, the soldiers are bots and trolls, and the casualties are not only political candidates but the trust of citizens. The line between legitimate persuasion and illegitimate manipulation grows ever thinner, while the costs of defending democracy escalate. The challenge is not simply to secure voting machines or police social media, but to rethink what electoral integrity means in a world where perception itself has become a contested terrain. *For democracies to endure, they must recognise that the defence of elections is no longer a seasonal task but a permanent campaign—one fought in real time, across borders, and within the minds of their citizens.*

Weaponizing Trust

The most effective weapon in modern politics is not a bomb or a bullet, but the deliberate corrosion of trust. Democracies rest upon the assumption that institutions, information flows, and public officials operate within a framework of relative honesty. Citizens need not believe everything they are told, but they must believe enough to engage—believe that their votes will be counted, that courts are impartial, that the media is not systematically deceiving them. Disinformation campaigns strike at this fragile architecture, not necessarily to replace one truth with another, but to make truth itself appear contested, irrelevant, or unknowable. The goal is not persuasion in the classic sense; it is disorientation. Once people cannot tell the difference between truth and falsehood, they lose confidence in the very possibility of shared reality. *At that point, the democratic system begins to corrode from within.*

What makes trust so exploitable is that it is both indispensable and inherently fragile. Unlike laws, which can be codified, or military forces, which can be measured, trust cannot be stockpiled. It exists only through ongoing belief and practice. This makes it an ideal target for adversaries: hard to defend, easy to destabilise. Consider the Russian strategy of "reflexive control," honed over decades of psychological operations. Rather than imposing one narrative, it saturates the environment with multiple contradictory narratives, leaving the audience confused and paralysed. When the downing of Malaysia Airlines Flight 17 over Ukraine in 2014 was linked to Russian-backed separatists, Moscow did not offer a single alternative explanation but dozens: it was a Ukrainian jet, it was a CIA plot, it was staged altogether. The purpose was not to convince the world of any one story but to ensure that no story could be trusted. This deliberate fragmentation of reality is now a template applied globally.

The corrosion of trust has cascading effects on institutions. When disinformation erodes confidence in elections, the judiciary, or the media, it reduces citizens' willingness to accept political outcomes they dislike. In the United States, a significant portion of the electorate still believes the 2020 presidential election was stolen, despite exhaustive evidence to the contrary. This belief is not merely an opinion; it shapes behaviour, from violent insurrection to routine refusal to accept lawful authority. Once trust breaks down, democratic mechanisms for resolving disputes—debate, compromise, and lawful opposition—begin to fail. Politics becomes zero-sum, and opponents become enemies. In this sense, disinformation does not simply mislead; it restructures the civic ecosystem into one where compromise appears naïve and violence appears rational. *The slow poison of distrust transforms political disagreement into existential struggle.*

Trust is weaponised not only against institutions but against the very idea of expertise. During the COVID-19 pandemic, coordinated campaigns cast doubt on scientific authorities, medical professionals, and public health agencies. Conspiracy theories flourished, not simply because people believed them, but because belief in the alternative—that institutions were competent and honest—was systematically undermined. Attacks on the World Health Organisation, on vaccine efficacy, and on national health services created an informational environment where every claim was suspect. The effect was deadly. Where misinformation spread most intensely, vaccination rates lagged, death tolls climbed, and political divisions deepened. This revealed the strategic potential of disinformation: by eroding trust in experts, adversaries can convert a public health crisis into a political one, destabilising societies without firing a shot.

In many democracies, the weaponisation of trust has been facilitated not only by hostile foreign actors but by domestic opportunists. Political leaders have discovered that undermining trust in institutions can serve their immediate interests. When a candidate insists that "the system is rigged" before an election even occurs, they inoculate themselves against defeat. If they win, they claim legitimacy; if they lose, they claim fraud. This strategy turns trust itself into a partisan weapon. The erosion of shared confidence is no longer merely an unintended consequence of disinformation but an explicit tactic wielded from within. *In this way, democracies become vulnerable not only to external manipulation but to self-sabotage by those seeking short-term advantage.*

The mechanics of this corrosion are intimately linked to the design of digital platforms. Algorithms prioritise engagement over accuracy, amplifying content that provokes outrage or fear. False stories, especially those confirming pre-existing biases, spread more rapidly than true ones. Studies of Facebook during the 2016 US election revealed that fabricated news stories were among the most widely shared political content, outperforming material from established news outlets. The architecture of these platforms is not neutral: it rewards sensationalism, fragments public debate into echo chambers, and accelerates the spread of disinformation. Trust, already fragile, is subjected to continuous stress. The problem is compounded by the opacity of platform governance. Decisions about content moderation—what is removed, what is labelled, what is allowed to circulate—are made by private companies with little transparency or accountability. As a result, *citizens no longer know whether the information they see is manipulated by foreign actors, domestic politicians, or platform algorithms themselves.*

What emerges is a paradox: trust must exist for democracy to function, yet in the digital age it can be so easily manipulated that defending it becomes nearly impossible. To fight disinformation effectively, democracies must strike a delicate balance. Efforts to regulate content can be portrayed as censorship, fuelling further distrust. Leaving platforms unregulated, however, allows malign actors to exploit them unchecked. Similarly, fact-checking can mitigate falsehoods, but when institutions themselves are distrusted, fact-checkers are dismissed as biased actors. This creates a vicious circle in which every corrective measure risks deepening the very scepticism it seeks to resolve. *The corrosion of trust is therefore not only a tactical victory for adversaries but a structural challenge for democracies.*

Yet there is another dimension often overlooked: the emotional basis of trust. Trust is not purely rational; it rests on feelings of identity, belonging, and fairness. Disinformation campaigns exploit emotional vulnerabilities by appealing to fear, resentment, and nostalgia. They do not need to offer coherent policy proposals; they need only to evoke feelings that make alternative viewpoints seem threatening or illegitimate. For example, disinformation surrounding migration in Europe has often focused less on factual debates about numbers or policy and more on evoking existential fear of cultural loss. Similarly, campaigns targeting minority groups or refugees often succeed not because they are believed factually but because they resonate emotionally. *When trust is displaced by fear, institutions can appear as enemies rather than protectors.*

Some analysts argue that democracies should focus less on countering individual pieces of disinformation and more on rebuilding the resilience of trust itself. This means investing in civic education, strengthening independent journalism, and creating transparency in digital governance. Countries like Finland, which have integrated media literacy into school curricula, have shown greater resilience against foreign propaganda. But resilience cannot be achieved overnight. It requires long-term investment and a political culture that values truth even when inconvenient. Democracies that treat information as a partisan battlefield, rather than a shared resource, risk accelerating their own decay. The defence of trust, in this sense, is not a technical challenge alone but a cultural and political one.

The weaponisation of trust reveals the deeper vulnerability of democracy: its reliance on voluntary belief. Authoritarian regimes can rule through coercion and fear, but democracies require the consent of the governed, and that consent depends on the conviction that institutions, however flawed, are fundamentally trustworthy. By turning trust into a target, disinformation strikes at the democratic heart. Its success does not lie in converting masses to one ideology or another, but in persuading enough people that no ideology, no institution, and no truth can be trusted at all. Once that threshold is crossed, the mechanisms of democracy remain in form but collapse in substance. *The ballot box still opens, the courts still convene, the press still publishes—but the belief that they matter, that they can be trusted, is gone.*

This is why the weaponisation of trust is not merely a problem of information security but a profound threat to political stability. It blurs the line between external attack and internal decay, between misinformation and civic breakdown. The corrosion of trust does not announce itself with the drama of a coup or an invasion; it advances quietly, through doubt, suspicion, and the slow evaporation of confidence. The challenge for democracies is not simply to resist disinformation campaigns but to recognise that trust itself has become the terrain of battle. *The future of democracy depends not on whether it can eliminate disinformation—an impossible task—but on whether it can preserve and rebuild the fragile faith that binds citizens to institutions, and institutions to truth.*

The Privatization of Censorship

The struggle over who controls information is no longer confined to governments or media outlets. In the twenty-first century, some of the most consequential decisions about speech, truth, and legitimacy are made in the boardrooms of technology companies. Platforms such as Facebook, Twitter (now X), YouTube, and TikTok have become the frontlines of modern political conflict, not only because they host the world's conversations but because they decide—largely in private—what those conversations can be. In doing so, they have assumed roles once reserved for courts, legislatures, or regulators. They have become *arbiters of truth in digital war zones*, exercising powers of censorship and amplification at a scale unmatched in human history.

The privatisation of censorship is striking because it emerges not from overt state repression but from the commercial architecture of digital platforms. These companies do not exist to safeguard democracy; they exist to maximise user engagement, data extraction, and advertising revenue. Their moderation policies are therefore shaped less by democratic principles than by reputational risk, political pressure, and the imperatives of profit. This has created a paradox: societies that prize free speech now outsource the boundaries of acceptable discourse to corporations whose interests are neither elected nor transparent. *The tension is no longer between state and citizen but between citizen and platform—an unaccountable gatekeeper with global reach.*

The consequences of this shift became starkly visible during the COVID-19 pandemic. In the face of viral misinformation about vaccines and public health measures, platforms were pressured by governments to act decisively. Content moderation escalated: posts flagged by fact-checkers were hidden, accounts spreading conspiracies were suspended, and algorithms were adjusted to promote official health guidance. Yet the interventions also raised thorny questions. Who decides what qualifies as misinformation? Scientific understanding evolves, and positions once deemed conspiracy—

such as debates about the origins of the virus—later entered legitimate inquiry. When platforms removed or suppressed such content, critics argued that corporate censorship narrowed public debate and undermined trust in institutions. Here the dilemma of privatised censorship crystallises: action is demanded, yet any action risks reinforcing the very scepticism it seeks to counter.

The political stakes are even higher in electoral contexts. During the 2020 US presidential election, social media firms intervened aggressively to stem the flow of disinformation about voting procedures and election fraud. Tens of thousands of posts were labelled, downranked, or removed. On the one hand, these measures likely limited the viral spread of baseless claims. On the other, they fed narratives of censorship among political factions already primed to distrust mainstream institutions. By blocking certain speech, platforms did not neutralise disinformation; they made themselves protagonists in the conflict. For many users, the spectacle was less about truth than about power: corporations deciding which voices counted. *The very act of censorship, however well-intentioned, became ammunition in the disinformation wars.*

Outside the United States, the power of platforms is even more pronounced because local institutions often lack the capacity to regulate or counterbalance them. In Myanmar, Facebook became effectively synonymous with the internet, providing the primary channel for news and political discussion. When hate speech and incitement spread on the platform in the years preceding the Rohingya genocide, the company failed to act decisively, citing resource constraints and cultural distance. By the time interventions were attempted, the damage was irreversible. In Ethiopia, similar patterns emerged, with social media fuelling ethnic violence. The unevenness of corporate censorship is not simply a matter of oversight but of structural priorities: content moderation is often most robust in wealthy Western democracies, leaving vulnerable societies exposed. *This reveals the geopolitical dimension of privatised censorship—decisions made in Silicon Valley reverberate across fragile states with life-and-death consequences.*

The privatisation of censorship also raises profound philosophical tensions about free speech. Traditional democratic theory views censorship as a function of state authority, constrained by constitutional protections, judicial oversight, and political accountability. When private platforms decide what may or may not be said, those safeguards disappear. Appeals processes are opaque, enforcement is inconsistent, and rules shift without public debate. Platforms often invoke their status as private companies to justify broad discretion, yet in practice they operate as global public squares. Citizens have no realistic alternative; exclusion from a major platform is equivalent to exclusion from political life. *Censorship without accountability is no less dangerous for being privatised.*

Some argue that platform censorship is not truly censorship at all, since users voluntarily enter private spaces governed by terms of service. Yet this view underestimates the monopolistic power of digital platforms. A handful of companies dominate the global information ecosystem, meaning that opting out is not a meaningful choice. Furthermore, the line between private and public has blurred: governments increasingly pressure platforms to remove content, and platforms in turn shape what governments and citizens can see. This fusion of state pressure and corporate discretion creates a hybrid regime of censorship—neither wholly public nor wholly private, but something in between. *In this hybrid space, accountability dissolves, and power hides behind layers of deniability.*

The most insidious effect of privatised censorship is its potential to normalise arbitrary control over information. Because content moderation is often framed as a technical challenge—solved through algorithms, AI filters, and trust-and-safety teams—it appears procedural rather than political. Yet every decision about what counts as misinformation, hate speech, or harmful content is inherently normative. When AI systems flag content for removal, they encode cultural assumptions and political judgements. When moderation is outsourced to low-paid workers in the Global South, those individuals are forced to enforce rules created far from their own societies. The process strips censorship of its visible politics while embedding it more deeply into daily communication. *The most powerful censorship is not overt silencing but the quiet engineering of attention, invisibly shaping what people see and believe.*

To understand the gravity of this shift, one must compare it to historical models of information control. In authoritarian states, censorship is explicit: publications are banned, broadcasters are shut down, journalists are jailed. In democracies, the line was traditionally drawn at direct state suppression, leaving the marketplace of ideas to operate freely. Today, the boundary is not enforced by governments but by private infrastructure: recommendation algorithms, content policies, automated detection systems. This is censorship by architecture rather than decree, and it is harder to contest because it hides behind technical design. Users rarely know whether a post was downranked by algorithm, removed by moderator, or never delivered at all. The absence of visibility means the absence of protest. *When censorship becomes infrastructural, resistance becomes nearly impossible.*

There is, however, a conceptual tension worth recognising. Democracies demand both free expression and safe discourse. Few would argue that child exploitation material, terrorist propaganda, or deliberate incitement to violence should circulate freely. The challenge lies in drawing lines around categories such as "disinformation" or "hate speech," which are deeply contested. Private platforms, tasked with balancing these tensions at scale, inevitably err—sometimes by over-censoring legitimate speech, sometimes by allowing harmful content to spread. Both errors undermine democratic trust. Critics who demand platforms "do more" against harmful content often overlook that every additional intervention increases corporate power over public discourse. *The paradox is that the more platforms intervene to safeguard democracy, the more undemocratic their role becomes.*

Some governments have begun to push back, introducing laws that attempt to reassert public oversight. The European Union's Digital Services Act requires platforms to disclose their moderation practices, provide explanations for content removals, and submit to independent audits. Yet even these measures leave the fundamental problem unresolved: the centralisation of power in private corporations whose business models depend on commodifying speech. Transparency and oversight may mitigate abuses, but they do not alter the structural reality that a handful of firms now govern the conditions of global conversation. The very framing of moderation as a technical service obscures the deeper question: should corporations be entrusted with defining the boundaries of truth in societies built upon free expression?

The privatisation of censorship is not a temporary aberration; it is a defining feature of digital politics. As long as the infrastructure of communication is privately owned, the rules of speech will be shaped by corporate interests and political pressures, not by collective deliberation. This does not mean democracies should abolish content moderation—an impossible and reckless proposition—but that they must recognise its political nature. *Censorship, whether public or private, is never neutral; it always expresses power.* The challenge is not merely to regulate platforms but to reimagine the relationship between speech, sovereignty, and corporate authority in a digital age where information itself has become the terrain of war.

What is at stake is not only who may speak but who decides who may speak. In that decision lies the future of democratic legitimacy. When platforms act as arbiters of truth, they inherit responsibilities for which they were never designed and are held to account by no one. When governments outsource information control to corporations, they surrender one of the most vital levers of democratic authority. The privatisation of censorship thus represents a structural shift in the architecture of power—subtle, invisible, and yet transformative. *The battle for democracy will not be fought only at the ballot box or on the streets, but in the hidden decisions of algorithms, moderators, and corporate boards that now police the boundaries of public truth.*

The Democratic Paradox

Democracies are uniquely vulnerable to forms of warfare that do not rely on tanks or missiles but on information, networks, and perception. Their very openness—the transparency of institutions, the plurality of voices, the freedom of speech and assembly—creates the vectors through which adversaries can penetrate and destabilise them. Where authoritarian regimes can impose firewalls, censor narratives, and tightly control political discourse, open societies leave the gates unbarred, trusting that the circulation of truth will overwhelm lies. Yet in the age of algorithmic warfare and stateless actors, this assumption is no longer secure. The paradox is stark: *the qualities that make democracies resilient in principle also render them fragile in practice.*

This vulnerability is not theoretical but evident in recent political earthquakes. The 2016 United States presidential election, targeted by Russian troll farms and bot networks, demonstrated how foreign adversaries could exploit divisions not by creating new grievances but by amplifying existing ones. Disinformation campaigns did not need to persuade voters of entirely new realities; they merely had to heighten polarisation, erode trust, and delegitimise institutions. Europe has witnessed similar tactics, from Brexit debates shaped by targeted misinformation to Eastern European states confronting disinformation that blurs the line between propaganda and domestic discourse. The paradox lies in the democratic commitment to free debate: what is celebrated as pluralism becomes weaponised as dissonance.

Algorithmic warfare magnifies these risks. Social media platforms, designed to maximise engagement, reward emotionally charged and polarising content. Algorithms privilege outrage over nuance, spectacle over substance, virality over verification. In authoritarian contexts, governments can co-opt these platforms directly, dictating what information circulates. In democracies, the manipulation comes less from top-down imposition than from bottom-up distortion, aided by algorithms indifferent to truth. The battlefield is not geographic but cognitive, fought in timelines and newsfeeds. *When algorithms amplify falsehoods faster than institutions can correct them, the democratic marketplace of ideas ceases to function as intended.*

What makes stateless actors particularly dangerous is their asymmetry. A small group of hackers, trolls, or cyber-mercenaries can destabilise a political process at a fraction of the cost of traditional warfare. They do not require territory, tanks, or armies; they require servers, fake accounts, and an understanding of cultural fault lines. Democracies, with their heterogeneous populations and contested identities, provide fertile ground. Every unresolved grievance—racial injustice, economic inequality, regional tension—becomes a potential weapon when magnified through coordinated disinformation. Authoritarian states, by contrast, are often less susceptible because dissenting narratives can be brutally suppressed before they gain traction. *It is easier to weaponise freedom than to weaponise censorship.*

The paradox extends into the legal and ethical realm. Democracies are constrained by commitments to human rights and civil liberties, which limit the tools they can deploy against stateless or algorithmic adversaries. When governments attempt to regulate or censor content, they risk undermining their own democratic ethos. When they hesitate, they leave themselves exposed. This double bind is exploited by adversaries who know that democracies are least effective when forced to choose between security and freedom. For instance, European states have struggled to counter extremist propaganda online without infringing on free expression protections, while authoritarian regimes face no such hesitation. The paradox is that restraint, a virtue in democratic governance, becomes a liability in asymmetric conflict.

Case studies illustrate the scope of this dilemma. In Taiwan, a society targeted relentlessly by Chinese disinformation campaigns, citizens have developed civic innovations such as crowd-sourced fact-checking and rapid public rebuttal networks. These grassroots measures reflect an effort to defend openness with openness rather than censorship. By contrast, in the Philippines, algorithmic manipulation during elections by networks of paid influencers and trolls reshaped political discourse with little resistance, demonstrating how fragile democracies can be when institutional guardrails are weak. The two examples show opposite ends of the spectrum: resilience requires adaptation, but adaptation is uneven, and the paradox remains—*the more open the system, the more vulnerable it is to manipulation unless deliberate countermeasures are embedded within that openness.*

Another layer of the paradox emerges in the geopolitical dimension. Democracies are most targeted precisely because they pose an ideological challenge to authoritarian regimes. Destabilising an open society through disinformation is not simply about electoral outcomes but about undermining the legitimacy of democracy itself. Each conspiracy theory that takes root, each contested election result, each surge of distrust in media and science erodes the credibility of democratic governance globally. The battlefield extends beyond any single country: democratic vulnerability in one state becomes propaganda fodder for authoritarian rivals elsewhere, who can point to chaos as evidence of democracy's dysfunction. *Undermining trust in one democracy destabilises faith in the model as a whole.*

One might ask whether democracies can ever fully reconcile this paradox. The instinct to defend openness through restriction—to regulate speech, censor harmful content, police algorithms—risks replicating the logic of authoritarianism. Yet the failure to act leaves societies exposed to manipulation that corrodes the foundations of trust. Some scholars argue that the solution lies not in censorship but in resilience: media literacy, transparency in political advertising, public investment in independent journalism, and civic infrastructure that strengthens trust. Others point to the need for structural regulation of platforms, forcing algorithms to prioritise accuracy over engagement. Yet even here, tensions abound: who defines accuracy? Who decides what counts as manipulation? *In solving the paradox, democracies risk entrenching new vulnerabilities.*

Ultimately, the democratic paradox cannot be "solved" in the sense of eliminated; it can only be managed. Open societies must continually balance between liberty and protection, plurality and coherence, transparency and security. What is required is not the abandonment of openness but its radical rethinking in light of digital and algorithmic realities. Democracies must ask whether their institutions, built for an analogue age, can withstand adversaries that exploit digital architecture with precision and persistence. They must consider whether legal frameworks, electoral systems, and civic norms can adapt quickly enough to an environment where narratives travel faster than laws. *The paradox is not a flaw in democracy but a condition of its survival: vulnerability is the price of openness, and resilience is the test of its endurance.*

The lesson for policymakers, citizens, and scholars is sobering yet urgent. Democracies under siege are not defeated by external armies but by internal corrosion, seeded and amplified by adversaries who exploit openness as weakness. Stateless and algorithmic warfare does not conquer territory; it conquers trust. And once trust collapses, the democratic edifice—built on consent, dialogue, and legitimacy—becomes hollow. The paradox, then, is not only that democracies are most vulnerable to these forms of attack, but that their survival depends on their ability to protect openness without betraying it. *How they navigate this balance will determine whether democracy remains a viable model in the twenty-first century or becomes an artefact of a less networked past.*

Chapter 10

The New Geography of Power

The political map of the world has always been a simplification, a series of bold lines and shaded territories that suggest clarity where there is none. For centuries, sovereignty has been anchored to geography, expressed in borders, fortified in territory, and legitimised by the state's claim to control what lies within those lines. Yet in the twenty-first century, these assumptions no longer hold. Conflicts are redrawing the map not by annexing land but by shaping the flow of information, capital, and allegiance. Power today is exercised less by tanks rolling across borders than by networks seeping invisibly through them. The question that follows is unsettling: *if geography no longer defines power, what will?*

One of the defining features of this new landscape is the prevalence of conflicts without borders. Proxy wars from Syria to Ukraine have demonstrated that control is measured not solely by territorial gain but by influence over populations, infrastructures, and digital domains. Russia's hybrid warfare exemplifies this shift: disinformation campaigns, cyberattacks, and the cultivation of loyal militias achieve effects comparable to conventional occupation, yet without the costs or liabilities of formal conquest. Similarly, Iran's use of militias across Iraq, Syria, and Lebanon extends its sphere of influence far beyond its borders, crafting zones of allegiance that operate independently of the traditional state framework. What we are witnessing is the replacement of cartographic certainty with *fluid spheres of influence*, where borders blur into channels of access and denial.

The redefinition of conflict is not abstract but vividly visible in global cities. Urban centres, once thought of primarily as hubs of commerce and culture, have become frontlines in geopolitical struggles. Kiev is not only the symbolic heart of Ukrainian sovereignty but also the testing ground for Russia's cyberattacks, aimed at disabling power grids and disrupting governance. Hong Kong has been a battleground of ideology and information, its streets contested as much by digital surveillance and propaganda as by physical clashes. Lagos illustrates another dimension: a metropolis vulnerable not only to insurgent violence in Nigeria's peripheries but also to digital extortion campaigns and the geopolitics of oil flows. Cities concentrate people, infrastructures, and narratives, making them irresistible targets for both kinetic assaults and algorithmic manipulations. *To control a city today is to control not only its territory but its symbolic resonance in the global imagination.*

This shift foregrounds the rise of stateless power brokers who no longer sit comfortably in the margins of international politics but rival states in reach and influence. Warlords have long challenged state authority in fragile regions, but the twenty-first century has added new players: tech executives who wield platforms larger than most nations, and hackers who can cripple economies from basements thousands of miles away. A single ransomware syndicate can extract more from a country's banking system than a traditional military raid. CEOs of technology firms decide which voices are amplified or silenced in public discourse, shaping elections and revolutions with algorithmic tweaks. Even private military contractors now negotiate with heads of state on near-equal terms, demonstrating how market forces have inserted themselves into the management of war. *Sovereignty is increasingly fragmented, parceled out among actors who command resources, attention, and legitimacy without the trappings of statehood.*

What this reveals is the fragility of sovereignty itself. For centuries, sovereignty implied control over territory and recognition by other states. Today, territory is less decisive than connectivity: pipelines, data cables, satellite constellations, and social networks form the arteries of power. A state that cannot protect its cyber infrastructure, or cannot prevent disinformation from undermining its elections, may technically exist on the map but functionally lose sovereignty in practice. Conversely, a non-state actor with control over key networks can project influence disproportionate to its size or geography. This inversion challenges not only international relations but also the assumptions of citizenship, legitimacy, and governance. *What does sovereignty mean when the power to govern is exercised through networks rather than borders?*

The implications are profound. If sovereignty is diluted, international law, diplomacy, and security strategies must all be reimagined. Defence ministries accustomed to thinking in terms of tanks and territory must now grapple with adversaries that control narratives rather than land.

Diplomats negotiating over borders must acknowledge that influence often extends beyond maps, spilling into diasporas, digital spaces, and transnational capital flows. Citizens, too, must reckon with the fact that their allegiances are being courted not only by their governments but also by corporations, religious networks, and online communities that operate across borders. The geography of power no longer coincides with the geography of the state.

What emerges, then, is not the end of geography but its reconfiguration. Power is still mapped, but the lines are invisible: fibre optic cables rather than trenches, viral memes rather than propaganda posters, influence campaigns rather than occupations. This new geography is unstable, contested, and deeply consequential. For some, it offers opportunities—small actors can exert influence previously unimaginable. For others, it signals a loss of control, as traditional sovereignties are hollowed out by forces they cannot contain. The challenge for the reader is not only to understand this transformation but to recognise its stakes: the very organisation of global order depends on how societies adapt to this shifting terrain. *The map of the future will not be drawn with borders but with networks, and those who master this cartography will define the century ahead.*

Conflicts Without Borders

When a state can extend its power without crossing a border, the very logic of sovereignty begins to unravel. The wars of the twenty-first century often leave maps untouched, yet their effects are no less profound than the great conquests of the past. No flags are raised over annexed lands, no new lines are etched into atlases, yet populations wake to find themselves living under the influence of powers far beyond their borders. Proxy wars and hybrid conflicts redraw not territories but allegiances, shaping how communities, economies, and information flows are governed. The borders that once defined international order are being replaced by *spheres of influence*—fluid, overlapping, and often invisible to the eye.

Consider Ukraine, where Russia's strategy has been less about territorial acquisition than about ensuring enduring dependence and instability. The 2014 annexation of Crimea was a visible land grab, but Moscow's more enduring victory has been in eastern Ukraine, where support for separatist militias, disinformation campaigns, and cyberattacks against infrastructure blurred the line between war and governance. Here, Russia exerted control without the burden of formal occupation, creating a region that was neither fully independent nor truly sovereign. The goal was not to replace Ukraine's borders but to hollow out their meaning, leaving the state formally intact but functionally compromised. *This is the hallmark of borderless conflict: not conquest, but corrosion.*

Elsewhere, Iran has mastered the art of influence without annexation through its support of militias and political movements across Iraq, Syria, Lebanon, and Yemen. These groups operate with autonomy, yet their actions often align with Tehran's strategic interests, effectively extending Iranian influence deep into the Arab world. Hezbollah in Lebanon exemplifies this duality: both a domestic political actor and an arm of Iranian projection, it occupies the paradoxical space of being local and foreign simultaneously. To understand this is to recognise that the map of the Middle East cannot be read only in terms of formal states; it must also be understood through the dense web of non-state actors that tie disparate geographies into coherent spheres of influence.

Digital conflict has intensified this erosion of cartographic certainty. Where once propaganda was constrained by borders, today influence operations travel instantaneously across continents. The so-called Islamic State demonstrated how digital tools could create a sense of belonging for individuals scattered worldwide, building a transnational community of fighters and sympathisers bound not by geography but by narrative. Similarly, Russia's interference in Western elections shows how a state can alter the political trajectory of another nation without firing a shot or crossing a frontier. By shaping information environments, adversaries achieve outcomes once thought possible only through direct invasion: the ability to sway leadership, alter policy, and destabilise institutions. *Control of narratives has become as decisive as control of land.*

The persistence of these conflicts without borders complicates the international system itself. Traditional war had a discernible end: territory gained or lost, treaties signed, borders adjusted. But proxy wars and digital campaigns rarely end in such clarity. They smoulder, shaping politics and economies for decades, while leaving international law groping for definitions that no longer apply. Is a cyberattack that shuts down a hospital an act of war or a criminal offence? When a militia aligned with a foreign power commits atrocities, who bears responsibility? These questions expose the inadequacy of frameworks designed for a world in which sovereignty was assumed to be bounded by geography.

To see how power is exercised today, one must look not to maps but to networks. Pipelines, fibre optic cables, satellite systems, and diasporas create channels through which influence flows. China's Belt and Road Initiative, for instance, is often described in terms of infrastructure, but its deeper significance lies in the political dependencies it fosters. A port in Sri Lanka or a railway in Kenya is not merely an economic asset but a lever of influence, binding nations into Beijing's orbit without the need for territorial annexation. Similarly, American dominance of internet infrastructure has created spheres of control that extend well beyond its borders, with private companies acting as both enablers and arbiters of global influence.

Critics argue that these developments merely reflect the continuation of imperial strategies by other means. Yet there is a distinction worth emphasising: empires historically sought territorial expansion, whereas contemporary powers often seek denial and disruption. Russia does not need to govern all of Ukraine to achieve its aims; it merely needs to ensure Ukraine remains unstable, incapable of aligning fully with the West. Likewise, China does not need to occupy the South China Sea islands to benefit strategically; it suffices that rival states remain uncertain about their rights and hesitant to act. *Influence, not ownership, is the currency of modern conflict.*

The consequence is a world of overlapping jurisdictions and perpetual ambiguity. A village in Iraq may answer simultaneously to a national government, a foreign-backed militia, and the economic interests of an international oil company. A social media user in Europe may unknowingly participate in a political campaign orchestrated by actors thousands of miles away. A city's power grid may depend on software maintained in another country, leaving its sovereignty contingent on the goodwill of unseen engineers. These entanglements demonstrate how the neat clarity of the Westphalian system is giving way to a reality where borders are porous, contested, and frequently irrelevant to the actual distribution of power.

Philosophically, this shift forces a reckoning with the very idea of sovereignty. If sovereignty implies supreme authority within a territory, then borderless conflict exposes its fragility. Authority is fragmented, dispersed among states, non-state actors, corporations, and networks. For citizens, this means the source of power shaping their daily lives may no longer be their government but a militia, a hacker collective, or a multinational firm. The battlefield is not elsewhere; it is everywhere, diffused into the structures that enable modern life. *The collapse of borders in conflict is also the collapse of borders in responsibility.*

The task for policymakers, scholars, and citizens alike is to adapt to this transformed landscape without retreating into nostalgia for a world of stable borders that no longer exists. The challenge is not only defensive—protecting against interference and disruption—but also conceptual, developing frameworks that acknowledge the realities of networked power. Without such frameworks, states will remain locked in outdated assumptions, perpetually surprised by adversaries who exploit the gaps. In a borderless conflict, the most dangerous vulnerability is not a weak frontier but an unexamined belief that frontiers still matter as they once did.

Cities as Battlefields

For much of human history, cities were considered prizes of war, coveted for their wealth, infrastructure, and symbolic importance. Armies marched across fields and mountains to besiege them, and their fall often marked the end of campaigns. In the twenty-first century, however, cities are no longer simply the objects of conquest—they are the battlefields themselves. From Kiev to Hong Kong to Lagos, urban centres have become theatres where kinetic warfare, digital conflict, and psychological operations converge. The defining struggles of our age are not taking place on remote frontiers but in the heart of global cities that embody political will, economic vitality, and cultural influence.

Kiev illustrates this transformation starkly. When Russia launched its full-scale invasion of Ukraine in 2022, its early military thrust aimed not at peripheral border towns but directly at the capital. The logic was clear: controlling Kiev meant controlling the state's political nerve centre. Yet the battles that followed were not confined to tanks rolling through suburbs or artillery flattening residential blocks. They extended into cyberspace, where Russian hackers targeted Ukraine's power grid and communications systems in an effort to paralyse governance and sow panic. The city thus became both a physical frontline and a digital one, with residents experiencing war through the shells that landed in their neighbourhoods and the blackouts engineered from hundreds of kilometres away. The defence of Kiev underscored a new reality: cities are not only symbols but systems, and disrupting their functioning can be as strategically decisive as occupying them.

The case of Hong Kong offers a different but equally instructive perspective. Here the battle was less about kinetic force than about the suppression of information and control of narratives. The 2019 pro-democracy protests demonstrated how a city can become a global flashpoint, with streets and public squares serving as contested zones between demonstrators and state security forces. Yet the struggle extended far beyond tear gas and barricades. Digital surveillance, misinformation campaigns, and cyber-harassment of activists were central to Beijing's strategy of eroding resistance. International attention magnified the stakes, with the city's fate becoming a litmus test for the resilience of liberal values under the shadow of authoritarian influence. In Hong Kong, the battlefield was the city itself: its transportation networks clogged by strikes, its financial sector shaken by unrest, its public discourse flooded with state-backed narratives. The city was not merely the backdrop but the weapon, its infrastructure and global visibility harnessed to wage war on dissent.

Lagos, too, demonstrates the vulnerabilities of megacities in the age of hybrid conflict. With over twenty million residents and sprawling informal settlements, Lagos embodies the challenges of rapid urbanisation in the Global South. Its size and density make it ungovernable in parts, leaving vacuums readily exploited by criminal networks, insurgents, and cyber actors. The #EndSARS protests in 2020 revealed how quickly grievances in an urban environment could transform into sustained movements that blend physical demonstration with digital mobilisation. Social media platforms turned Lagos into a stage visible to the world, amplifying both the voices of protesters and the state's attempts at repression. In such contexts, *urban disorder becomes both a domestic threat and an international event*, raising questions about how fragile cities can withstand pressures that exploit their very interconnectedness.

What unites Kiev, Hong Kong, and Lagos is that their significance is not derived from their borders but from their centrality. They are nodes in political, economic, and digital networks whose disruption has ripple effects far beyond local geography. A blackout in Kiev sends signals across European energy markets. Protest suppression in Hong Kong reverberates through global debates on democracy. A demonstration in Lagos, livestreamed to millions, alters international perceptions of Nigeria's governance. In each case, the city serves as a multiplier of strategic effect, magnifying both the risks and the rewards of conflict.

This shift toward cities as primary battlefields also highlights a profound asymmetry. States and powerful actors exploit urban density to magnify fear: a single explosion in a crowded market, a cyberattack that cripples hospital systems, or an information campaign that spreads panic across neighbourhoods. By contrast, defending cities requires extraordinary resources—securing infrastructure, maintaining trust, and preserving daily life in environments where disruption is easy but stability is fragile. The adversary can weaponise chaos; the defender must preserve order. *This imbalance makes cities not only vulnerable but strategically irresistible to those seeking leverage.*

There is also a symbolic dimension to the urban battlefield. Cities are not just administrative centres; they embody identities. Kiev is not only Ukraine's capital but the cradle of its historical narrative. Hong Kong is not just a metropolis but a symbol of contested futures between East and West. Lagos is more than a city; it is an emblem of African dynamism and fragility. To strike at a city is to strike at what it represents. Modern conflicts thus exploit cities as both physical and psychological terrain, recognising that the image of a skyline under siege can alter perceptions globally, often more powerfully than the capture of remote territory.

Importantly, the urban battlefield is not solely kinetic or digital but hybrid. Cities today are wired into global systems, which means an attack on their infrastructure reverberates across borders. Cyberattacks on Kiev's grid affect European energy security; disruptions to Hong Kong's financial markets ripple through global supply chains; instability in Lagos strains international investment confidence in West Africa. The line between local conflict and global consequence has thinned, if not disappeared. Cities therefore represent points of leverage where controlling or destabilising them can yield influence far out of proportion to their geographic size.

Some argue that this transformation is inevitable in an era of mass urbanisation. With more than half of the world's population now living in cities, it is unsurprising that wars migrate to where people, infrastructure, and power are concentrated. Yet this explanation alone is insufficient. What makes the contemporary moment distinctive is not simply urbanisation but connectivity. Cities are not isolated metropolises; they are embedded in transnational flows of finance, data, culture, and politics. To attack a city is therefore to weaponise its connections, disrupting not only its internal order but the networks to which it belongs. *The battlefield is the city, but the war is fought through the systems that sustain it.*

Philosophically, this raises unsettling questions about sovereignty and governance. When a city becomes the frontline of global conflict, is it still under the control of its state, or has it become a contested space subject to external manipulation? In Kiev, the defence of the city was as much a defence of Ukraine's statehood as of its geography. In Hong Kong, the erosion of autonomy highlighted the city's vulnerability to external will, even under the façade of "one country, two systems." In Lagos, state authority contends daily with forces that blend the political, the criminal, and the digital, making governance a constant act of negotiation. Sovereignty in the twenty-first century may increasingly hinge not on controlling borders but on maintaining authority within cities that serve as both assets and liabilities.

The future trajectory suggests this trend will only intensify. As cities grow larger, denser, and more technologically dependent, their exposure to hybrid conflict will deepen. Artificial intelligence will enable new forms of digital manipulation; drones will make urban warfare more precise yet more pervasive; disinformation will spread faster through increasingly polarised digital communities. Cities will remain at the centre of this struggle not only because they concentrate people and power but because they project influence outward, shaping how the world interprets conflict. The spectacle of an urban battlefield—whether through images of resistance in Kiev, repression in Hong Kong, or mobilisation in Lagos—carries a weight that rural or peripheral conflicts rarely achieve.

To grasp the geopolitics of the twenty-first century, one must understand cities not just as places where people live and work, but as contested spaces where sovereignty, influence, and legitimacy are fought over daily. They are both prizes and weapons, vulnerabilities and strengths. The battlefield is no longer a distant plain; it is the metropolis itself, lit not only by streetlights but by the glow of screens that carry its struggles to the world.

The Rise of Stateless Power Brokers

Power in the twenty-first century is no longer confined to the borders of states or the corridors of traditional government. It has slipped into the hands of actors who command influence not through flags or constitutions, but through networks, capital, and technology. These *stateless power brokers*—warlords who dominate resource-rich territories, corporate executives whose platforms shape public life, and hackers who can paralyse governments with a few keystrokes—are increasingly rivalling, and at times surpassing, states in their ability to project authority, command loyalty, and impose consequences. What distinguishes them is not only their autonomy but also their adaptability; they thrive precisely because they operate outside the formal architectures of international order.

The archetype of the warlord demonstrates how authority can be derived from control over violence rather than recognition from the international community. Figures like Khalifa Haftar in Libya or the Taliban's regional commanders before their formal seizure of power illustrate how sub-state leaders can wield coercion and patronage to command legitimacy among populations. Their power is sustained less by the trappings of statehood and more by the ability to distribute security, extract resources, and impose order amid chaos. In fragile states, these figures often enjoy more immediate legitimacy than distant governments, because they provide what the state cannot: protection, economic opportunity, and a sense of belonging. This authority is highly localised but deeply resilient, as it rests on social contracts built in warzones rather than the halls of diplomacy. *The lesson here is stark: the monopoly of violence, once assumed to be the defining feature of the state, is increasingly shared with entrepreneurs of conflict.*

At the other end of the spectrum, corporate executives have emerged as geopolitical players whose influence is grounded in technological infrastructure rather than guns. When Elon Musk's SpaceX provided Starlink internet access to Ukraine during the Russian invasion, it became clear that the decisions of a single individual could alter the course of a war. Tech companies now determine how information flows across borders, which voices are amplified, and which are silenced. Their platforms shape elections, manage critical communication infrastructures, and decide—through algorithmic design—what billions of people perceive as reality. This concentration of power is not mediated by parliaments or treaties but by corporate governance structures and the personal choices of CEOs. The rise of these corporate figures raises a pressing question: *when unelected individuals control the arteries of global communication, does sovereignty still reside with states, or has it migrated to boardrooms?*

Hackers, too, embody the rise of stateless influence, but their power is diffuse, decentralised, and often invisible until it is unleashed. Groups like Anonymous, state-aligned collectives such as Russia's Killnet, or ransomware gangs operating out of safe havens in Eastern Europe demonstrate how coding skills can be weaponised to disrupt entire economies. A successful cyberattack does not require armies or supply lines; it requires expertise, coordination, and anonymity. The Colonial Pipeline attack in the United States in 2021, which disrupted fuel supply for millions, was orchestrated not by a rival state but by a criminal group seeking financial gain. Yet the geopolitical impact was indistinguishable from state-level aggression: panic buying, government intervention, and international security negotiations. Cyber actors thus blur the line between crime and war, revealing that stateless groups can shape national security agendas without firing a shot.

These actors—warlords, CEOs, hackers—do not operate in isolation. Their power often overlaps, reinforcing one another in a complex ecosystem. Warlords may fund operations through illicit mining that feeds global supply chains overseen by corporations. CEOs may negotiate with non-state actors in conflict zones to secure infrastructure or resource access, legitimising them as de facto authorities. Hackers may be hired by both governments and corporations as mercenaries of code, shifting allegiances fluidly between state and non-state employers. This convergence illustrates a profound transformation: *power is no longer binary, divided neatly between states and rebels; it exists on a spectrum where alliances and rivalries transcend traditional categories.*

Yet the rise of stateless power brokers also exposes tensions that defy easy categorisation. They thrive on deniability. States often find it convenient to outsource sensitive operations to these actors precisely because their statelessness provides cover. Russia's use of the Wagner Group in conflicts across Africa and the Middle East exemplifies this dynamic: Moscow reaps strategic benefits while disavowing direct responsibility. Similarly, governments tacitly tolerate ransomware gangs operating within their borders, treating them as useful irritants against adversaries. For corporations, the calculus is different but equally consequential: by controlling information flows, they shield themselves behind the rhetoric of free speech and innovation while exercising quasi-sovereign power over what constitutes public truth.

What makes stateless power brokers particularly significant is their capacity to mobilise legitimacy without relying on traditional markers of sovereignty. Warlords frame themselves as protectors of ethnic or tribal identity. CEOs cultivate narratives of technological progress and global connectivity. Hackers adopt the language of justice, anonymity, or anti-establishment rebellion. Each appeals to constituencies who find in them a form of representation absent from formal politics. This legitimacy is crucial, because it transforms raw influence into sustainable power. Without it, these actors would be dismissed as criminals or opportunists. With it, they become figures who rival states in the loyalty they command and the disruption they can orchestrate.

There is also an economic dimension to their power. Warlords extract rents from mines, trade routes, or smuggling operations, weaving their authority into global supply chains. CEOs manage platforms whose market capitalisation dwarfs the GDPs of many countries, granting them leverage in negotiations with states. Hackers operate in an informal economy that generates billions annually, siphoning wealth from corporations and governments alike. *In all three cases, control over flows—of resources, data, or capital—supersedes control over territory as the foundation of power.*

Critically, the rise of stateless power brokers forces a reconsideration of accountability. States are, at least theoretically, answerable to their citizens and subject to international law. Stateless actors, by contrast, operate in a legal grey zone. Warlords are seldom prosecuted unless they lose their local power bases. CEOs face regulatory pressures, but these are often reactive and fragmented, far behind the pace of technological innovation. Hackers are pursued by law enforcement, yet anonymity and jurisdictional barriers make enforcement uneven. This accountability vacuum allows these actors to operate with remarkable impunity, shaping global outcomes without the checks that constrain formal governments.

Some analysts see this diffusion of power as destabilising, eroding the state system that has underpinned international order for centuries. Others argue that it reflects the adaptive logic of a networked world, where decentralisation is inevitable. What cannot be denied is that these stateless power brokers expose the limitations of frameworks built for a state-centric age. The Westphalian assumption that borders delineate authority is increasingly undermined by actors who operate in spaces where borders are irrelevant: cyberspace, global markets, and transnational networks of loyalty and identity.

Looking forward, the influence of these figures is unlikely to diminish. On the contrary, technological advances and geopolitical fragmentation create conditions ripe for their expansion. Artificial intelligence will amplify the power of hackers to conduct autonomous attacks. The continued retreat of governance in fragile states will open new opportunities for warlords. The growing dependence of societies on digital infrastructure will elevate the authority of tech executives to unprecedented levels. Unless states find ways to adapt, the future will belong not to the monopolists of territory but to the brokers of flows.

The rise of stateless power brokers does not signal the end of the state, but it does mark the end of its uncontested supremacy. Authority today is plural, dispersed among actors who do not need flags to command influence. Their existence challenges not only how we understand power but how we imagine accountability, legitimacy, and sovereignty itself. To study them is not to look at the margins of global politics but at its new centre, where the forces shaping the twenty-first century converge without regard for borders.

The Future of Sovereignty

Few concepts have been as enduring in global politics as sovereignty, the principle that a state has supreme authority over its territory and population. Yet, the twenty-first century has exposed its fragility in ways few could have anticipated. The decline of territorial centrality and the rise of networks—economic, digital, and cultural—are reshaping the foundations upon which sovereignty has rested for centuries. The shift is not simply a matter of borders becoming porous; it is a deeper reorganisation of power, legitimacy, and control. *If sovereignty was once measured in miles of land and armies under command, it is now increasingly assessed in the capacity to shape flows of data, finance, and allegiance.*

The traditional Westphalian state system, formalised in the seventeenth century, enshrined territory as the cornerstone of political authority. Sovereignty meant recognition of a state's control over defined borders, the monopoly of violence within them, and the legitimacy to govern without interference. That model has proved resilient, but today it confronts challenges that go beyond the usual breaches of international law. Cyberattacks, transnational corporations, global supply chains, and diasporic movements do not merely test sovereignty—they reconfigure it. Borders remain on maps, but networks now dictate the dynamics of power. The ability of a government to command loyalty, regulate behaviour, or even tax its citizens increasingly depends on flows that it does not control.

Consider digital infrastructure. When a corporation like Meta can determine the circulation of information for billions, or when Elon Musk can decide whether a nation at war retains satellite internet access, sovereignty no longer rests exclusively in the hands of governments. The power to define who communicates, what is amplified, and what is silenced shifts from parliaments and ministries to algorithms and corporate boards. For states, this is an existential dilemma: *they have ceded not just technical capacity but normative authority to entities that owe them no allegiance.* In a networked age, control over information is more decisive than control over territory, because narratives shape legitimacy, and legitimacy shapes power.

Finance illustrates a similar transformation. Cryptocurrencies and decentralised finance challenge the monopoly of central banks, enabling actors—from insurgents to tech entrepreneurs—to move capital across borders without oversight. Sanctions, once a tool of statecraft, are circumvented through digital tokens or shadow banking systems. The Russian economy's resilience in the face of Western sanctions highlights how globalised markets dilute sovereign leverage. Meanwhile, small states like El Salvador, by adopting Bitcoin as legal tender, signal a pivot away from monetary sovereignty towards entanglement with transnational networks of digital finance. Sovereignty in this sense becomes not a shield but a negotiation, where the lines between autonomy and dependence are blurred.

Security, too, is no longer territorial. States once derived legitimacy from providing protection to their populations. Yet today, non-state actors, from private military contractors to cyber armies, erode that monopoly. The Wagner Group projected Russian influence from Syria to Mali, blurring the distinction between state and private force. Hackers, operating from safe havens or under tacit state protection, can cripple infrastructure thousands of miles away. These examples demonstrate that *violence has been untethered from geography.* A strike on a power grid does not require tanks crossing borders; it requires malware in a network. The battlefield is everywhere, and thus sovereignty is nowhere in particular.

One might argue that sovereignty is not disappearing but mutating. States are adapting by co-opting networks rather than resisting them. China's Great Firewall, for instance, represents an attempt to reassert control over digital space by nationalising the internet within its borders. The European Union, through its General Data Protection Regulation (GDPR), imposes standards that effectively extend its sovereignty into the global digital economy. These efforts suggest that sovereignty is being redefined less as territorial control and more as regulatory capacity over flows. A state is sovereign to the extent that it can set the terms of access to its networks, whether of data, finance, or trade.

Yet such adaptations expose a paradox. Sovereignty was once grounded in universality—the idea that each state was equal in principle, however unequal in practice. In the networked age, sovereignty is stratified. Large powers with technological capacity—China, the United States, the European Union—retain the ability to project authority across networks. Smaller states, however, find themselves dependent on infrastructures controlled by others, from undersea cables to cloud servers. Their sovereignty becomes contingent, not absolute, existing at the discretion of actors beyond their borders. In this asymmetry, sovereignty risks becoming less a principle of equality and more a reflection of digital hierarchies.

Philosophically, the challenge to sovereignty goes deeper still. At its core, sovereignty rests on the belief that political communities can be defined by geography: those within borders form a polity, those outside do not. But networks cut across these boundaries. Diasporas engage politically in home countries through remittances and online mobilisation. Activists coordinate transnationally on encrypted platforms. Global corporations treat citizenship as irrelevant to their customer base, operating across dozens of jurisdictions simultaneously. In such a world, belonging is not determined by territorial membership but by networked affiliation. *The community of loyalty is no longer national; it is algorithmic, financial, or ideological.*

The implications for democracy are profound. States derive legitimacy from representing their citizens, yet in a networked age, citizens are influenced, mobilised, and even governed by actors outside their state's reach. Election interference demonstrates this vividly: votes cast within national borders can be swayed by disinformation campaigns orchestrated abroad. When citizens' sense of truth, identity, or belonging is shaped by transnational platforms rather than local institutions, sovereignty loses its democratic foundation. It may persist as a legal fiction, but it no longer guarantees the state's ability to represent its people.

Some analysts see these shifts as heralding the end of sovereignty altogether, a descent into a post-Westphalian order where networks replace states as the primary loci of authority. Others argue that sovereignty will endure precisely because states remain indispensable: they still issue passports, raise taxes, and command armies. What both perspectives miss is that the real struggle is not about survival or extinction, but about transformation. Sovereignty will neither vanish nor remain unchanged; it will be reconstituted. It will be less about commanding territory and more about orchestrating networks, less about defending borders and more about managing interdependence.

The question, then, is not whether sovereignty will survive, but what form it will take. If it is to remain meaningful, it must adapt to a world where power lies in flows rather than frontiers. States that cling to territorial definitions of sovereignty will find themselves outmanoeuvred by actors—whether corporations, hackers, or transnational movements—who operate without regard for geography. Conversely, those that can regulate, channel, and harness networks will find new forms of authority that may prove as consequential as the territorial sovereignty of the past. *The future of sovereignty is not in the map but in the matrix of connections that shape how we live, trade, fight, and believe.*

In this reconfigured order, sovereignty will endure, but it will no longer be the immutable principle of territorial absolutism that defined the modern age. Instead, it will be contested, plural, and negotiated, reflecting the realities of a world where territory is not irrelevant but no longer decisive. The state remains, but it now shares the stage with actors who wield power through networks, forcing sovereignty to reinvent itself if it is to retain any relevance at all.

Chapter 11

Living in a Proxy World

The most unsettling truth about twenty-first century conflict is not its scale but its intimacy. Wars without flags no longer remain at the periphery of daily life, confined to remote battlefields or the pages of foreign news reports. They seep into the devices we carry, the companies we patronise, and the networks we inhabit. Ordinary people—citizens who neither wear uniforms nor fire weapons—find themselves living inside wars they cannot see but can nevertheless feel. From the glitch of a banking app during a cyberattack to the quiet normalisation of surveillance software embedded in consumer products, conflict has threaded itself into everyday routines. *The battlefield is no longer elsewhere; it is everywhere, and everyone is already enlisted.*

For citizens living under the shadow of militias or criminal groups, this reality has long been tangible. In parts of Nigeria, Afghanistan, or Colombia, to name only a few, individuals have had to negotiate daily life amid the competing presence of state forces, paramilitaries, cartels, and mercenary firms. Security becomes fragmented, and loyalty often a calculation of survival rather than conviction. But the digital age has generalised this condition. Today, even in supposedly stable democracies, civilians are caught in invisible wars waged through misinformation campaigns, ransomware, and algorithmic manipulation. When hackers shut down the Colonial Pipeline in the United States, it was not generals who queued at petrol stations but ordinary families unable to drive to work or school. The effects of stateless warfare are not abstract—they manifest in the disruption of commutes, the inflation of food prices, or the silencing of journalists targeted by spyware.

This entanglement has produced a new form of insecurity: one where *the citizen is both the target and the terrain.* Unlike conventional war, where armies clash and civilians are collateral, proxy wars and cyber conflicts deliberately exploit civilian spaces. Voting systems, energy grids, personal data—these are not auxiliary zones but primary targets. The blurring of war and peace means that civilians now live in what might be called a "permanent grey zone," where the absence of open conflict does not mean safety, and where daily routines are quietly shaped by forces beyond their perception. In Ukraine, for instance, the kinetic bombardment of cities has been paired with a constant cyber onslaught aimed at destabilising institutions and exhausting public trust. But the same playbook—less visible, more insidious—has been adapted in peacetime societies to fracture democracies and polarise populations.

Faced with such conditions, individuals and organisations increasingly adapt through what can only be described as a stateless security market. Where once the state was assumed to provide protection, people now assemble their own defences. Wealthier citizens hire private security contractors in cities like São Paulo or Johannesburg, creating enclaves of safety that deepen inequality. Businesses turn to private cyber firms to protect against ransomware, paying retainers to digital mercenaries who patrol firewalls and networks rather than streets. Even at the household level, digital self-defence has become routine: encrypted messaging, VPNs, and biometric locks are no longer niche tools for activists but everyday practices for parents, students, and professionals who sense that security has shifted from public provision to private purchase. *Safety has been commodified, and survival often depends on one's ability to afford it.*

Yet adapting to this environment is not only about security; it is also about ethics. Every consumer decision becomes entangled with conflict. To download a social media app may mean accepting the intrusion of foreign intelligence services. To purchase a smartphone may indirectly fund supply chains controlled by armed groups in mineral-rich regions. To buy petrol may finance states whose proxy militias destabilise neighbours. The citizen thus faces an impossible calculus: *how to live an ordinary life when the ordinary itself feeds extraordinary violence.* Even silence is a choice with consequences, as failing to contest disinformation online enables its spread. In this sense, daily behaviour—mundane, unpolitical, banal—becomes a form of participation in proxy war, whether one wishes it or not.

What makes this condition so destabilising is not simply that conflict has come home, but that it has arrived invisibly. Unlike the obvious markers of traditional war—uniforms, weapons, frontlines—proxy conflicts and algorithmic warfare remain hidden beneath the surface of consumer life. Surveillance technologies are disguised as conveniences. Misinformation is packaged as entertainment. Even violence itself is mediated through abstractions like "service disruption" or "platform outage," leaving many unaware of the conflicts shaping their lives. This invisibility makes preparation difficult, for how does one build resilience against a war that cannot be easily recognised? And yet resilience is precisely what is required. To live in a proxy world is to accept that conflict will reach you digitally, economically, or psychologically before it ever arrives physically.

Resilience, however, must be reimagined. It is no longer enough to think of resilience as stocking supplies or fortifying homes. It must include the capacity to discern truth from manipulation, to protect data as much as property, and to cultivate trust within communities fragmented by disinformation. At the organisational level, resilience means not only safeguarding infrastructure but also ensuring adaptability to disruptions that may never be claimed by an adversary yet bear the fingerprints of one. For individuals, resilience demands new literacies: digital hygiene, critical media awareness, and an understanding of how personal choices ripple through global conflicts. To prepare for the unseen is not paranoia but prudence in an age where invisibility is a weapon.

Ultimately, living in a proxy world requires a different conception of citizenship itself. No longer shielded by the presumed monopoly of state protection, citizens are both more vulnerable and more responsible than before. They inhabit a landscape where violence is outsourced, trust is weaponised, and survival is increasingly privatised. The question is not whether this condition can be avoided—it already defines our present—but how it can be navigated with clarity, responsibility, and foresight. The citizen of the proxy world must learn to live not in denial of these wars, but with an awareness that transforms passive vulnerability into active resilience. *The wars without flags are fought around and through us; to pretend otherwise is to surrender without knowing it.*

How Ordinary People Are Caught in Invisible Wars

The most enduring feature of modern conflict is not its spectacle but its silence. Wars without flags are not always marked by columns of tanks or the thunder of missiles; they are woven into the ordinary rhythms of daily life. The first sign that someone has become a participant may be the failure of their bank card, a sudden blackout in their city, or the quiet knowledge that their phone is listening when it should not be. Conflict today is ambient, distributed, and, most unnervingly, invisible. Ordinary people have become the terrain upon which power struggles are fought—not only in warzones where militias patrol the streets, but in apartment blocks in

Berlin, offices in Lagos, and households in San Francisco. What defines this age is not the absence of violence but its transmutation into forms so subtle they often go unrecognised until the consequences are undeniable.

For those living in regions where militias, warlords, or private security firms operate alongside fragile states, this condition is hardly new. In parts of Iraq or the Democratic Republic of Congo, civilians have long been forced to navigate multiple overlapping authorities—government soldiers by day, armed gangs by night, foreign mercenaries in between. To survive means to master the choreography of divided loyalties, paying bribes at checkpoints, obeying curfews imposed by non-state actors, and constantly recalculating which group controls which stretch of road. Yet the digital age has globalised this predicament. Citizens of wealthy democracies now experience their own version of divided sovereignty—not through guns at street corners, but through the competing control of data, networks, and information. A ransomware attack on a hospital in Düsseldorf in 2020 led to the death of a patient redirected to another facility. The perpetrators were never clearly identified. The lesson was stark: ordinary people no longer need to live in a failed state to suffer the costs of invisible war.

Surveillance has become one of the most intimate expressions of this reality. Where authoritarian governments once relied on visible tools of coercion—secret police, overt censorship—today's power brokers use systems embedded in the very technologies civilians embrace. Smartphones double as tracking devices; social media feeds act as vectors for disinformation; consumer apps gather data as currency in global competitions for influence. Pegasus, the spyware developed by the Israeli firm NSO Group, was marketed as a tool for governments to combat terrorism, yet investigations revealed it had been deployed against journalists, lawyers, and activists across multiple continents. For those targeted, the war arrived not with a raid at dawn but with a compromise of the most personal object they owned. *The battlefield, in this sense, is not external territory but the intimate geography of private life.*

Artificial intelligence adds another layer of opacity. Civilians increasingly move through environments where algorithms—designed by corporations, deployed by states, and sometimes manipulated by hostile actors—make consequential decisions invisible to them. Credit scoring systems, predictive policing software, and automated content moderation are not framed as tools of conflict, yet they can be exploited to suppress communities, silence dissent, or marginalise individuals under the guise of efficiency. In Xinjiang, AI-enabled surveillance has been used to monitor, categorise, and control the Uyghur population with unprecedented precision. Cameras, biometric scanners, and digital checkpoints do not announce themselves as weapons, yet their combined effect is the creation of an open-air prison. The paradox is unsettling: technologies that appear to serve order and convenience can be weaponised to wage war against trust, autonomy, and identity.

For many, the daily experience of this invisible war is not the drama of sudden attack but the steady erosion of confidence in systems once taken for granted. The internet connection becomes suspect—was that outage accidental, or a test by a foreign adversary? News stories provoke doubt—does this headline reflect fact, or the agenda of a bot-driven campaign? A neighbour's allegiance becomes uncertain—do they genuinely hold these views, or have they been radicalised online? This creeping distrust corrodes the fabric of community. When every institution, from banks to elections, can be hacked, the collective sense of safety dissolves. *War without borders breeds fear without clarity, leaving civilians uncertain of where the line between normal disruption and hostile act truly lies.*

The ethical choices of civilians are also entangled with these conflicts in ways few can escape. A consumer downloading a messaging app may inadvertently submit their communications to surveillance by foreign powers. A parent buying a cheap smartphone for their child may be funnelling money into supply chains dependent on forced labour overseen by militias. Even the act of sharing a video online can amplify disinformation designed to destabilise democracies. Citizens, often unaware, become vectors in larger struggles, not by intent but by design. This is what makes modern wars so difficult to resist: participation is not chosen but engineered. *To live in a proxy world is to be implicated by default.*

Yet civilians are not only victims; they are also forced into strategies of adaptation. In cities like Johannesburg or São Paulo, private security firms now guard middle-class neighbourhoods because citizens no longer trust the state to provide safety. In Mexico, entire communities have organised armed self-defence groups against cartels, blurring the line between civilian and combatant. In cyberspace, individuals turn to encryption, VPNs, and pseudonyms to reclaim a semblance of privacy. Each of these adaptations underscores the same reality: survival now depends less on the protection of the state and more on the ingenuity and resources of the individual. Safety has been outsourced, and those unable to afford it are left exposed.

What makes this condition uniquely destabilising is its invisibility. Wars once announced themselves; now they disguise themselves as glitches, policies, or market choices. Civilians are caught in a paradox where the very tools they rely upon—smartphones, electricity grids, social media—double as conduits of conflict. To live in such an environment is to inhabit a permanent low-level state of war without ever formally recognising it as such. The consequences are profound: democracy weakens when citizens cannot trust information, economies falter when systems are perpetually under cyber threat, and communities fracture when fear and suspicion replace solidarity.

The reality is stark: ordinary people are no longer outside observers of conflict but its primary participants, whether they wish to be or not. The wars they are caught in are invisible by design, engineered to bypass conventional defences and exploit the mundane. This is the true cost of stateless warfare—it transforms everyday life into contested ground, where civilians carry the burdens of battles they never declared. *To understand contemporary conflict, one must begin not with generals or strategies, but with the daily uncertainties of the citizen who wakes up each morning in a world at war, and yet cannot always see it.*

Adapting to a Stateless Security Market

The assumption that the state is the sole and sufficient guarantor of security is no longer credible. Across much of the world, individuals and organisations now purchase, negotiate, or improvise their own protection, not because they distrust authority in the abstract, but because the authority they once relied on has proven absent, weak, or compromised. This shift has not occurred in a vacuum; it is the product of global insecurity that is at once political, technological, and economic. From private security patrols in affluent Johannesburg suburbs, to corporate cyber-defence teams in Silicon Valley, to community militias in rural Mexico, the trend is unmistakable: security is becoming commodified, fragmented, and increasingly privatised. *To live in this world is to accept that protection is no longer a universal right but a differentiated good—purchased by those who can afford it, improvised by those who cannot.*

The most visible manifestation of this market is in physical protection. In societies where state policing is unreliable or mistrusted, private guards have become the de facto frontline of order. In Brazil, the number of private security personnel now exceeds that of public police officers, reflecting a broader dynamic in which the affluent contract armed protection while the poor rely on fragile community arrangements. The industry is booming not only in unstable regions but also in advanced economies. Wealthy

Americans employ private security details during election cycles when political violence spikes, while European football clubs hire firms to manage crowd control in ways once considered a sovereign responsibility. This outsourcing is not simply about safety; it reconfigures the social contract. *Security is no longer delivered by citizenship but by transaction.*

Digital security represents an even more transformative dimension of this trend. The proliferation of ransomware, state-sponsored hacking, and mass data breaches has created an environment where corporations and individuals alike must assume that their digital infrastructures will be attacked. Cyber insurance has become one of the fastest-growing sectors of the insurance industry, while companies such as Microsoft and Google increasingly act not just as service providers but as de facto cyber-defence agencies. When Microsoft took unilateral action to dismantle elements of the Russian-linked SolarWinds attack infrastructure in 2020, it demonstrated a striking inversion: a private corporation effectively acted in place of the state to defend critical systems. This was not an isolated event but part of a larger pattern in which *the guardians of cyberspace are more likely to be engineers in corporate headquarters than intelligence officers in government facilities.*

The adaptation extends to individuals, who now practice forms of digital self-defence once reserved for spies or activists. Encryption apps like Signal, once niche, have become mainstream, while VPN services and password managers are staples of personal security. In Hong Kong's 2019 protests, civilians coordinated through mesh networks that bypassed government-controlled telecommunications. In authoritarian regimes, citizens adopt pseudonyms, encrypted chatrooms, and coded language to survive within hostile digital environments. These practices are not fringe behaviours; they represent a mass migration towards self-protection in the digital realm. *Where once locks and alarms guarded the home, encryption keys and firewalls now guard the self.*

This shift, however, raises profound inequalities. The capacity to adapt to a stateless security market is not evenly distributed. Large corporations can build in-house cyber-defence teams, hire former intelligence officers, and pay millions in ransoms if necessary. Small businesses and individuals, by contrast, face existential risk when attacked, often collapsing under the costs of breach recovery. The same applies in physical space: wealthy neighbourhoods can fund private patrols, while poorer districts suffer the neglect of both state and market provision. The commodification of security thus stratifies protection along familiar lines of wealth and privilege. *Security becomes a mirror of inequality, reinforcing divisions rather than bridging them.*

There are also ethical dilemmas inherent in this adaptation. Private security firms often operate in a legal grey zone, with limited oversight and accountability. Their actions may suppress threats, but they can also escalate violence, entrench corruption, or intimidate communities. In cyberspace, companies that dominate defensive infrastructures also wield enormous power to determine what constitutes legitimate traffic, acceptable speech, or acceptable risk. When Facebook or Twitter remove disinformation campaigns, they act as arbiters of truth in ways that affect entire societies. These decisions are often opaque, raising questions about legitimacy: who authorised these companies to police public discourse, and to what extent do they act in the interest of society rather than their own shareholders? *The outsourcing of security is also an outsourcing of sovereignty.*

Adaptation is not always voluntary; sometimes it is forced. In parts of Nigeria, communities have formed vigilante groups to defend themselves from Boko Haram and bandit gangs, not because they wished to militarise civilian life but because no alternative existed. Similarly, in Eastern Ukraine before Russia's full-scale invasion, civilians navigated a complex patchwork of local militias, foreign fighters, and quasi-state authorities, often paying multiple groups for protection. These arrangements illustrate the darker side of adaptation: survival may mean engaging with armed actors who exploit insecurity for profit. To adapt in such contexts is not to achieve safety but to navigate risk in a perpetual state of negotiation.

The rise of a stateless security market also transforms the psychology of security itself. Where the state once promised a collective shield, citizens now internalise the notion that they are personally responsible for their own defence. This cultural shift manifests in the proliferation of home surveillance systems, cybersecurity awareness campaigns, and community watch groups. It creates resilience, but it also fosters paranoia and a retreat into privatised fortresses. When individuals and organisations no longer expect the state to guarantee safety, the sense of shared obligation weakens. Societies risk becoming not communities of mutual protection, but archipelagos of private security arrangements.

What makes this transformation historically significant is its permanence. This is not a temporary stopgap until states "catch up" with new threats; it is a structural reconfiguration of how security is organised. Technology ensures that cyber warfare will remain decentralised, while globalisation guarantees that non-state actors will continue to wield influence across borders. The stateless security market is not an aberration but a new equilibrium. The pressing question, therefore, is not whether individuals and organisations will adapt, but how—and at what cost to social cohesion, political accountability, and the very meaning of citizenship.

To adapt successfully requires more than tools or guards; it demands a new mindset. Individuals must think of themselves not only as consumers but as custodians of their own resilience, balancing convenience with vigilance. Organisations must recognise that their survival depends not only on compliance with regulation but on anticipating threats that regulators themselves cannot manage. And societies must grapple with the paradox that while adaptation brings security, it also fragments the collective bonds upon which long-term stability depends. *The stateless security market is not only reshaping how people defend themselves—it is redefining what it means to live together in an age where war is everywhere and nowhere at once.*

The Ethical Dilemmas of Everyday Choices

Few citizens imagine that their morning routines—downloading an app, ordering from a global retailer, or clicking "agree" to a new set of digital terms—could feed conflicts unfolding continents away. Yet the cumulative weight of consumer behaviour increasingly funds, legitimises, or normalises the machinery of proxy wars. *The frontlines of conflict are not only in contested cities or shadowy cyber domains; they are embedded in the devices we carry, the platforms we trust, and the brands we endorse.*

Consider the seemingly innocuous act of installing a social media app. Behind the convenience of messaging friends or watching videos lies an ecosystem of data extraction and surveillance. Some applications are backed by corporations deeply entangled with national security interests, or even directly aligned with state power. By sharing personal data, users may be unwittingly feeding the intelligence operations of rival powers. For instance, concerns surrounding TikTok's links to Beijing or the long-standing suspicion of Russian platforms like VK highlight how apps function not merely as tools of entertainment, but as extensions of geopolitical rivalry. To use them is not a neutral choice; it is to participate—however indirectly—in battles over influence, data sovereignty, and cultural dominance. *Consumer choice in digital markets is rarely detached from questions of national strategy.*

The dilemma extends to commerce. Modern supply chains are not only intricate but often inseparable from conflict zones. Electronics assembled in East Asia may contain rare earth minerals mined under exploitative conditions in Central Africa, controlled in part by armed groups or mercenary outfits. The device purchased in a London shop or New York mall might, therefore, carry within it the financial imprint of warfare thousands of miles away. The ethical weight of such choices is heavy, yet obscured by layers of corporate branding and marketing. This creates a moral paradox: individuals want affordable, innovative technology, but meeting that demand sustains systems in which coercion, corruption, and violence thrive. The very logic of consumer capitalism collides with the aspiration for ethical distance from war.

Even digital services marketed as "neutral" or "apolitical" can be weaponised. Cloud storage companies, internet service providers, and content-hosting platforms frequently find themselves at the centre of proxy conflicts. Hosting decisions—whether to allow a controversial website or to de-platform extremist groups—have implications far beyond the corporate realm. When Amazon Web Services withdrew hosting for Parler in 2021, it was more than a business decision: it shaped the information ecosystem of a polarised United States. Similarly, when Facebook and Twitter removed state-sponsored disinformation networks linked to Russia or Iran, they altered not just discourse but the battlefield of perception itself. *Private corporations are now arbiters of legitimacy in the digital sphere, and consumers who fund or legitimise these platforms indirectly empower their geopolitical role.*

Yet the moral burden is not confined to corporations; it filters down to individual decision-making. Consumers often face subtle but consequential trade-offs between convenience and principle. Choosing to use encrypted apps may protect personal privacy but could also be portrayed by some governments as a refusal to cooperate with law enforcement, raising tensions over the balance of rights and security. Opting for products marketed as ethically sourced often carries higher costs, effectively pricing ethical participation in global markets as a privilege. These everyday decisions reveal a stark truth: *ethics in consumer behaviour is no longer only about sustainability or labour rights but about complicity in the conduct of modern war.*

The dilemmas become sharper when corporations and consumers occupy contested information environments. Boycotts, for instance, have become a tool of both solidarity and warfare. Calls to boycott companies operating in occupied territories or in markets accused of human rights abuses can signal political alignment. Yet boycotts are themselves double-edged:

they may punish offending corporations but also harm workers with little influence over corporate decisions. Similarly, targeted sanctions on technology companies accused of supporting authoritarian regimes often leave consumers with limited alternatives, forcing them into complicity even when they wish to abstain. *The illusion of choice hides the reality that many consumer markets are entangled with conflict by design.*

At the individual level, digital engagement itself has become a terrain of ethical struggle. Sharing or amplifying disinformation, even inadvertently, contributes to psychological operations designed to destabilise societies. Liking a page, joining a group, or reposting an article can provide legitimacy to networks that spread propaganda and polarisation. The boundary between passive consumption and active participation is blurred, and the consequences reverberate far beyond the user's screen. Citizens become not only consumers but vectors in wars of perception. The dilemma is acute: abstaining from engagement feels impossible in hyperconnected societies, yet participating risks fuelling the very dynamics that undermine democratic institutions.

Corporations, too, face their own forms of ethical compromise. Technology giants are frequently caught between markets and principles. Apple, for example, has been criticised for complying with Chinese state regulations that restrict user freedoms, while simultaneously marketing itself as a champion of privacy in Western markets. These contradictions filter down to consumers, who are asked to purchase devices that embody conflicting values depending on geography. Similar tensions arise in the defence technology sector, where firms supplying AI systems for civilian use may also license their tools for military applications. Purchasing a product from such companies inadvertently strengthens their capacity to service warfare markets. *Consumers are, in effect, subsidising technologies that blur the boundary between civil utility and instruments of conflict.*

The moral challenge is compounded by the opacity of modern supply chains and platform governance. Few consumers have the time, resources, or expertise to trace the origins of every product or the ultimate use of their data. This informational asymmetry absolves individuals of immediate guilt while still implicating them in broader systems of violence. It creates a quiet complicity: people know they may be indirectly fuelling conflict, but the scale of the system makes ethical abstention feel futile. Ethical consumption in a proxy war economy is less about clean choices and more about negotiating compromises in which no option is entirely innocent.

Philosophically, this raises the question of agency in modern warfare. Traditional theories of just war presuppose that civilians, unless directly taking up arms, remain outside the moral calculus of conflict. Yet in a proxy world where financial flows, digital signals, and consumer markets shape the battlefield, this distinction collapses. Civilians become implicated, not as deliberate agents of violence but as participants in networks that sustain it. The moral innocence once associated with ordinary consumption is no longer tenable. *The battlefield has expanded to encompass wallets, clicks, and choices made at checkout counters.*

At the same time, this does not absolve states or corporations of responsibility. It highlights instead a need for greater transparency, regulation, and accountability in the intersection between markets and conflict. Ethical consumption cannot substitute for governance, but it can serve as a form of pressure, signalling public demand for systems that minimise complicity. The challenge lies in building mechanisms—certification schemes, regulatory frameworks, and civic accountability structures—that make consumer choices less fraught and more genuinely ethical. Without such frameworks, individuals will continue to navigate impossible dilemmas, shouldering responsibility for conflicts far beyond their control.

Everyday choices have never been free from politics, but in the age of proxy wars and algorithmic conflict, they have become inescapably geopolitical. To download, to purchase, to share—these are not neutral acts but decisions embedded in global struggles over power, influence, and survival. *The ethical dilemmas of modern consumption remind us that war is no longer confined to armies and borders: it is carried in pockets, streamed through feeds, and woven into the fabric of daily life.*

Preparing for the Unseen

The most destabilising threats of the present century are those that arrive without the sound of sirens or the sight of soldiers. A blackout in a financial hub may not be caused by ageing infrastructure but by a foreign hacker manipulating energy grids. The sudden disappearance of trusted news sources may stem not from journalistic collapse but from a disinformation campaign eroding the foundations of truth. What is striking is not merely the invisibility of these attacks but the fact that they strike citizens before governments recognise them. *The first victims of digital conflict are often ordinary people, not armies or officials.*

Resilience in such a world cannot be defined by the traditional imagery of bunkers, stored provisions, or physical fortifications. Instead, it requires preparedness for disruption that is psychological, informational, and infrastructural. One of the most sobering lessons from cyber incidents—from the NotPetya malware that crippled Ukrainian institutions and spread worldwide, to ransomware attacks on hospitals during the COVID-19 pandemic—is that societies function on assumptions of invisible trust. We assume our bank balances will remain accurate, our medical records intact, and our communications authentic. When those assumptions are undermined, panic and paralysis spread faster than the actual attack. *The fragility of trust is the unseen vulnerability on which digital aggressors rely.*

For individuals and organisations, resilience therefore begins with rethinking the architecture of everyday life. Digital literacy is no longer a matter of convenience or employability; it is a civic defence mechanism. Recognising a phishing attempt, verifying the source of information, or maintaining secure digital practices can mean the difference between being a passive conduit for hostile influence and serving as a barrier against it. Yet the burden cannot fall on citizens alone. The state and private sectors must cultivate resilience as a shared responsibility, building systems that assume failure is inevitable and recovery essential. A society prepared for the unseen does not expect to stop every attack; it expects to withstand them without collapse.

The paradox of digital warfare is that the most advanced societies are often the most vulnerable. Countries with integrated online economies and highly connected populations benefit from efficiency but pay in fragility. Estonia's experience in 2007 remains instructive: a sustained cyberattack paralysed banking, government, and media services, demonstrating how a small state at the cutting edge of digital governance could be held hostage without a single missile launched. The lesson was not that connectivity is dangerous, but that resilience depends on distributing capacity. Estonia responded by pioneering data embassies—backups of state records stored abroad—ensuring continuity even if local servers were destroyed. *Resilience, in this sense, is not isolation but redundancy; survival rests on the ability to restore function even after disruption.*

At the individual level, resilience must also be reimagined in psychological terms. Digital warfare is as much about perception as about infrastructure. Disinformation campaigns aim not only to spread falsehoods but to seed cynicism, convincing citizens that no source is trustworthy and no fact verifiable. The effect is corrosive: societies fracture into tribes of suspicion, paralysed by the impossibility of consensus. Preparing for the unseen, then, requires cultivating mental resilience against manipulation. This is not simply media literacy but a deeper discipline of discernment—resisting the allure of outrage, questioning the origin of information, and recognising when emotions are being engineered. *In the digital battlespace, psychological immunity is as critical as firewalls and encryption.*

Organisations too must adapt. The private sector, especially those that manage critical infrastructure—energy, finance, healthcare, logistics—cannot rely solely on governmental defence. Increasingly, corporations are treated as de facto military targets by hostile actors. Attacks on supply chains, such as the SolarWinds breach, reveal how deeply interconnected vulnerabilities are. Firms must build what security experts call "assumed breach" strategies, operating on the expectation that adversaries are already inside systems and focusing on containment, detection, and rapid recovery. The days of static defence lines are over; resilience is iterative, adaptive, and dynamic.

Yet resilience is not only about systems but about communities. Societies under attack reveal a crucial truth: the stronger the social fabric, the harder it is for external actors to fracture. During the early stages of the Russian invasion of Ukraine, local communities demonstrated extraordinary resilience by maintaining communications, supporting displaced families, and improvising logistics even when formal systems faltered. This illustrates that resilience is not simply technological or institutional but deeply human. Trust networks—families, neighbourhoods, local associations—are the true redundancies of society. Preparing for the unseen therefore requires investing not only in cybersecurity and infrastructure but in the cohesion of communities that can absorb shocks together.

The difficulty lies in convincing citizens and policymakers alike to prepare for threats that have no fixed timeline. Unlike hurricanes or earthquakes, digital and informational attacks cannot be predicted by meteorological models or seismic sensors. They strike when politically advantageous, often masked until too late. The natural impulse is complacency—until disruption arrives. Yet this complacency is precisely what aggressors exploit. The challenge is cultural: to instil habits of preparedness without lapsing into paranoia, to live in awareness of risk without succumbing to fatalism. *The unseen cannot be eliminated, but it can be anticipated and survived.*

Philosophically, this raises questions about the meaning of security itself. For much of modern history, security was equated with the state's ability to defend borders, deter invasions, and maintain territorial sovereignty. But when conflicts arrive invisibly, bypassing borders and striking individuals first, security becomes diffused. It is no longer the monopoly of governments but a shared condition of networked societies. This does not mean the state is irrelevant, but that its role is transformed: not to promise absolute protection but to orchestrate resilience, enabling citizens and institutions to adapt. *Security in the digital age is not a fortress but a choreography of interdependence.*

Looking forward, resilience must be seen not as a reaction to crises but as a cultural orientation. Just as societies once built fire drills, disaster preparedness kits, and civil defence exercises into daily life, so too must they normalise practices of digital and psychological readiness. Schools must teach not only history and science but the skills of discernment and digital hygiene. Companies must view cybersecurity as core to their existence, not as a peripheral cost. Citizens must internalise that every click, every password, every piece of shared information carries significance in the broader conflict ecosystem. This is not a call to paranoia but to a pragmatic recognition: in a world of invisible wars, resilience is citizenship.

The unseen cannot be avoided, but it can be prepared for. Ordinary people will remain the first targets of digital aggression, yet they can also be the first line of defence. Resilience is not about perfection but about continuity—the ability to bend without breaking, to adapt without surrendering, and to recover without forgetting. *The societies that thrive in this century will not be those that promise to avoid disruption, but those that learn to live with it, prepare for it, and emerge stronger each time it arrives.*

Chapter 12

After the Flag: Power Beyond the Nation-State

The modern international order was built on the assumption that the flag defined the boundaries of power. Territory, marked by borders and recognised through treaties, was meant to determine who governed whom and under what authority. Yet as we move deeper into the twenty-first century, that assumption no longer holds. The flag is still raised, but it is no longer the primary marker of sovereignty or the decisive instrument of control. Instead, states and non-state actors alike operate in a system where influence radiates outward not through occupation but through networks of proxies, data flows, corporate leverage, and algorithmic reach. *The language of sovereignty remains, but the logic of empire has returned in disguised form.*

Consider the major conflicts of recent decades. In Syria, Libya, and Yemen, competing powers have funded and armed militias, mercenaries, and political factions without ever formally annexing land. Russia's Wagner Group, American contractors, Iranian militias, and Turkish-backed forces each carved influence not by planting flags but by managing proxies. The United States' use of drone warfare, often coordinated with local partners, projects force globally without establishing colonial structures. China's Belt and Road Initiative, while not framed as imperial, creates strategic dependencies across continents, tying infrastructure, ports, and digital networks to Beijing's long-term reach. *The result is a form of empire without the name: spheres of influence built on flexible alliances, contractual dependencies, and private enforcers rather than territorial conquest.*

This new configuration reveals why proxy conflicts so rarely resolve. Unlike conventional wars, which end with treaties or territorial settlements, proxy wars perpetuate themselves by design. They allow states to pursue influence without risking open confrontation, making them politically cheaper and strategically sustainable. When one proxy falters, another can be armed or funded; when one battleground cools, another can be ignited elsewhere. The incentives for resolution diminish because instability itself becomes the resource—an environment in which competing powers can test tools, shift costs, and weaken rivals indirectly. The outcome is less like the definitive wars of the past and more like rolling contests with no natural conclusion. *Instability has become the currency of modern power, and civilians pay its price indefinitely.*

The difficulty is compounded by the absence of rules. International law was designed to govern states, armies, and borders. It has little to say about deniable militias, cyber armies, or AI-driven operations that blur the lines of agency and accountability. Treaties crafted in the twentieth century are ill-suited for twenty-first-century conflicts where attacks can be launched from private laptops, covert financial flows can bankroll armed groups, and autonomous systems can act faster than human oversight. Attempts to apply the Geneva Conventions to digital and proxy warfare reveal how inadequate existing frameworks are. The fog is not only of war but of law: who can be held accountable when violence is outsourced, data is weaponised, and decision-making is automated? *The old architecture of rules is collapsing under the strain of conflicts designed to avoid regulation altogether.*

This is not merely a problem for governments but for societies, businesses, and individuals navigating a security environment where threats no longer arrive under a state flag. Tech platforms decide which voices are amplified and which are silenced, effectively becoming arbiters of truth. Multinational corporations control infrastructure as vital as energy grids, satellites, and undersea cables, making them targets in geopolitical struggles. Communities face manipulation campaigns that corrode democratic processes not by tanks at the border but by tailored narratives on social media feeds. In such a context, the question of security shifts dramatically: how does one stay safe in a world where the frontlines run through servers, shopping platforms, and even household devices?

If the flag is no longer the guarantor of safety, resilience must be reimagined beyond the nation-state. Societies must confront that their well-being is tied not only to the competence of governments but also to the robustness of networks, the accountability of corporations, and the adaptability of citizens. Businesses cannot see security as an external concern; they are embedded in the conflict ecosystem and must act accordingly. Individuals, too, cannot assume protection as a passive right but must cultivate forms of digital literacy, information resilience, and community solidarity. *Security in this age is plural: distributed across actors, technologies, and scales of action that no single state can monopolise.*

The chapter that follows examines these shifts in depth. It interrogates the silent return of empire in the form of proxy networks, where states wield power less through conquest than through manipulation of dependencies. It dissects the logic of endless proxy conflict, showing how instability itself becomes a tool of strategy. It explores the void in international governance, where the absence of enforceable rules enables private armies, cyber militias, and algorithms to shape events without accountability. Finally, it advances a vision of how security can be reimagined: not by returning to the outdated monopoly of state power but by designing frameworks of shared resilience fit for a stateless age.

The decline of the flag as the ultimate symbol of authority does not mark the end of politics but the transformation of its terrain. Just as empires once rose and fell through shifting alliances, tributary networks, and spheres of influence, today's world is being redrawn through digital conduits, financial leverage, and the outsourcing of violence. The stakes for ordinary people are profound: their economies, freedoms, and even identities are shaped by conflicts they cannot see and by powers they did not elect. The challenge, therefore, is not to mourn the passing of the old order but to recognise what is emerging in its place. *To understand life after the flag is to grasp the future of power itself—how it will be exercised, resisted, and lived with in the decades ahead.*

The Return of Empire, Without the Name

For centuries, empire was the dominant structure of world politics, a system in which great powers extended control far beyond their borders through conquest, colonies, and tributary arrangements. By the mid-twentieth century, empire appeared to have collapsed under the weight of decolonisation, self-determination, and the triumph of the nation-state. The flag replaced the crown, sovereignty replaced imperial hierarchy, and international law declared the equality of nations. Yet beneath the veneer of this supposedly post-imperial age, empire has quietly returned—though it no longer looks like its historical predecessor. States are rediscovering imperial logic, not through the planting of flags or annexation of land, but by building webs of proxies, dependencies, and networks that achieve dominance without formal ownership. The map still shows national borders, but real power increasingly flows through influence, contracts, and covert alliances that transcend them.

Nowhere is this more evident than in the Middle East and Africa, where rival states use mercenary forces, local militias, and private military companies to shape conflicts while avoiding the costs of formal rule. Russia's Wagner Group carved out zones of influence across Syria, Libya, and the Sahel by embedding itself with local regimes, trading military support for resource concessions, and ensuring Moscow's reach without direct responsibility. The United States, long reliant on local partners in Iraq and Afghanistan, built an architecture of security contractors, special operations forces, and allied militias that allowed Washington to withdraw troops while maintaining influence. Turkey's reliance on Syrian fighters deployed to Libya and Nagorno-Karabakh reflects the same logic: *outsourcing war not to annex territory but to engineer leverage.* These arrangements achieve many of the same ends as empire—access to resources, political leverage, and geopolitical reach—without the costs of garrisons, colonies, or imperial administration.

China's model extends the pattern into the economic and digital domains. Its Belt and Road Initiative has built a network of ports, railways, fibre-optic cables, and financial dependencies that tether states to Beijing's strategic orbit. While no Chinese flag flies over Sri Lanka's Hambantota port or Pakistan's Gwadar, their financial and logistical realities mean those assets cannot easily escape Beijing's grip. At the same time, Chinese technology companies provide surveillance infrastructure and digital ecosystems across Africa, Central Asia, and beyond, embedding states into a technological dependency that resembles the imperial practice of shaping not just economies but the very architecture of governance. *This is empire built on infrastructure and code rather than colonies and governors.*

What distinguishes today's empire is deniability and flexibility. The old colonial empires made sovereignty explicit: colonies were marked on maps, subjects were administered by imperial officials, and the costs of rule—rebellions, famines, administrative expense—were borne openly. By contrast, modern empire avoids formal responsibility. If a proxy militia commits abuses, the patron state disclaims accountability. If a private company manipulates data or controls infrastructure, it is dismissed as market activity rather than geopolitical leverage. This shift creates a system in which power is exerted without liability, allowing states to enjoy influence without absorbing the reputational and legal burdens of colonialism. It is an imperialism designed for an age of global media, human rights advocacy, and international law—one that hides behind the rhetoric of sovereignty while hollowing it out in practice.

Yet, this new imperial form is not uncontested. It thrives precisely because international law has failed to adapt. The United Nations was built on the principle of equal sovereignty, but in practice it struggles to respond to wars fought by mercenaries, conflicts manipulated through cyber warfare, or coercion exercised through economic leverage. When Russia annexed Crimea in 2014, it faced sanctions but retained the territory. When Iran supports militias across Iraq, Syria, and Lebanon, it shapes regional politics without triggering conventional war. When the United States conducts drone strikes in countries it is not formally at war with, it exercises imperial reach without admitting imperial intent. *The gap between law and practice creates a grey zone where empire flourishes unseen yet undeniable.*

For ordinary citizens, the return of empire is experienced less in symbols than in vulnerabilities. A villager in Mali may find his local economy tied to Russian security contractors and Chinese mining firms. A Hong Kong resident lives at the intersection of Chinese authoritarian reach and Western financial interests, his freedoms curtailed not through annexation but through legal and digital pressure. A voter in Europe or the United States may unwittingly participate in imperial contests when their data is harvested by foreign powers to manipulate elections. The apparatus of empire now operates through the flows of money, information, and mercenaries—its presence diffuse but its consequences intimate.

Critically, the new empire thrives on a paradox. States loudly defend sovereignty in principle while simultaneously undermining it in practice. Russia invokes sovereignty to shield itself from Western criticism while violating Ukraine's sovereignty through proxy militias and hybrid war. The United States affirms self-determination while its military and intelligence agencies shape outcomes abroad. China champions non-interference even as it locks states into economic dependencies that reduce their autonomy. *Empire today does not need to deny sovereignty; it redefines it, making weaker states formally independent but substantively constrained.*

One must also consider the role of private actors in sustaining this imperial logic. Corporations with global reach—whether energy giants, defence contractors, or tech platforms—act as power brokers that rival states in their influence. Meta's decisions about content moderation shape political discourse in countries far beyond its American headquarters. Energy firms determine the viability of governments dependent on resource revenues. Private security companies stand as parallel armies in fragile states. In this context, empire no longer belongs solely to governments but to a hybrid ecosystem of public and private power that jointly produces networks of control. *Empire has been privatised as much as it has been revived.*

The implications are profound. Unlike the empires of the nineteenth century, which eventually collapsed under the pressures of nationalism and anti-colonial struggle, today's empires are more resilient because they are less visible. They cannot be toppled by independence movements because sovereignty has not been formally taken away. They are harder to oppose because they operate in diffuse domains—finance, digital networks, security outsourcing—rather than fixed territories. And they are more sustainable because they are cheaper: maintaining a proxy militia or digital surveillance infrastructure costs far less than sustaining colonial administrations and standing armies abroad. *Invisibility and deniability are the survival strategies of modern empire.*

To grasp the return of empire is to see international politics as a contest less about borders and more about influence. Maps still matter, but not in the way they once did. The decisive frontiers are pipelines, undersea cables, data centres, and proxy armies, not the coloured boundaries of national atlases. Empire has returned not with crowns or colonies but with contracts, militias, and networks that achieve similar ends under a different name. It is not nostalgia for empire that drives this system but cold pragmatism: states find in proxy networks and private arrangements the flexibility to project power in a world where overt conquest has become too costly and politically toxic.

Understanding this shift is vital for anyone seeking to make sense of twenty-first-century geopolitics. To look only for flags on maps is to miss where power now flows. Empire has not disappeared; it has been reconfigured. And until international governance adapts, it will remain the default architecture of global competition—hidden in plain sight, denied in words, but enacted in deeds.

The Logic of Endless Proxy Conflict

Wars once had identifiable beginnings and endings: declarations of war, campaigns fought to exhaustion, treaties signed, borders redrawn. Proxy conflicts, however, resist such neat closure. They are wars without definitive victories, waged through surrogates rather than regular armies, structured less around achieving resolution than maintaining influence. They persist not because they cannot be solved, but because too many actors benefit from their continuation. To understand modern instability is to understand why proxy wars almost never end, why they metastasise across regions, and why they create legacies that outlast the original grievances.

At the heart of proxy conflict lies asymmetry of interest. For local actors, the conflict is existential—about survival, territory, or political control. For external patrons, however, the war is instrumental, a lever to constrain rivals, expand influence, or secure access to resources. This mismatch means that external powers often prefer the war not to end but to remain at a simmer, providing just enough support to prevent their proxies from collapsing but rarely enough to secure a decisive victory. Syria provides a stark example. Russia, Iran, the United States, Turkey, Israel, and Gulf states all intervened in the conflict, but none desired a comprehensive settlement that would either empower adversaries or remove their leverage. The result is a war that has not ended in more than a decade, mutating into zones of foreign influence where no single actor has either the capacity or the incentive to impose closure. *Proxy wars persist because they are designed not to resolve but to remain useful to those who fuel them.*

Unlike conventional wars, proxy wars create networks of dependency that self-perpetuate. Militias funded and armed by external powers develop interests in sustaining their role. Leaders who gain weapons, salaries, or political recognition from patrons rarely surrender them willingly. The Afghan mujahideen in the 1980s were empowered by U.S. and Saudi support to fight Soviet forces, but the infrastructure of militias, weapons, and foreign sponsorship did not vanish when Moscow withdrew. Instead, it mutated into civil war, warlordism, and eventually the Taliban. Proxy conflicts generate ecosystems of violence where commanders, smugglers, contractors, and intelligence services all have a stake in avoiding final settlements. Peace becomes threatening not only to political elites but to entire wartime economies.

The logic of endless proxy conflict is also technological. Cyber operations, disinformation campaigns, and the use of autonomous systems have created ways of conducting proxy war without heavy financial or political costs. Unlike large-scale military interventions, these operations carry low visibility, low risk of casualties, and high deniability. For example, Russian interference in the 2016 U.S. presidential election was not designed to produce immediate territorial gains but to undermine confidence in democratic processes at minimal cost. Similar operations have targeted European elections, African information environments, and Asian political movements. These conflicts unfold indefinitely because they do not require the mobilisation of armies or the risk of national prestige. *So long as the tools are cheap and the deniability high, the incentive to end such operations is almost non-existent.*

Proxy conflicts also evade traditional diplomatic frameworks. Peace treaties require identifiable parties who can negotiate on behalf of combatants and deliver compliance. But in proxy wars, accountability is diffused: local militias take direction from multiple patrons; states deny their involvement; private contractors operate in grey zones of legality. In Yemen, for instance, the war involves Houthi rebels backed by Iran, a Saudi-led coalition, Emirati-supported southern separatists, al-Qaeda factions, and a range of mercenary outfits. Negotiating an end requires not just bringing Yemeni actors to the table but also reconciling Saudi-Iranian rivalry, Emirati ambitions, and broader regional politics. The complexity guarantees stalemate, as external patrons can always spoil settlements that threaten their strategic interests.

Another driver of endlessness is the asymmetry of accountability. Democracies face domestic pressures to justify casualties and expenditures, but proxy strategies allow them to pursue interests without directly endangering their own populations. The United States' reliance on drone warfare, contractors, and local militias in Afghanistan and Iraq prolonged both conflicts by reducing the domestic urgency for resolution. For authoritarian states, meanwhile, proxies provide a way to wage war while shielding their populations from the consequences altogether. This reduces the political cost of endless conflict, making it sustainable even over decades. *Proxy wars are protracted not only because they are complex but because they are politically convenient for those waging them by proxy.*

Importantly, proxy conflicts are self-reinforcing in the way they produce new security dilemmas. Arming one militia prompts rival states to counter-arm another. Funding cyber disinformation campaigns leads adversaries to launch their own in response. The Syrian conflict became so enduring not simply because of local grievances but because each external intervention triggered counter-interventions: U.S. support for Kurdish forces prompted Turkish incursions; Iranian support for Assad deepened Saudi and Israeli involvement; Russian intervention hardened U.S. positions. Once locked into these cycles, proxy wars acquire a momentum that makes de-escalation almost impossible. Each step taken to secure advantage generates reactions that further entrench instability.

The economics of proxy war reinforce the cycle. Local actors often depend on war economies for survival—smuggling, extortion, taxation of aid convoys, and control of resources. External patrons exploit these networks, securing access to oil, minerals, or trade routes through their proxies. Wagner's operations in Africa illustrate this: military support for fragile regimes is exchanged for lucrative mining concessions, creating an incentive for both the patron and the client to sustain instability rather than resolve it. Peace would dismantle the networks that enrich both sides, making perpetual low-level conflict more attractive than resolution.

There is also a cultural and psychological dimension. Proxy wars foster identities defined by resistance and loyalty to external sponsors, identities that endure beyond battlefield necessity. Lebanese Hezbollah has long outlived the original conflicts that birthed it, becoming a political and military actor precisely because Iranian patronage sustains it as a symbol of resistance. In such cases, proxies become entrenched not only as military forces but as political identities embedded in communities. Ending the conflict would require dismantling entire narratives of belonging and legitimacy—a task much harder than signing an accord.

Critically, endless proxy wars are not accidents but strategies. They allow great powers to exhaust rivals, destabilise regions, and prevent the consolidation of hostile regimes. The Cold War demonstrated this logic vividly. The U.S. and Soviet Union rarely confronted each other directly but fought through proxies in Angola, Afghanistan, Nicaragua, and elsewhere. These conflicts did not produce decisive outcomes but served the purpose of tying down adversaries, draining resources, and spreading instability. The modern multipolar world replicates this logic: Iran uses proxies to stretch U.S. and Saudi commitments across the Middle East; Russia sustains frozen conflicts in Georgia, Ukraine, and Moldova to prevent Western integration; Turkey leverages militias in Syria and Libya to extend its influence. The wars drag on because endurance, not victory, is the point.

The consequences are devastating. Proxy conflicts rarely yield stable post-war orders. Instead, they create fractured states unable to reconstitute coherent sovereignty, zones of lawlessness where crime and extremism thrive, and populations traumatised by wars that have no endpoint. Afghanistan, Somalia, and the Democratic Republic of Congo illustrate how proxy interventions leave legacies of violence that persist across generations. Citizens grow up in conditions where war is normalised, governance is fragmented, and external actors shape their fates without accountability. *Endlessness becomes not just a feature of the conflict but a condition of life.*

The logic of endless proxy conflict is, therefore, both rational and perverse. Rational for the external powers who gain influence without bearing the costs of conquest, rational for the proxies who benefit from wartime economies and political legitimacy, but perverse for the societies trapped in perpetual instability. Breaking the cycle would require addressing not only the local grievances but also the structural incentives that make endlessness profitable and convenient. Until then, proxy wars will remain less about resolution and more about perpetuation—conflicts designed not to end but to endure.

New Rules for a World Without Rules

The defining challenge of our century is not that rules are absent, but that they are being systematically outpaced by the kinds of violence they were never designed to contain. The twentieth century's architecture of global governance was built to regulate states: treaties sought to limit nuclear proliferation, conventions codified the treatment of prisoners, and the United Nations offered a forum where sovereigns negotiated their rivalries. Yet power today is exercised in ways that slip the grip of these frameworks. Violence is no longer monopolised by the state nor confined to traditional battlefields. It is private, digital, outsourced, and often algorithmic—harder to attribute, harder to regulate, and infinitely easier to deny. *The world still has rules; the problem is that they no longer apply to those wielding the most disruptive forms of power.*

Consider how the Geneva Conventions, the cornerstone of humanitarian law, assume combatants who wear uniforms, belong to identifiable chains of command, and engage on visible battlefields. But how does one apply such principles when an autonomous drone operated by contractors strikes in a grey-zone conflict, or when a botnet hijacks millions of civilian devices to paralyse another nation's infrastructure? The problem is not only enforcement but ontology: the law struggles to define who the combatants even are. When a multinational tech firm decides to deplatform political figures or entire movements, is that a private act of content moderation or a form of political intervention? Global governance cannot answer because its categories are still anchored to state sovereignty, while the violence being inflicted belongs to a post-sovereign landscape.

One of the most pressing areas of failure is attribution. Traditional deterrence depends on identifying the aggressor, but in a world where ransomware gangs operate under loose toleration by host states, where disinformation campaigns are layered through cut-outs and troll farms, and where AI-generated propaganda can be plausibly denied by governments, responsibility evaporates. The SolarWinds cyber intrusion exposed vulnerabilities across U.S. federal agencies and corporations, yet the line between state-backed espionage and criminal activity was deliberately blurred. This ambiguity is not incidental; it is strategic. By cultivating ecosystems of deniable proxies, states and private actors alike exploit the fact that international law requires clarity of responsibility to trigger accountability. *Without attribution, there is no accountability, and without accountability, governance collapses into irrelevance.*

The privatisation of violence further complicates the terrain. Mercenary firms like Wagner or its successors in Africa, and their equivalents in the Middle East and Latin America, are not rogue actors outside global politics; they are extensions of statecraft executed through corporate form. They sign contracts, collect payments, and hold concessions, while simultaneously engaging in military operations indistinguishable from those of regular armies. Yet because they are corporations, they fall into regulatory gaps: too private to be considered official combatants, too politicised to be treated as neutral commercial entities. The Montreux Document, a non-binding initiative meant to establish best practices for private military companies, has no enforcement teeth. Meanwhile, these firms redraw conflict zones and reshape governments. *The rules lag not because they are absent, but because they refuse to acknowledge the hybrid nature of contemporary power.*

Algorithmic violence poses an even more profound challenge. When Facebook's algorithms amplified hate speech in Myanmar, contributing to the persecution of the Rohingya, the architects of the violence were not generals in uniform but engineers designing engagement-maximising systems. When Twitter's manipulation policies affect the visibility of political movements, it is not neutral technology but a form of private governance that shapes political outcomes. Algorithms weaponise attention, invisibly privileging certain voices, marginalising others, and in doing so, constructing realities that can destabilise entire states. Global governance, built for treaties and summits, lacks both the jurisdiction and the conceptual vocabulary to regulate such diffuse, automated decisions. *What is violence when it is executed not through bullets or bombs but through the manipulation of belief itself?*

Some argue that national regulation could fill the gap, pointing to the European Union's General Data Protection Regulation (GDPR) or its proposed AI Act as evidence that states can still impose rules on global corporations. Yet the reality is that regulatory patchworks fail in a world defined by transnational networks. A Russian troll farm can influence African elections through American-owned platforms, using servers in Southeast Asia, targeting voters in Europe. Which jurisdiction prevails? Whose courts apply? And how does enforcement occur when the actors are shielded by layers of plausible deniability? National regulations address fragments, but violence does not respect borders. The mismatch is structural: *a global threat cannot be meaningfully governed by parochial frameworks.*

If governance is to evolve, it must reimagine both the agents and the arenas of accountability. One potential path is recognising platforms as political actors, not merely private firms. Their power to shape discourse, moderate speech, and enforce norms exceeds that of many states. A system of international oversight—akin to how arms control treaties recognise categories of weapons—may be necessary to regulate algorithmic architectures. Another is establishing legal responsibility for states that knowingly harbour or tolerate proxy actors, whether mercenary firms or ransomware gangs. Just as states are responsible for preventing terrorism within their borders, they could be held liable for the digital violence launched from their territory.

Yet even these frameworks encounter resistance because they threaten the flexibility that makes proxy and algorithmic violence attractive in the first place. States exploit proxies precisely because they offer deniability; corporations deploy algorithms because they drive engagement and profit. Governance that removes these incentives will face opposition from the very actors whose cooperation is essential. Here lies the paradox: rules must evolve, but those empowered by the absence of rules are least likely to support their creation.

A more radical rethinking involves shifting governance away from the state-centric model altogether. Civil society coalitions, multinational corporations, and even technical communities already exercise forms of governance in cyberspace. The norms around responsible disclosure of software vulnerabilities, for instance, emerged not from treaties but from agreements among engineers, security firms, and platforms. Similarly, the Christchurch Call to Action—an initiative led jointly by governments and tech firms to curb online extremism—demonstrates how governance can emerge from hybrid coalitions that include non-state actors as equal partners. *The future of rules may not be about states regulating others, but about distributed networks setting standards together.*

Still, the danger of fragmentation is real. Without coherent global frameworks, governance risks devolving into competing spheres of influence: Chinese cyber-sovereignty doctrines, American tech-led liberal norms, European regulatory models, Russian and Iranian models of digital authoritarianism. In such a fractured landscape, rules become less about universal principles and more about blocs enforcing their preferences. The result would not be the absence of rules but the multiplication of incompatible ones, creating further instability.

The necessity, then, is not just new rules but new legitimacy. Any framework to address private and algorithmic violence must be seen as impartial, not as a cover for one power bloc to entrench its dominance. This requires global buy-in, which is difficult in an era of mistrust. But precedent exists. The Geneva Conventions were not born in an era of harmony but in the aftermath of brutal wars, when adversaries nevertheless recognised shared interest in regulating violence. Today's equivalent may need to emerge from the recognition that unchecked algorithmic and proxy violence threatens not just rivals but the system itself. *No actor benefits in the long term from a world where war is invisible, endless, and unaccountable.*

The "world without rules" is, therefore, not an anarchic vacuum but a contested field where outdated rules no longer constrain those most willing to exploit them. Addressing this requires governance that transcends states, that confronts the hybridity of modern power, and that treats algorithms and proxies as forms of violence deserving regulation as much as tanks or missiles. Without such an evolution, global governance risks irrelevance, ceding the future to actors who thrive precisely because the rules do not reach them. The choice is not between rules and no rules, but between rules that adapt to new forms of power and rules that collapse under their obsolescence.

Reimagining Security

The idea of security has always been bound to territory. Armies guarded borders, fortresses shielded cities, and sovereignty was measured by the ability of a state to defend its land. That assumption, once so deeply ingrained that it was scarcely questioned, now feels increasingly obsolete. In a stateless age defined by networks rather than frontiers, security is no longer a matter of walls and weapons but of resilience, adaptability, and shared responsibility across layers of society. *To feel secure in the twenty-first century is less about living inside a protected border and more about surviving in an interconnected environment where threats can materialise without crossing a single checkpoint.*

The first step in reimagining security is recognising that its foundation is no longer exclusively a state's monopoly. Individuals and organisations now participate in their own defence in ways unimaginable to earlier generations. A citizen may deploy end-to-end encryption, biometric authentication, or virtual private networks in the same way that a medieval villager once relied on the walls of a castle. Small businesses hire cybersecurity firms to patrol their networks as attentively as mercenaries once patrolled city gates. Multinational corporations manage threat intelligence units that resemble miniature intelligence agencies, tracking disinformation campaigns, criminal syndicates, and geopolitical risks. Security has become a distributed practice, layered across private and public spheres. *The monopoly of the state has been replaced by a marketplace of protection where trust, competence, and technology matter more than citizenship.*

Yet this diffusion of responsibility also creates new vulnerabilities. The reliance on private companies for digital and physical protection risks deepening inequalities. Wealthier individuals and corporations can afford premium security solutions—ranging from hardened compounds in Lagos to AI-driven threat detection systems in Silicon Valley—while ordinary citizens are left exposed. In fragile democracies, this stratification of protection corrodes the very notion of equal citizenship, producing societies where safety is determined less by legal rights than by purchasing power. The result is a world that resembles the early modern period, when private guilds, militias, and mercenaries safeguarded trade routes while peasants and workers bore the brunt of insecurity. Security in the stateless age threatens to become not a universal right but a luxury good.

At the same time, the proliferation of self-defence technologies blurs the line between protection and provocation. Encryption, firewalls, and digital anonymity tools empower individuals to safeguard their privacy, but they also provide cover for criminal networks and authoritarian actors. Drones, marketed as consumer products, can be repurposed for surveillance or even improvised attacks. The technologies that enhance resilience for some become instruments of insecurity for others. *Security in the twenty-first century is not a neutral shield—it is a contested resource whose deployment can generate as much risk as protection.*

Societies, therefore, must cultivate a new ethic of security: one that recognises interdependence. Unlike in the past, when armies could repel an invader at a border, today's threats cascade through networks. A single weakly secured company can become the vector for a ransomware attack that paralyses hospitals and transport systems. A single piece of misinformation amplified by algorithms can destabilise an entire election. This interdependence means that resilience cannot be purely individual. Collective norms—such as adopting shared cybersecurity standards, regulating algorithmic transparency, or embedding digital literacy into education—are as crucial as tanks and missiles once were. In a world where threats are distributed, security can only be sustained if protection is distributed as well.

Businesses occupy a particularly complex position in this reimagined landscape. They are both targets and arbiters of security. A financial institution is attacked not simply for profit but because destabilising trust in a bank can ripple across national economies. A technology company, by adjusting its moderation algorithms, can unintentionally shift the tenor of political discourse. Corporations thus carry responsibilities that extend far beyond their balance sheets: their decisions influence not just their shareholders but the sovereignty of states themselves. *The line between economic actors and security actors has eroded to the point where companies may now be more consequential guardians of stability than national armies.*

For individuals, reimagining security requires a mindset shift from passive recipients of protection to active participants in resilience. This does not mean every citizen must become a cyber expert or private soldier. Rather, it means understanding that daily behaviours—choosing which platforms to use, which data to share, which sources to trust—feed into larger systems of stability or instability. The "everyday" now intersects with the geopolitical: a single click can fuel surveillance capitalism, foreign disinformation campaigns, or the financing of militias. *To live securely in a stateless age is to accept that one's private choices are never entirely private; they are micro-decisions with systemic consequences.*

This awareness also demands a new conception of sovereignty. If sovereignty has traditionally meant the authority of a state to guarantee safety within its borders, then its contemporary equivalent must mean the ability of societies to protect their networks, data, and shared information ecosystems. Sovereignty is no longer measured by how much territory a nation controls but by how resilient its citizens are to disruption. Estonia's digital society, for instance, offers a glimpse of this new model: through distributed data embassies and robust cyber education, it has sought to secure its sovereignty not through military might but through the resilience of its digital infrastructure and its citizens' preparedness. Sovereignty becomes less about walls than about *systems that can survive attack, adapt quickly, and recover trust.*

Crucially, security must also be reimagined at the cultural level. Resilience is not just technical but psychological. Disinformation exploits polarisation and erodes trust precisely because it targets emotions and identities. A resilient society is not one that prevents all attacks but one that prevents attacks from shattering its cohesion. This means investing in civic trust, institutional credibility, and shared narratives that can withstand manipulation. In the same way that past societies fortified their walls, present societies must fortify their *sense of belonging.* Without it, even the most advanced digital protections will crumble under the weight of division.

The stateless age thus requires a layered approach to security that integrates individuals, businesses, and societies into a shared ecosystem of resilience. States still matter, but they are no longer the sole custodians of safety. The future will belong to those communities that can combine technological defence, cultural trust, and ethical awareness into a coherent practice of security. Such a practice will not eliminate risk—indeed, risk is now an unavoidable condition of interconnectedness—but it can manage risk in ways that prevent collapse.

Reimagining security in this context is not about designing perfect shields but about cultivating adaptive systems: systems that bend without breaking, societies that can absorb shocks without imploding, and individuals who understand that their choices contribute to the safety of the collective. The measure of sovereignty in the stateless age will not be the power to prevent every incursion but the capacity to endure and adapt when incursions inevitably come. *Security is no longer the promise of invulnerability; it is the practice of resilience in a world where the unseen is always at the door.*

About the Author

Rowan Hale writes on the collision of privatized force, cyber power, and artificial intelligence—how conflict escapes borders and enters markets, networks, and everyday life. His work blends field reporting, open-source investigation, and interviews with private contractors, militia organizers, and threat-intelligence teams to map how "wars without flags" actually operate on the ground and online. Hale has briefed humanitarian groups and corporate risk leaders on deniable warfare and information manipulation, and curates a widely read newsletter on AI and conflict. He is driven by a simple aim: make fast-moving security shifts legible to thoughtful readers so they can separate signal from noise, challenge easy narratives, and make better real-world decisions.

www.ingramcontent.com/pod-product-compliance
Lightning Source LLC
Chambersburg PA
CBHW031324230926
51848CB00001B/86
9789390349692